D1325346

Students of social science will recognize in the contributors outstanding scholars and theorists in the field:

Gordon T. Bowles, Prof. of Anthropology, Syracuse Univ.

Paul Meadows, Prof. of Sociology, Syracuse Univ.

William C. Lehmann, Prof. Emeritus of Sociology, Syracuse Univ.

John W. Bennett, Prof. of Anthropology, Washington Univ.

Earl W. Count, Prof. of Anthropology, Hamilton College

Robert E. L. Faris, Prof. of Sociology, Univ. of Washington

Carl J. Friedrich, Prof. of Government, Harvard Univ.

Talcott Parsons, Prof. of Sociology, Harvard Univ.

John F. Manfredi, Prof. of Sociology, Univ. of Massachusetts

Ernest Becker, formerly Asst. Prof. of Anthropology, State Univ. of New York Upstate Medical Center in Syracuse

T. F. McIlwraith, Prof. of Anthropology, Univ. of Toronto

Morris E. Opler, Prof. of Anthropology, Cornell Univ.

E. S. Craighill Handy, formerly Research Associate in Anthropology, Bishop Museum, Honolulu

Alfred Rodman Hussey, Commander (ret.), U.S. Navy

Fact and Theory in
Social Science

Fact and Theory in Social Science

EARL W. COUNT
GORDON T. BOWLES

Editors

SYRACUSE UNIVERSITY PRESS • 1964

Manufactured in the
United States of America

DEDICATED TO

Douglas Gilbert Haring

Essays presented in his seventieth year

FOREWORD

THE INSPIRATION to honor Douglas Haring by presenting him with a collection of essays first came from some of his former students shortly before his retirement in 1961 from the Maxwell Graduate School of Citizenship and Public Affairs, Syracuse University. At that time Dean Harlan Cleveland initiated the plan, proposed a general theme for the volume, and undertook to assure funds for its publication. The plan has been carried forward unchanged since Dean Cleveland resigned to become Assistant Secretary of State.

A *Festschrift* seems a fitting tribute to a Syracuse University scholar of national and international repute who has given thirty-four years of service to his university, served his government unstintingly during and after the war, and been deeply involved in numerous state and local welfare enterprises. In these three categories of excellence, then—teaching, scholarship, and community service—Douglas Haring has had an outstanding record.

As a person, Douglas Haring has always been outspoken, as was dramatically illustrated during the stormy years before World War II when his pessimistic predictions about Japan's hostile attitude and warlike preparations were little appreciated and less understood. Together with two other Syracuse University professors, he was burned in effigy on the campus in 1940 and accused by a number of intemperate students of being a warmonger.

In scholarly circles, he is best known for his studies in personality and culture—describing personality differences in individual behavior as reflections of differences in culture. While his emphasis has been on Japanese civilization and on Japanese society in particular, he has also studied Americans and, largely due to the influence of Franz Boas in his earlier days, American Indians. His most notable contribution to sociological theory has been ably summarized by Professor Paul Meadows, Chairman of the Department of Sociology and Anthropology, Syracuse University, in "The Action-System Theory of Social Behavior."

Professor Haring has also left his mark on the research interests of the university. After World War II, he had been posted by the U.S. Army Civil Affairs Division to Amami Oshima (Northern Ryukyu Islands). The research which he commenced in this area at that time and has continued since then has made Syracuse University one of the centers for Ryukyuan studies.

Syracuse University has recognized Douglas Haring's services by awarding him the title of professor emeritus and by conferral of the LL.D. degree. Colgate University, his alma mater, conferred on him the D.Sc. degree.

This *Festschrift* could not have come into being without the tireless efforts of editors Professor Earl W. Count of Hamilton College and Professor Gordon T. Bowles of Syracuse University. Thanks are due to all of the contributors. Most of the work for this volume has been volunteered as an expression of affection and admiration for a great teacher, scholar, and American.

STEPHEN K. BAILEY
Syracuse University

January, 1964

EDITORS' PREFACE

When Dean Harlan Cleveland of the Maxwell Graduate School of Citizenship and Public Affairs initiated the idea of a *Festschrift* to honor Douglas Haring and assigned the task of editorship, he expressed the hope that the volume might be something other than a mere collection of miscellaneous essays. He hoped, rather, that it would center on such a theme as the character of significant fact in social science, a topic which Haring himself has emphasized and developed. Unavoidable delays in publication have made the task of editing greater than had been originally foreseen, and such measure of approximation to the Dean's expectations as has been realized must be credited more to the authors than to the editors.

From the start, the plan has been to include essays from Professor Haring's personal friends and colleagues which collectively would represent the full spectrum of his activity. We believe this has been realized. Among the contributors, one is a former Syracuse student (Becker); one had been a teaching colleague at Syracuse (Faris); one combines associations at Syracuse and Columbia (Lehmann); two were colleagues at Harvard (Friedrich and Parsons); two were students at Harvard (Manfredi and Hussey); one was in the Civil Information and Education Section of the Occupation in Japan (Bennett); three are colleagues and friends of long standing, teaching in upstate New York and neighboring Ontario (Opler, Count and McIlwraith); and one was a Syracuse neighbor and professional colleague (Handy).

The theme of this volume, the role of fact in social science, clearly has facets of philosophical principle, of social theory, and of practical application. And there is the added truth that the participants in any culture give factual interpretation to phenomena according to the thought-idiom in which they have been brought up.

Consequently, it has gratified the editors that the wide spectrum of respondents to the invitation should nevertheless have converged upon the assignment as effectively as they have done. Imperfections and some imbalance exist but, these notwithstanding, the arrangement of the essays has come about inductively and we believe there is a general progression of theme.

We have grouped the essays in four parts. The first is devoted to the life and work of Douglas Haring. The second part is concerned with definitions and with the limiting aspects of sociological thought,

ix

the historical stages in the development of definable cultural elements, "facts" and their relevance to behavioral science; the third relates mainly to theories concerning the structure of society and social behavior both recent and current; and the fourth provides examples reflecting the interpretation of "facts" in particularized cultural settings.

While Bowles' biographical sketch of Douglas Haring traces the events which stimulated the man's interest in sociology and anthropology, changing the course of his career, Meadows' analytical résumé of Haring's work summarizes the major themes and theories which Haring has developed, over a lifetime of observation and study, as a major contribution to his field. Meadows' analysis is a tribute to his ability to grasp the significance of Haring's contribution to sociological theory, and it sets the tone for the symposium. A bibliography of Haring's writings reveals the scope of his work.

Occidental thought (using Theodore Merz' sense of the word) is itself a cultural-historical process. Appropriately, Lehmann's study of one of the seminal minds of nineteenth century Europe was selected to open the second part of the symposium with a consideration of Herder's sociohistorical "facta."

Bennett's essay brings the reader to the present and shows anthropology criticizing itself. He has no illusions about the hiatus between what it has done or should have given promise of doing and what it has been delivering, in both theory and application. What he says may suggest to many of us why anthropology has become a shrewd rather than a profound discipline, one which has suffered often and unduly from the limited perspective and biases of the unique observer.

Considering "fact" as a matter of definition within a culture pattern, Count argues that its scientific definition has its own peculiar restriction, and that anthropology faces the problem of such definition while maintaining nonetheless its humanistic identification and the perspective of history which first gave it rise.

Faris demonstrates that what often passes for social fact is all too often pseudo fact because of the failure to consider and conceptualize all the relevant variables, so that the data inevitably yield spurious reality.

From dimensions and definitions the critique passes in the third part of the symposium to theory. By utilizing the Human Relations Area Files, Friedrich, a political scientist, confronts the anthropologists who have authored them with the sobering doubt that the analytic categories they employ have yet achieved the needed cultural neutrality and operational universality. He follows his question with a constructive suggestion by means of a sample operation based primarily on processual rather than structural categories.

Parsons, himself a leader in the direction he describes, reviews recent evolution in sociologic theory in the United States with particular reference to the lines of tradition emanating from Weber and Durkheim. His article is the English version of an article which appeared in German in 1963 in the *Kölner Zeitschrift für Soziologie.*

Dealing with problems of convergence, Manfredi attempts to show that in measure as cultures unrelated to each other (as filiates from a common and earlier original) become complex, their freedom of choice of new mechanisms narrows—an inherent feature of the situation, whence their convergence upon seemingly identical resolutions.

While Becker's consideration of the "Oedipus complex" has its own intrinsic point, in wider context it asserts the principle that social science, in diametric distinction from physical science, possesses factors of quality in its foundation *a natura rei.*

The fourth group of essays illustrates vividly the cultural relativity of observable phenomena. From his field experience among the Bella Coola Indians, McIlwraith suggests that what is regarded as "fact" in any culture proceeds from certain axioms of the world view, and this in itself becomes a valid subject of study.

From North India, Opler's field research documents rather precisely how social roles, beliefs, and goal structuring of a people are an effective reality which reform measures can never afford to ignore. His principal examples are those of women's position and the valuation placed upon child producing as these bear upon policies of population control.

Handy, drawing his illustration from the now Occidentalized Hawaiians, details an example of an environmental phenomenon retaining undiminished its ancient, pre-Christian interpretation, and its pragmatic treatment, by virtue of its being tremendous and uncontrollable.

Finally, the wide range of experiences which confront Americans living abroad in a variety of alien cultures and equipped with what their own culture has made of them induces Hussey to attempt an explanation of Americans to themselves, and to indicate their particular problems in these circumstances and what adjustments Americans as individuals must be prepared to make in the present and in the future.

In any symposium covering such a span in time and range of subject matter there is always the problem of satisfactory integration. The present instance is no exception, and that the lacunae are greater than the substance we readily admit. But we have been concerned with a theme, not an encyclopedia. It appears to us that, taken together, the essays do indicate the kind of thinking about social man that is generally current in twentieth century America.

EARL W. COUNT
Hamilton College

GORDON T. BOWLES
Syracuse University

January, 1964

ACKNOWLEDGMENTS

THE EDITORS express their appreciation to the contributors whose generosity and cooperation have made this symposium possible. At times the limited theme may have imposed strictures upon freedom of expression, but the accommodation to its frame of reference has been both unusual and gratifying.

Special mention must be made of the late Professor Clyde Kluckhohn of Harvard University who died before he could complete his essay. Other colleagues of Douglas Haring, including A. I. Hallowell, also expressed a desire to contribute but could not because of unforeseeable circumstances. Hallowell's comments on the essays are reflected, however, in the organization of the symposium.

We wish to thank the following publishers for granting permission to quote from their publications: American Association for the Advancement of Science (*Science*); *American Scientist*; Harper & Row, Publishers, Inc.; Human Relations Area Files; McGraw-Hill Book Company; *The New Republic*; New York University Press; Prentice-Hall, Inc.; and The University of Chicago Press (*The American Journal of Sociology*). Complete references to the works cited are given in the Notes following each chapter.

Thanks are also due to Mrs. Marian A. Borst for expert typing, and to the Paul H. Appleby Research Fund for defraying part of the expenses of manuscript preparation. The patience and editorial advice of the Syracuse University Press is especially appreciated by all who have worked on the manuscript.

Finally, to Professor Haring himself we are most grateful. Throughout the past several months of collation and editing he has placed his time, memory, and advice unstintingly at our disposal. One of us (Count) has valued him as a colleague and close personal friend for over thirty years. The other (Bowles), as a youngster, first knew Haring in Tokyo in 1917, later in government, and more recently as a professional colleague.

E. W. C.

G. T. B.

CONTENTS

FOREWORD .... *Stephen K. Bailey* vii

EDITORS' PREFACE .... *Earl W. Count* and *Gordon T. Bowles* .. ix

ACKNOWLEDGMENTS xiii

Part One. Douglas G. Haring: Man and Scholar

    I.   Earlier Years and Scholarly Career 3
        GORDON T. BOWLES

    II. The Action-System Theory of Social Behavior 9
        PAUL MEADOWS

    III. Bibliography: The Writings of Douglas G. Haring ... 24

Part Two. Dimensions of Sociological Thought

    IV. Sociological and Cultural-Anthropological Elements in the Writings of Johann Gottfried von Herder 35
        WILLIAM C. LEHMANN

    V.   Myth, Theory and Value in Cultural Anthropology: Questions and Comments 67
        JOHN W. BENNETT

    VI. Dimensions of Fact in Anthropology 85
        EARL W. COUNT

    VII. Some Issues of Relevance of Data for Behavioral Science 107
        ROBERT E. L. FARIS

Part Three. Developments in Social Theory

    VIII. The Uses of Anthropological Materials in Political Theory 127
        CARL J. FRIEDRICH

    IX. Recent Trends in Structural-Functional Theory 140
        TALCOTT PARSONS

X.   Societal Complexity and Limited Alternatives   159
JOHN F. MANFREDI

XI.   The Validity of "Oedipus Complex" as an Abstract
Scientific Construct   165
ERNEST BECKER

Part Four. Cultural Relativity

XII.   Facts and Their Recognition Among the Bella Coola   183
T. F. McILWRAITH

XIII.   Cultural Context and Population Control Programs in
Village India   201
MORRIS E. OPLER

XIV.   Active Vulcanism in Kau, Hawaii, as an Ecological
Factor Affecting Native Life and Culture   222
E. S. CRAIGHILL HANDY

XV.   The American Official Overseas   230
ALFRED RODMAN HUSSEY

Part One

Douglas G. Haring: Man and Scholar

GORDON T. BOWLES

Chapter I: Earlier Years and Scholarly Career

Douglas Gilbert Haring was born in 1894 in Watkins Glen in Central
New York. In 1899 his parents moved to Buffalo, the scene of his
childhood and early youth. His father, a devout Baptist, was a lifelong
pillar of the church, albeit with no sectarian boundaries around his
catholicity of practice. His mother, poetically inclined and not without
literary ability, devoted much time and thought to fostering good
habits of speaking and writing in her only child. Her constant hope,
however, was that her son might become a foreign missionary.

Significantly for an important period in his adult life, the grade
school boy in Buffalo knew as a visitor in his home a high school
classmate of an aunt who had lived for a year in the Haring home:
her closest friend, Ruth Fulton, later known in anthropological circles
around the world as Ruth Benedict.

At Colgate University, Haring majored in mathematics and chemistry in addition to being employed as a laboratory assistant in physics.
He was absorbed in the "exact" sciences and received the B.S. degree
in 1914. It was no surprise to his parents, however, that he decided
to enter Rochester Theological Seminary (now Colgate-Rochester
Divinity School) for three years of graduate study. During college
and seminary years, he spent several summers working as a laborer
in the Bureau of Water at Buffalo gaining experience in the practical
aspects of engineering. He cherished a hope that somehow engineering and theology might be combined to make him a useful Christian
missionary in China. The Baptist Mission Board, however, held other
ideas.

In August 1917 Haring was appointed by the American Baptist
Foreign Mission Society a missionary to Japan—a country that had
not figured in his ideas for the future. En route he met Ann Teasdale
Howell, a pianist graduate of the Juilliard School of Music, who was
bound for China to teach music. She spent one year in Ningpo and
came to Japan in 1918 where they were married in the mountain
resort of Karuizawa. Both attended the School of Japanese Language
and Culture (in which Haring already had completed the first year)

3

and then lived for a year in Himeji where they met few English-speaking people. In 1920, Haring was appointed principal of a small school for underprivileged boys in Yokohama, a situation which served to stimulate in him recognition of the commonality of urban social problems and understanding of a non-Christian civilization. This cross-cultural experience ultimately transformed his thinking and, most important, his feelings about life.

On furlough from Japan in 1922-23, Haring turned to graduate study at Columbia University to find some intellectual light for his questions about the meaning of cultural contrasts. After taking general courses at Teachers College and studying general psychology with Woodworth and finally sociology with Giddings, he obtained the M.A. in sociology with a thesis on militaristic propaganda in Japanese official primary school readers. In 1923 he also completed the B.D. requirements at Rochester.

A decision to delay the scheduled return to Japan until after the birth of their second child fatefully changed the Harings' lives. Their daughter was born on September 1, 1923, the day of the great earthquake and holocaust in Tokyo and Yokohama. Haring's house and possessions, in the heart of the burned area in Yokohama, were included in the virtually total destruction of that city. Immediately dropping other commitments, Haring spent the next few months traveling across the United States to raise relief funds for the earthquake victims. Early in 1924 he was recalled to Japan to take over the various relief and reconstruction tasks of his fellow missionaries who by then were exhausted. It was particularly in the rebuilding operations that Haring's engineering experience and training proved useful.

By 1925, Haring was able to return to teaching; and in the temporary absence of his friend and mentor, Daniel C. Holtom, the great Shinto scholar, he served as acting professor of history at Tokyo Gakuin. But two events were to disrupt his missionary career. One was the threat of dismissal from the mission, foreshadowed by vigorous agitation against "heretics" in the Baptist churches in America; and the other was acquisition of a few books on anthropology which were purchased with funds given him to help replace his lost library. In 1926 Haring was recalled to the United States where he stood trial before the Mission Board for heresy; after a protracted investigation he was found guilty of doctrinal heresy and was dismissed from the missionary organization. The bitterness of this experience was relieved, however, by his introduction to anthropology and, in particular, to the writings of Kroeber. Haring found what he had been seeking—a discipline devoted to the comparison of differing cultures.

Employment in the United States, after eight years' absence from his homeland and with no previous full-time job at home, posed a new problem. In search of a solution, he turned to his old friend, Marc Rose, then editor of the *Buffalo Evening News*. Haring had written a fortnightly column on Japan for that paper since 1923. Rose encouraged him to select essays from these columns for re-editing in book form. The result was Haring's first major publication, *The Land of Gods and Earthquakes*.

By a fortunate series of events, Haring encountered an old friend and classmate in the Tokyo Language School—Thomas Elsa Jones. Jones had just received the Ph.D. in sociology from Columbia and had been named president of Fisk University. It was on Jones' advice, after an all-night conversation beside the Hudson, that Haring was persuaded to aim for a career as a university teacher; and it was Jones' recommendation that secured him a lectureship at Columbia in sociology. He taught half time under the Columbia Extension Service in the Brooklyn Law School and at the same time carried a full load of study in anthropology.

Haring's first formal courses in anthropology were taught by Leslie Spier. Coincidentally, the Harings were living next door to the Spiers, and daily commuting from Spuyten Duyvil to Columbia gave Haring an opportunity to know one of the most unique and brilliant minds in American anthropology. The following autumn, he began to study under Franz Boas and Ruth Benedict, discovering to his astonishment that Ruth Benedict was the person he had known as Ruth Fulton in his childhood. By that year (1926-27), Franz Boas' seminar was attracting not only graduate students but numerous anthropologists already established in the profession: among others, frequent attenders were Margaret Mead, Melville and Frances Herskovits, Otto Klineberg, Gladys Reichard, Paul Radin, A. A. Goldenweiser, Pliny Godard, Carl and Erminie Vogelin, Thorne Deuel, Ruth Bunzel, May Mandelbaum, Dorothy Keur, Ruth Underhill, Melville Jacobs, Ruth Sawtell, Alexander Lesser, and Gene Weltfish. This exposure to a group of inquisitive, brilliant, and varied minds provided a major experience and stimulus for Haring.

In autumn of 1927, Haring was invited by Dean William E. Mosher to teach anthropology and Asian studies at what is now the Maxwell Graduate School of Citizenship and Public Affairs, Syracuse University. Actually, the exigencies of the economic depression that ushered in the 1930's required Haring to teach statistics for a decade;

there seemed slight room in the academic curriculum for more than one anthropology course and one Asian course at a time. His early efforts to develop courses on China and Japan were warmly assisted by an old friend and Japanese Scholar Dr. Ernest Clement, who had been a teacher in Japan for forty years. In addition to teaching statistics and sociology and initiating the teaching of anthropology at Syracuse as well as the Asian Studies Program, Haring devoted much of his energy for more than a decade to developing an examination technique for the course, Introduction to Responsible Citizenship. He subsequently contributed nine chapters to the textbook of the same title which Dean Mosher edited. Three times he has served temporarily as Chairman of the Department of Sociology (later called the Department of Sociology and Anthropology).

Between 1927 and 1938, Haring engaged actively in several research projects. In 1933-34, he prepared the statistical data for a study of work relief in Onondaga County, a study which influenced the setting up of the W.P.A. as a measure of depression relief. A few years earlier he had served as consultant and joint editor of a study of the national Y.M.C.A. and Y.W.C.A. organizations directed by Dr. H. N. Shenton. In 1937-38, he acted as consultant, statistician, and general editor of a voluminous study by the New York State Division of the National Youth Administration, involving a detailed analysis of a wealth of data on over 10,000 youths from relief families. For Haring, the initial fifteen-year period at Syracuse was a time of intellectual development and broadening of contacts. Most of his lasting friendships with professional colleagues originated during this period.

For Mrs. Haring, the period meant also the opening up of a new and rich career. In 1930, the Harings lost their eldest daughter during a polio epidemic. The shock and sorrow was deep and lasting. For Mrs. Haring the tragedy was also a challenge. Moving from her earlier devotion to music, she completed an M.A. in biology and was unwittingly on her way to a career as medical technician and bacteriologist. She qualified as one of two county specialists in the identification of polio, using the serum techniques of the day. Thus, with the passage of time, Ann Haring's training and specialization completed for the family a full cycle of experience.

Beginning in 1932, after the Japanese army had moved decisively into Manchuria and northeastern China, Haring's former reputation as an uncompromising pacifist was shattered by his vigorous proclaiming of the facts: namely, Japan's preparation for war and her obvious ambitions of conquest. After Pearl Harbor he traveled extensively in the United States to lecture about Japan in Army camps.

In 1944, Haring was invited to the Civil Affairs Training School at Harvard University as Visiting Lecturer on Japan and, after the termination of hostilities on V-J Day, to lecture for a term in Harvard College. It was through his connection at Harvard that he met as colleagues or students a number of the contributors to this volume.

Returning to Syracuse for the spring semester of 1947, he continued teaching until his retirement in the spring of 1961. It was especially during these sixteen years and the immediately preceding wartime period that Haring carried out his major research and writing.

In 1948, as a recipient of a post-doctoral Viking Fund Fellowship, he collaborated with W. Tsuneishi in translation of part of M. Takikawa's *Social History of Japan*. In 1951 and 1952, he was a research associate of the Pacific Science Board of the National Research Council and initiated an Ethnographic Field Survey of Amami Oshima in the northern section of the Ryukyu Island chain. He also received a four-month research grant from the Wenner Gren Foundation to edit motion picture films of Amami Oshima and parts of the adjacent islands of Japan. A subsequent grant from the Rockefeller Foundation made possible the processing of much of the data secured during 1951-52—a work as yet unpublished and forming only a part of a more extensive study on which he is presently engaged.

During and shortly after the war, Haring served as consultant to the Assistant Secretary of the U.S. Army, adviser and lecturer to officers of the Civil Information and Education Section under the Occupation, consultant to the Japanese Universities Project of the American Council on Education (1954-55) and delivered numerous lectures before university audiences in Japan and the United States. His membership in professional societies has been extensive, and he has carried his full share of responsibility in their administration.

Douglas Haring's life has been varied, unusual and uncertain; it has also been one of great personal satisfaction. He has seen the university to which he devoted so many years of his life grow not only in size but even more so in stature, and he has received the love and admiration of his students, thousands of whom have come and gone through his classes. Probably his greatest satisfaction has been derived from tributes from his alma mater and the university with which he was associated for nearly thirty-five years. In 1962, just after retirement, Haring was recipient of the D.Sc. Honorary

Degree from Colgate University and the LL.D. from Syracuse University which also conferred upon him the title of emeritus professor for rendering outstanding services to the university. For his lifelong dedication and significant contributions to the theoretical realm of the social sciences, Douglas Haring can take equal satisfaction.

PAUL MEADOWS

Chapter II: The Action-System Theory of Social Behavior

Douglas Haring's social science career combined in its mixture of practical and humanitarian interests and theoretical scholarly pursuits two major themes that appear in his writings: the convergence of facts from many fields in the understanding of a single human fact, and the employment of an action-system theory in the description and explanation of human social behavior. This résumé of his work, which follows only some of the more interesting trails of his general social theory, will cover these subjects: (1) the identification of significant social fact, (2) the nature of the action approach to human social behavior, (3) the dimensions of social being, (4) the problems of structure and order and of behavior and possibility, (5) the relationship between human response indeterminacy and social change, (6) organic stability and cultural transcendence, and (7) science itself viewed as pluralistic behavior.

I.

Order and Possibility in Social Life, co-authored with Mary E. Johnson (to whom Haring has always attributed many of his ideas) and appropriately dedicated "to the late Franklin H. Giddings," is unquestionably the most complete statement of Douglas Haring's social theory, both as an anthropologist and as sociologist. The volume is organized into six books; the introductory comments on each are very helpful. Book I contains "descriptive data without interpretive comment." Books II-III present "selected biological findings descriptive of the human persons who compose societies." Book IV deals with societies, defined "in terms of persons and their activities and a scientific approach to social phenomena. . . ." Book V treats of "various aspects of human societies." And Book VI develops "implications of a scientific study of social life."

These economical comments which sketch out the scope of inquiry of this volume do not, of course, reveal much about its dominant perspective. That appears in the following comment: "In the discovery of what man *can* do, the data of the biological sciences are pertinent; in the discovery of what man *does,* the social sciences provide descriptive data. In practical decision as to what a specific individual or group of individuals *wish to do,* the limitations and possibilities of human nature and of social order are definitive."[1] Order is a pervasive theme. "Human beings seek and find an essential integrity in the sequential experience of living. If life appears whole, such unity founds in the subjective orderliness of events which each individual attains through evaluation and rationalization in the process of growing up. Since all behavior is sequential expenditure of energy, his existence has for him continuity."[2] But possibility is an equally persuasive perspective. "The complementary nature of individual differences, organic and behavioristic, is the basis of endless variety in human relationships, a phenomenon more or less formalized and organized in every society."[3] Reciprocals of one another, order and possibility have a common matrix. "Pluralistic or multi-individual behavior evidences an order that founds in orderly sequences of individual behavior."[4] The theme is inherently a dynamic one. "Study of the action system of an organism is study of sequences of change in dynamic equilibrium and structural arrangements, perceptible as sequences in a pattern of motion."[5]

In a significant sense this concern with order is part of the universal human concern with patterns. "Man thinks in patterns; he organizes his social living according to patterns; he seeks for orderly patterns of historical change. . . . So in the study of himself as an organism he attempts to describe the configurations and patterns of structure, of growth and change, which are perceived in observation of human organisms, and to compare these with the patterns of organization perceived in the study of other living things."[6] The discovery of patterns is a slow, uneasy and hard-won process of careful observation. "A society," we are reminded, "is not a spatial arrangement of parts mechanically linked in a single structure. . . ."[7] Hence the discovery of societal patterns must be regarded "in any instance" as "the hard-won result of intellectual synthesis of detailed data obtained in particularized studies."[8] There is indeed no single significant social fact. "What is it important to know about a people? The history of scientific investigation demonstrates that in the long run no fact is too trivial, no research too laborious."[9]

It is important, however, to keep in mind that even monumental efforts at minute observational details fall short. "In human behavior the indefinite range of individual modifiability in pattern of response emphasizes the dynamic hiatus between stimulation and the form of the response. . . . Attempted mathematical formulations of the relation between a stimulating situation and a pattern of response provide little more than symbolic statements of an analogy or of a capricious probability—something basically different from equations descriptive of physical and chemical events."[10]

The following generalizations, taken seriatim from an impressive formal statement on "Science and Social Phenomena," frame a neat, precise view of the human landscape as seen from the perspective of an action-system theory.

1. All significantly related events of social phenomena are dynamically inequivalent.

2. All social phenomena are sequential.

3. Every human community, grouping or social situation is unique.

4. A central problem in social science is description of the circumstances that attend relative societal stability.

5. Cultural behavior is observable and scientifically definable.

6. Differing patterns of cultural behavior are incommensurable.

7. Cultural behavior involves purposeful selection of patterns of response in terms of subjective criteria.

8. Human beings never behave socially in ways whose patterns they have not learned.

9. In any locality individuals manifest patterns of cultural behavior that are current among their associates.

10. The objective unit of observation is a human being behaving.[11]

II.

Haring's acute sensitivity to people—and their behavior—as the ultimate "stuff" of the social sciences led him to reject analogies generally, physical analogies quite especially. "The complexity of the human personality is more adequately revealed in objective description of organic phenomena than in analogies drawn from physics."[12] Elsewhere he comments in a similar vein: "The self-activating character of the individual units contrasts sharply with the transmission of electrical currents in a telephone system"[13]—one of the more fashionable "models" of the interwar period.

Like so many social scientists trained in the heydey of Childs, Jennings, Sherrington and Herrick, Haring pinpoints the utter uniqueness—and towering importance—of the human nervous system, *i.e.,* "the phenomenal development of the cerebral cortex" from which derives "the self-stimulating" character of the human organism.[14] Cortex-dominated, the human organism is the persistent frame of reference for Haring's action-system theory of human social behavior. Developed by Jennings as a way of coping with the conceptual and methodological problems created by the collapse of instinct doctrine, the action-system concept is described in the statement that the "motions characteristic of any species are termed the action system of that species."[15] The phrase refers, following Jennings, to the "habitual mode of reaction to the environment which is determined wholly or in part by its inherited organization."

This conceptualization of behavior is of course inherently systemic, as Haring knew. Thus he writes: "The concept of organic regulation, to the end of continued existence, leads to scientific description of behavior as motions of organisms in process of self-maintenance; in other words, behavior is progressive re-adjustment of a dynamic system disturbed by changes incidental to processes of growth and metabolism, and by alterations in the environing energy complex."[16] However, there is a brief but powerful disclaimer to input-output system-model thinking now current: "Behavior is effected by the stored energy of the organism, not with energy derived from the stimulus." Nonetheless, being generally system-oriented, an action theory of behavior lays heavy stress on organism-environment interactive equilibrium. Behavior, Haring observes, may be described as "the sequential motions and changes in organisms, to readjust and thereby to maintain internal constancy of functioning in the face of varying environmental conditions."[17] He is, to be sure, critical of the equilibrium image, which he finds "inadequate to denote this dynamic continuum" of organic behavior; this latter he identifies in terms of the "self-restoring dynamic balance of the living organism."[18]

Well before the post-World War II vogue of cybernetics Haring wrote of the "complexity of the dynamic processes of the organism" that "they are describable ultimately in terms of the laws of thermodynamics."[19] The readjustment of organic equilibrium which he calls behavior and which he insists is "always sequential" has many radiant lines of significance—e.g. the struggle for existence which is the struggle for maintaining stability of individual organism integration. Moreover, what is often called organism plasticity, a term which Haring avoids, must be seen analogically as a way of viewing the "self-maintaining dynamic process" of the organism.[20] There is, so to speak, a bonus value in the equilibrating interaction of organism and environment. "The more complex the organism and the more specialized its parts for particular functions, the more highly coordinated is behavior and the wider are the range and diversity of environmental relations."[21] Herein lies the possibility of the extension of the human "sustentation field" which has characterized—which indeed made possible—the rise of cities and thus of civilization. Environmental adaptation is thus conceived of in its most dynamic sense, as a function of the conversion, constraint, depletion and transformation of environment-organism energy complexes.

Human societies tend to be "ecotypes" (borrowing Boas' little-known term)—stable life-form adjustments to relatively stable "sustentation fields." Human organisms develop, as do other organisms (but more variably and modifiably in time), similar responses to relatively homogeneous environmental contexts (rendered homogeneous by selective attention and selective response). Capable of learning from one another (whether individual, groups of individuals or generations of individuals) and possessing at best what must honestly be described as a limited number of models in any local situation, a "modal" personality pattern among a population emerges in time. Moreover, it is possible that "among the simpler peoples, at least, types of personality may be distributed geographically and could be represented on maps just as house forms . . . and other cultural phenomena are shown on the distribution maps that delimit culture areas."[22] Nonetheless, he calls attention to a serious risk in the personal character approach to behavioral interpretations. "The conclusions proclaimed by Boas and his generation of anthropologists, namely, that race, language, and general culture vary independently and do not explain each other, probably will be amplified by adding another independent variable. For styles of personal character also appear to vary independently of race, language, and broad cultural patterns of social organization, religion and technology."[23]

In general, Haring enters a quiet but firm and vigorous disclaimer to "culture" as an interpretive construct of human social behavior. An action-system theory, being organism oriented, is not a culture-system theory; but both, as an *action-system-culture-system complex*, are meaningless apart from each other. In his trenchant and relevant article published in the *American Sociological Review*, "Is 'Culture' Definable?" the following statements form a fairly definitive expression of his basic perspective.

In any inductive definition of cultural phenomena the *genus* or inclusive category should be *human behavior*. . . .

If human behavior be accepted as the major category, the

features that differentiate the specifically cultural from the non-cultural are amenable to descriptive statement. The same organisms behave both culturally and otherwise; sometimes the same act involves both aspects. The basis of differentiation lies in the phenomena of individual modifiability and invariability in behavior. . . .

Broadly viewed, in some species most of the observable behavior follows patterns relatively invariable in the species; in other species, notably *homo,* most of the observable behavior is modifiable in the individual. . . .

Cultural behavior, therefore, is differentiated from other behavior by the fact that its patterns are learned individually from models provided by other persons. Viewed as cultural, interest centers in the pattern and only incidentally on the behaving organism. Viewed as behavior, interest centers on the fact of learning. . . .[24]

Haring spotlights the behaving organism. When interest turns to the process of organism behavior, culture seems an appropriate reference context. When interest turns to the dynamics of the behavior, then the psycho-neural mechanisms seem to be a functional context of interpretation. "Behavior denotes any dynamic change in a living organism, not merely those external motions that are apparent to the untrained eye."[25] What is usually called the "culture" of a people may also be thought of in terms of the range of behavior choices available to a population in a given area—what Haring calls their "cultural repertory"—"the range of possible behavior alternatives as circumscribed by the accessible sources of knowledge."[26] In action-system terms, "culture" must be replaced by "cultural behavior," thus making it cognate with the general vocabulary of what is now called, with grand ambiguity, the behavioral sciences.

III.

The ultimate dimensions of social being in Haring's thinking are clear and precise: "Study of human life is study of *people* as organic and behavior kinds, and study of their *cultural behavior.*"[27] Elsewhere he expresses the matter even more bluntly. "The varied phenomena of a human society may be reduced ultimately to two aspects: (1) populations and (2) cultural behavior."[28]

It comes as no surprise that such specificity should also be linked with rejection of large-scale, global statements about the general

nature or process or dynamics of behavior. For example, he evaluates
the universal cultural pattern concept this way. The concept is really
"a classification of interpretations of society rather than a classification of facts of behavior, since the periphery of the cultural forms
included in any category differs with each observer."[29] No student
of Giddings, no reader of Childs or Jennings or Sherrington could
fail to emphasize the presence and indeed the prevalence of resemblances among living organisms, including man. "Likemindedness" is
also "likeness-mindedness," and among pluralistic organisms such
as man it is also "likewise-mindedness." Haring develops seven
postulates concerning speciate similarity.

    1. Man the organism resists environmental forces: "What
man does about his environment outweighs anything that environment does to him, short of violent death."

    2. Human nervous systems provide for indefinite modifiability
of individual behavior involved in environmental adjustment.

    3. Identical mechanical functioning of sensory organs under-
lies some "cultural universals."

    4. Human beings perceive their bodies alike and generally
hit upon similar analogies of body and environment.

    5. Some cultural "universals" result from physical limitations:
i.e., "rule of the road."

    6. Other "cultural universals" demonstrably result from dif-
fusion of ideas.

    7. Some alleged "universals" cited by psychoanalysts require
further verification.[30]

It is the presence of these prevailing similarities that constitutes
the basis of "essential social unity." In an imaginative phrase Haring
puts the matter this way: "As in a net, each activity is caught and
linked to every other."[31] The essential social unity which appears in
a given population is partly a function of the generic organic stability
of the human species, but it is also a function of the nature of the
"human action system and the similarity of social situations in which
habits are developed."[32] Though he always returns conceptually to
the "action-system" of the species, nonetheless Haring finds tremendous significance in the fact suggested in the following statement
about human learning. "If human beings exhibit similar responses,
such likeness is in consequence of learning. The preponderance of
patterns of behavior learned from his fellows, in contrast to behavior
stereotyped in pattern by organic structure, or learned in individual
trial and error, sets man apart from other species."[33] Learning, partic-

ularly social learning, as cultural behavior, becomes for him a
crowning theme, as the following attempt at a summary statement
of the conditions of social being shows:

> The existence of human societies is conditioned upon (1) in-
> dividuation whereby organisms, physically detached, move about
> and remain together at will; (2) the development of mentality,
> whereby such organisms are able to learn and to go on learning;
> and (3) the learning of similar patterns of behavior, including
> language, so that facility in coordination of activities is possible.[34]

IV.

The problems of structure and order and of behavior and possibility dominate much of Haring's social theory. His answer, in action-
system terms, is twofold: the emergence of habitual responses, by
structurally similar organisms, to continuing and recurrent and relatively similar environmental contexts; but at the same time the
capacity of the human organism, as the unique *human* organism, to
respond to its own internal stimulations, existing as stored energy
or as internalized and stored experiences in the form of symbols.
At one point the idea is expressed in these terms: "Through habit,
behavior is knitted into a sequential whole, in which deviations in
any specific situation are deviations from a usual performance—a
performance . . . which his fellows come to depend upon, an expect-
ancy in behavior which he himself accepts."[35] Playing a lead role in
the emergence and continuity of order is structure. "All behavior is
limited by the structure of the organism."[36] This latter concept may
be spelled out as "the continuity of the organism" or as the totality
of the organism (*i.e.*, "the organism functions as a whole").

This heavy accent on structure and order can easily be misleading.
For novelty competes with uniformity and possibility with routine
in human affairs. In dynamic terms, the action system of the organism
is characterized by creative moments. The idea of the present
experience rupturing the past is suggested in the conception of
growth. Growth is conceived of "as a continuum in which interaction
of genetic factors and environment produce a constantly changing
organism."[37] Growth and development remove some of the stigma
of routine which clings to the dominance of habit. As Haring points
out: "The nature of growth and development and the manner in
which the action system becomes integral, distinctively characteristic
of each human individual, impart to the concept of habit a meaning
vastly more comprehensive than that current in popular usage."[38]

Order and possibility, it may be suggested, form the foci of the ellipse of his action-system theory of human social behavior. Attention is carefully and rewardfully paid to both foci. Thus, in the original mimeographed version of the volume on *Order and Possibility* there appears Miss Johnson's statement: "Man, a highly plastic organism capable of being conditioned in a variety of ways, is conditioned by the cultural situations in which he participates. Personality, the human organism plus experience, is developed through such conditioning. Sociology, then, is the scientific description of those cultural situations which condition the highly plastic human organism."[39] The structure of organism action is not merely a structure of limitation but is one of possibility: freedom *within* as well as *of* the structure.

V.

The roots of social change lie in great part in the response indeterminacy of human beings themselves. There are several sources for this view of human behavior. One is the creativity of internal organism behavior—the incredibly networked storage and retrieval of human acts in endless combinations and permutations. Another is the cortical development so distinctive of the human organism: the phrase "man, the thinking animal," has done much damage by engulfing the fantastic treasures of symbolic behavior in a casual and stereotypical cliche. Another source of the conception of the creative character of human response indeterminacy is the universal fact of human "multi-individual, or pluralistic, response in stimulating situations."[40] Pluralistic response reflects the sequentiality (as opposed to coexistentiality) of human behavior. "All social phenomena," it is pointed out with frequency, "begin, continue, and end in time, a fact that invalidates so-called cross-section studies of social behavior."[41] The action system of human organisms "is unchanged in the range of possible responses, but the sequence or pattern of motions of response is modified and increased efficiency in maintenance of steady internal states results."[42] This may be spelled out in terms of the details of the human nervous system. "In the higher vertebrates, the higher correlation centers of the nervous system function to permit the combination and recombination of simple elements of response into new patterns. The constancy of structural pattern of the organism insures order in behavior; and insofar as its functioning provides the basis of individual modifiability, it introduces an element of possibility which reaches its climax in man."[43]

Herein, then, lies the nature of human possibility, the ultimate form of change: "the fact that the forms of human response are indeterminate. . . ."[44] The major clue here is "the highly specialized integrative function of the neural equipment."[45] In the contexts of multi-individual or pluralistic situations, a similar integrative activity occurs as human beings devise new cultural forms—"invention" is the word Haring prefers—for mediating organism-environment interaction. Cultural forms define behavior kinds, and the reconditioning and revising and reformulation of behavior (a process called learning) *is* social change. This process is of course greatly aided, among other possible variables, by the size of "the culture base" of a given population. Thus, "the more extensive and varied the cultural base and the greater the population participating in a common social life, the more readily are further inventions achieved."[46] The stress on participation in the preceding statement suggests the possibility of the sorting out within a given population (or populations in a given "culture area") of "central" and "peripheral" human beings or groups—a "central place" theory of social change!

Haring, statistician as well as ethnologist and sociologist, is not unmindful of the role of that other ultimate variable of social existence, the aggregate of human organisms generally called a population. There is in his writings a strong suggestion of a tendency toward demographic determinism—or conditioning, a milder and more accurate word—in his social theory. The demographic emphasis is understandable. The action-system approach begins with the structure of responses and response mechanisms characteristic of the species. The organism is forever in focus. People can be located and counted; they can be discriminated and classified; and endless varieties of enumerative tabular sorts are possible. But there is more: the behavior constitution of a society is a function of the demographic structure of the society. However, the reverse is no less true: demographic structure is a function of behavioral constitution. Age-sex composition shifts, occupational and marital changes, ethnic and educational trends, migration patterns and rates, locational quotients of peoples and services, these are indeed variables of social change. In fact, one gets the impression that in a sense the most precise predictive and analytic phases of his social theory center in the population dimension of social existence. "Societal changes," he comments, "are changes in population and in multi-individual cultural behavior, in the composition and constitution of a society as distinguished from the daily comings and goings of individuals that effect no modification in the general outlines of societal patterns."[47]

VI.

In action-system theory the organic and the behavioristic are reciprocals of one another: behavior is a function of the organism, and the organic is responsive to the behavioristic. Further, the organism is identified with structure and order, behavior of the organism with diversity and possibility. Although acknowledging that "the psychological periphery of personal history is never transcended,"[48] just as the organic boundaries of speciate endowment are never crossed, even so, in cultural behavior through learning, man does indeed transcend organic limitations. His newly invented environment—an internal environment of collapsed acts stored as symbols and retrieved as parts of actions, a psychosocial environment, as a contemporary of Haring's put it[49]—provides the human being with his margins and degrees of freedom, his utility and indifference curves, his creative moments. But herein lies a paradox: cultural behavior is itself order, one that "men devise in transcendence of the limitations of their own existence."[50] For man, a creature of cortex dominance, of anticipatory vulnerability and of anticipated gratification, and of all the interactional amplifications of pluralistic behavior, cultural transcendence of organic limitation is a learning, dialectic process, peculiar to him; it is an extraordinary because human treasure.

Cultural transcendence itself roots in the sequentiality of human action. "The motions that constitute behavior are sequential; all former activities are integral in present behavior and pervade future behavior. The more closely the inherent limitations of behavior may be defined in terms of organic structure and function, the more closely will the range be visualized within which deviations or new patterns may be expected."[51] Aided and abetted by "the innovative fall-out" of biological evolution, cultural transcendence adds behavioral continuities to the structural continuities of human genetics: one may speak of social heredity as well as biological, of behavioral genetics as well as biochemical, of cultural as well as genetic transmission of traits. (Whether one really adds anything by the use of this univocacy to the human dialogue on this matter is a moot point.)

And yet, like human heredity, so cultural transcendence *of* time or place is always limited by the facts of human learning *in* a time or place. For "every act, every human relationship, every idea or artifact has meaning only in relation to the cultural resources and social behavior of the people among whom it is observed."[52] The extent to which human responses can become themselves a kind of structure and order far more rigid and limiting than the organic order interested Haring prior to, during, and following the war years. His interest in and interpretations of Japanese culture, for which he is perhaps best known, reflect this preoccupation (not obsessive or blinding, I must add) with the manner in which Japanese culture behavior (perhaps more, perhaps less than other cultures in certain respects) represented this establishment of structure of responses— an order, a culture order, with obvious and powerful limitations and with no less obvious and powerful possibilities. In this connection it is still urgently important to hear these words, written just after World War II: "The Japanese of modern times are products of a dictatorship that foreshadowed the totalitarian police states of the twentieth century."[53] In this tragic light the problems raised by cultural transcendence of human organic limitations can only be seen as very far from solution.

VII.

Finally, we should pay some attention, in terms of an action-system theory of human social behavior, to the overwhelmingly obvious fact that science, being a kind of human behavior, must likewise be seen as an instance of pluralistic and multi-individual behavior; equally imperative is that it be seen in the light of the order and possibility of human action generally. This is an area which it is now fashionable to call "meta-science;" Haring does not use this term, but his approach is no less refreshing or provocative for that failure. "To the scientific mind," he observes, quoting Giddings, "the universe is order; to the practical mind it is possibility. Both minds, however, know that order and possibility are compatible. . . ."[54] However, unlike most pluralistic behavior, science involves enormous critical distinctions: for example, the distinction between "consensus of opinion" and "convergence of facts." Truth in science is not a show of hands. The distinction which separates fact from value and opinion from science also separates science as a kind of cultural transcendence that is always hard to achieve, even harder to maintain, and impossible to match in any other area of human social behavior.

And it is at the same time a forever incomplete behavior. In the Foreword to the original mimeographed version of *Order and Possibility* (1928) occurs this beautiful and apt image of science as a knowing kind of behavior: "As sunshine through tree branches, on the surface of a forest pool, leaves unilluminated shadow-spattered areas of blackness, so there are many phases of human life as yet imperfectly described."[55] As a scientist there is for Haring obvious pleasure in this imagery of an endless adventure which mingles the clear and the unclear, which links the known with the unknown, and which finds in the sequential human search the creative moments of human transcendence.

NOTES

1. Douglas G. Haring and Mary E. Johnson, *Order and Possibility in Social Life* (New York: Richard R. Smith, 1940), pp. vii-viii.

While this chapter was being written, Douglas Haring, in a personal communication, wrote the following comments concerning the volume *Order and Possibility:*

"*Order and Possibility in Social Life* was written (mostly between 1928 and 1936) as a result of a request from Dr. Herbert N. Shenton (Chairman, Department of Sociology at Syracuse, 1927-1937) that Haring and Miss Johnson prepare a basic introductory course for sophomores at Syracuse. Since Dr. Shenton had been brought to Syracuse because of his commitment to the general approach identified with the late Franklin H. Giddings, and both Chancellor Flint and Dean Mosher of the then School of Citizenship and Public Affairs had requested that the Giddings approach be developed at Syracuse because of its orientation to practical issues of public policy, the new book was to present this approach. This was a commitment to Giddings' scientific goals rather than to any system or dogma. Both authors shared a conviction that students of sociology at that time lacked the general background of related sciences whose findings set the limits of 'order and possibility' (Giddings' phrase: see his *Studies in the Theory of Human Society*). Certain principles were developed by the authors to guide their writing: (1) the book would not present a system of sociology, or even pose as sociology per se, but would summarize the background knowledge that students should acquire before taking advanced courses; (2) material from related sciences would be presented in the words of specialists who had contributed richly to their fields; (3) quoted materials should be fundamental papers that had pointed the way for further research, without attempting to provide the 'latest dope.'

"It should be noted that the book does not pose as a text in sociology or anthropology—it does not contain the word 'sociology' except in quoted materials or used as an adjective. When the biological materials in Books II-III were written, anthropology was still relatively innocent of genetics, and members of the biological faculty at Syracuse protested formally to the dean against the inclusion of material on genetics because the authors of the book were not biologists and they had shown their ignorance by quoting material written by a scientist of dubious status (Thomas Hunt Morgan!). The inclusion of material by C. J. Herrick was similarly protested by another colleague on the ground that Herrick's work had been misrepresented. Herrick later wrote that we had made excellent use of his ideas.

"Giddings criticized much of our manuscript and expected to sponsor the book with an Introduction—a plan that his untimely death negated. After his death we made bold to branch out on our own; we accepted his general approach, but deviated from his published works—first on some matters with respect to which he had changed his mind ('I wish I never had coined that phrase, "consciousness of kind;" everyone parrots it and ignores what I wrote'); second, we broke with him on the value of statistical data, from which he had expected to derive sociological 'laws.' But the book remains a restatement of Giddings."

2. *Ibid.*, p. 602.
3. *Ibid.*, p. 603.
4. *Ibid.*, p. 437.
5. *Ibid.*, p. 439.
6. *Ibid.*, p. 189.
7. *Ibid.*, p. 442.
8. *Ibid.*, p. 443.
9. *Ibid.*, p. 8.
10. "Science and Social Phenomena," *American Scientist*, XXXV (Summer 1947), 352.
11. *Ibid.*, pp. 352ff.
12. *Order and Possibility*, p. 353.
13. *Ibid.*, p. 334.
14. *Ibid.*, pp. 346-347.
15. *Ibid.*, p. 285. (Jennings' definition is quoted on p. 288.)
16. *Ibid.*, p. 313.
17. *Ibid.*, p. 313.
18. *Ibid.*, pp. 314, 315.
19. *Ibid.*, p. 316.
20. *Ibid.*
21. *Ibid.*, p. 317.
22. Douglas G. Haring, editor, *Personal Character and Cultural Milieu* (3rd ed.; Syracuse: Syracuse University Press, 1956), p. 23.
23. *Ibid.*
24. *American Sociological Review*, XIV (February 1949), pp. 28, 29.
25. *Ibid.*
26. *Ibid.*, p. 31.
27. *Order and Possibility*, p. 461.
28. *Ibid.*, p. 418.
29. *Ibid.*, p. 624.
30. Based on "Anthropology: One Point of View" in *Personal Character and Cultural Milieu*, pp. 24-28.
31. *Order and Possibility*, p. 623.
32. *Ibid.*, p. 399.
33. *Ibid.*, p. 393.
34. *Ibid.*, p. 398 (presented as a summary of Giddings).
35. *Ibid.*, p. 377.
36. *Ibid.*, p. 381.
37. *Ibid.*, p. 366.

38. *Ibid.,* p. 368. Elsewhere Haring defines habit: "The term habitual here denotes any behavior which an individual has learned to the point of being able to repeat it, whether the behavior be overt or implicit." W. E. Mosher, *et al., Introduction to Responsible Citizenship* (New York: Henry Holt and Co., 1941), p. 104.

39. *Ibid.,* p. ix.

40. *Ibid.,* p. 388.

41. *Ibid.,* p. 445.

42. *Ibid.,* p. 325.

43. *Ibid.,* p. 331.

44. *Idem.*

45. *Ibid.,* p. 371.

46. *Ibid.,* p. 494.

47. *Ibid.,* p. 664.

48. *Ibid.,* p. 712.

49. L. L. Bernard, *Introduction to Social Psychology* (New York: Holt, 1926).

50. *Ibid.,* p. 751.

51. *Ibid.,* p. 375.

52. *Personal Character and Cultural Milieu,* p. 17.

53. "Japanese National Character," *Yale Review,* XLII (1953), p. 382.

54. F. H. Giddings, *Studies in the Theory of Human Society,* p. 127.

55. *Order and Possibility,* p. ix (written by Miss Johnson).

DOUGLAS G. HARING

Chapter III: Bibliography of Writings, 1920–1963. Compiled by the Author.

1920

ARTICLE: Unsigned, "What of Japan? A View from Within," *World Tomorrow,* June and July.

1922–1927

Fortnightly column on Japan, *Buffalo Evening News.*
Numerous articles in religious and missionary journals and reports.

1926

ARTICLES: Three articles on study and teaching of the Japanese language; two in *Japan Advertiser,* Tokyo, March 18, 19. Third, a translation of "The study of Japanese" by Y. Matsumiya, in *Japan Advertiser,* January 22.

FOREWORD: In *Mastering Japanese* by Y. Matsumiya, Tokyo.

REVIEWS: *The Missionary Idea in Life and Religion* by J. F. McFadyen. *Buffalo Evening News,* August 14.

Imagination and Religion by S. P. Cadman. *Buffalo Evening News,* August 21.

Powdered Ashes by Geoffrey Theodata. *Buffalo Evening News,* October 23.

1928

ARTICLES: "The Ethnological Point of View," Syracuse University Summer School *Educational Radiograms,* Syracuse.

"Asiatic Culture and the Social Sciences," *The Critical Crown,* Vol. *1,* No. 1.

1929

BOOK: *The Land of Gods and Earthquakes.* N.Y.: Columbia University Press, 203 pp.

REVIEW: *The Japanese Enthronement Ceremonies* by D. C. Holtom. *American Anthropologist, 31*: 792-795.

1930

Consultant and joint editor, unpublished study conducted by H. N. Shenton for YMCA and YWCA national boards. Confidential.

1931

ARTICLE: "Social Aspects of Marriage," *Syracuse University Lectures,* pp. 40-45.

REVIEW: *History of Japanese Religion* by M. Anesaki, in *The Baptist,* November 14.

1932

REVIEWS: *Konkokyo, Die Lehre Von Konko* by W. Roth. *Sociologus* (Leipzig), Vol. 8, No. 4: 478.

History of Japanese Religion by M. Anesaki. *American Anthropologist,* 34: 158ff.

1933

Statistical section and collaboration on report, *Emergency Employment in Onondaga County,* by M. E. Johnson, H. O. Belknap, and D. G. Haring. Syracuse.

Statistical section, 96 pp. *Sociological Study of Certain Aspects of Onondaga County Emergency Work Bureau,* M. E. Johnson, Director. Syracuse. Privately circulated.

REVIEWS: *Transactions, Asiatic Society of Japan,* Ser. 2, vol. 8. *American Anthropologist,* 35: 190ff.

Culture Contacts of the U.S. and China by G. H. Danton. *American Anthropologist,* 35: 195.

Japan, A Short Cultural History by G. B. Sansom. *American Anthropologist,* 35: 192ff.

1936

ARTICLE: "Young Americans show interest in Things and People of Asia," *Japan Advertiser,* Tokyo, August 26.

ARTICLE AND STUDY OUTLINE: "Social and Cultural Life," *Japan Society Syllabus,* 8th ed., Japan Society, N.Y., pp. 38-52.

1937

REVIEW: *Transactions, Asiatic Society of Japan,* ser. 2, vols. 9-13. *American Anthropologist,* 39: 350ff.

1938

Personnel Record Study, National Youth Administration, New York State, 1938. 1,071 pp. Typed copies in U.S. Government files; not released to public.

1940

Book: *Order and Possibility in Social Life,* jointly with M. E. Johnson. N.Y.: R. R. Smith, 772 + xii pp.

Review: *Suye Mura* by J. Embree. *American Anthropologist, 42:* 680ff.

1941

Nine chapters in *Introduction to Responsible Citizenship,* ed. by W. E. Mosher. New York: Henry Holt and Co.

Suggestions for Teachers, for use with *Order and Possibility in Social Life.* Mimeo. N.Y.: R. R. Smith, 55 pp. (Jointly with M. E. Johnson.)

Letter: "Prof. Haring Argues Another War is Necessary," *Syracuse Post-Standard,* August 28.

Article: "The Position of the Ruler in Japan, a Comparison with certain Polynesian Data with reference to Hocart's Hypothesis of Divine Kingship," *Proceedings, Sixth Pacific Science Congress,* Vol. *IV.* Berkeley. (Paper read in 1939.)

1942

Articles: "Photography is an art," *American Photography,* January, pp. 34-35.

Three articles. *Syracuse Post-Standard,* March 22, August 30, December 2.

1942–1943

Member, Executive Committee, Syracuse University Rumor Clinic which published regular materials and analyses in *Syracuse Post-Standard* to educate citizens in criticism of wartime rumors.

1943

Book: *Blood on the Rising Sun.* Philadelphia: Macrae-Smith Co., 235 + xii pp.

Article: "Note Concerning Integration," *Bulletin, American Association of University Professors,* Vol. 29, No. 5.

1944

Article: "Look Westward, America!" *Bulletin,* Pennsylvania State School Directors' Association, Vol. 8, No. 1: 9-10.

Reviews: *Burma: Gateway to China* by H. G. Deignan. *Far Eastern Quarterly,* 3: 288-289.

School and Church, The American Way by C. H. Moehlman. *Syracuse Post-Standard,* June 27.

1945

ARTICLES: "God-Kings & Cosmic Government," *Christian Leadership and World Society*, ed. by J. Nixon & W. Hudson. Rochester, N.Y.

"Military Government for Japan," jointly with C. J. Friedrich. *Far Eastern Survey, 14*: 37-40.

REVIEWS: *Japanese Militarism* by J. Maki. *New Europe*, July-August, pp. 49-50.

Through Japanese Eyes by O. Tolischus. *New Europe*, July-August, p. 49.

1946

BOOK: Editor and contributor, *Japan's Prospect*. Cambridge, Mass.: Harvard University Press, 474 + xiv pp.

ARTICLE: "Aspects of Personal Character in Japan," *Far Eastern Quarterly, 6*: 12-32.

REVIEW: *Shinto the Unconquered Enemy* by R. O. Ballou. *Far Eastern Survey, 15*: 64.

1947

PAMPHLET: *Racial Differences and Human Resemblances*. Syracuse, 24 pp. (Revised edition of same, September, 1947.)

ARTICLES: "The Administration of Occupied Japan," *Introduction to Responsible Citizenship, Part III*, Syracuse University (Offset, in pamphlet), pp. 202-224.

"Science and Social Phenomena," *American Scientist, 35*: 351-363.

1948

BOOK: Compilation, *Personal Character and Cultural Milieu*. 1st edition, Ann Arbor, 540 + vi pp.

REVIEW: *Kingship and the Gods* by H. H. Frankfort. *Church History*, December 1948.

1949

BOOK: Revised edition of compilation, *Personal Character and Cultural Milieu*. Syracuse: Syracuse University Press, 670 + x pp.

ARTICLES: "Is Culture Definable?" *American Sociological Review, 14*: 26-32.

"Japan and the Japanese" in *Most of the World*, edited by Ralph Linton. N.Y. Columbia University Press, pp. 814-875.

REVIEWS: *Kokutai No Hongi: Cardinal Principles of the National Entity of Japan* by Gauntlett and Hall. Far Eastern Survey, *18*: 298-299.

Prospects for Democracy in Japan by T. Bisson. *Pacific Historical Review, 18:* 418-420.

The Proper Study of Mankind by S. Chase. *American Sociological Review, 14:* 167-169.

1950

ARTICLE: "The Social Sciences and Biology" in *Beitrage zur Gesellungs und Völkerwissenschaft, Prof. Dr. Richard Thurnwald zu Seinem Achtzigsten Geburtstag Gewidmet.* Berlin.

REVIEW: *The United States and Japan* by Reischauer. *Pacific Historical Review, 19:* 450-452.

Shushin: The Ethics of a Defeated Nation by R. Hall. *Far Eastern Quarterly, 10:* 106-107.

1951

CHAPTER: "Way of Life" in *Japan,* edited by Hugh Borton. Ithaca: Cornell University Press.

Idem in article "Japan," *Encyclopedia Americana,* New York.

ARTICLES: "Cultural Contents of Thought and Communication," *Quarterly Journal of Speech,* Vol. 37, No. 2: 161-172. (Address before Speech Association of America, New York, December 1950.) Reprinted in part, *News Bulletin,* Institute of International Education, Vol. 27, No. 3 (1951).

"Re: Ethnocentric Anthropologists," *American Anthropologist, 53:* 135-137.

REVIEWS: *Cooperation Among Animals* by W. C. Allee. *American Sociological Review, 16:* 588.

The Koreans and Their Culture by C. Osgood. *American Anthropologist, 53:* 389-391.

Time of Fallen Blossoms by A. Clifton. *Syracuse Post-Standard,* March 10.

Death of a Science in Russia by C. Zirkle. *Russian Review 10:* 64-66.

1952

MONOGRAPH: *The Island of Amami Oshima in the Northern Ryukyus.* Mimeo. Washington, D.C.: Pacific Science Board, National Research Council (Supporting data for return of Amami Islands to Japan by U.S., 1953).

ARTICLES: "Amami Gunto, Forgotten Islands," *Far Eastern Survey, 21:* 170-172.

"Amami Oshima ni kita Minzokugakusha," *Kyoiku To Bunkwa,* Naze, Vol. 6, No. 1: 29-32.

"Makoto no Amami Oshima wo sekai ni shirasetai," *Nankai Nichinichi Shimbun*, Naze, Ryukyu Islands, January 1, 1952. (This and preceding item in Japanese.)

1953

ARTICLES: "The Noro Cult of Amami Oshima," *Sociologus* 3: 108-121.

"Japanese National Character: Cultural Anthropology, Psychoanalysis, and History," *Yale Review*, 42: 375-392. Reprinted in *Japan Society Forum*, N.Y., November 1953 and in *Japan Christian Quarterly*, Tokyo, January 1954; in *Personal Character and Cultural Milieu*, 1956.

"Speculations on Japanese Communism," *Far Eastern Survey*, 22: 10-12.

EDITED ARTICLE: "Japan Looks Back on the Occupation" translated by V. Otake, a symposium from *Bungei Shunju*, Tokyo, June 5, 1952; *Far Eastern Survey*, 22: 26-32.

1954

ARTICLES: "Comment on Field Techniques in Ethnography; Illustrated by a Survey of Amami Oshima" *Transactions of the New York Academy of Sciences, 16*: Article 3.

"Fanatic," *Encyclopedia Americana*.

"Comment on Field Techniques in Ethnography: Illustrated by a Survey in the Ryukyu Islands," *Southwestern Journal of Anthropology, 10*: 255-267.

"Amami Archipelago: Reversion and After," *Far Eastern Survey, 23*: 156-158.

PAMPHLET AND PHONOGRAPH RECORD: *Japanese Buddhist Ritual*. Ethnic Folkways Library P449.

PAMPHLET AND PHONOGRAPH RECORD: *Folk Music of the Amami Islands*. Ethnic Folkways Library, P448.

REVIEWS: *Social Anthropology in Melanesia* by A. P. Elkin, and *Social Anthropology in Polynesia* by F. M. Keesing. *Far Eastern Quarterly, 14*: 130-132.

The Force of Women in Japanese History by Mary R. Beard. *American Journal of Sociology, 60*: 196-197.

Takashima: A Japanese Fishing Community by E. Norbeck. *Far Eastern Survey, 23*: 176.

1955

TRANSLATED REPUBLICATION: Japanese translation of "The Noro Cult of Amami Oshima" originally published in *Sociologus, 3*: 108-121 (1953); translated by K. Fukagawa, titled "Amami Oshima no norokyo," in *Chireki Kenkyu,* No. 3 (November 1955), pp. 51-62. Kago-shima, Japan. (*Chireki Kenkyu: Studies in Local History.*)

ARTICLE: "Changing Cultural Patterns," Section 12 in article, "Japan," *Encyclopedia Americana.*

BIBLIOGRAPHY: Books on Japan. Dittoed. 34 pp. Syracuse, N.Y.

REVIEWS: *Report from Hokkaido* by George A. Lensen. *Russian Review, 14:* 168-169.

Buddhist Texts Through the Ages by E. Conze *et al. American Anthropologist, 57:* 368.

Understanding the Japanese Mind by James Clark Moloney (N.Y., 1954). *Pacific Affairs, 28:* 176-180.

1956

BOOK: Editor, compiler and contributor, *Personal Character and Cultural Milieu.* 3rd revised edition, Syracuse, N.Y.: Syracuse University Press. 834 and xi pp.

ARTICLE: "Land and Men in Asia, a Review Article," *Far Eastern Survey, 25:* 13-16. (Including review of *Japan—Land and Men, An Account of the Japanese Land Reform Program,* 1945-1951. Ames, Iowa, 1955.)

BIBLIOGRAPHY: *Books on Japan, a Reference List.* Revised edition. Dittoed. 49 pp. Syracuse, New York.

REVIEW: *The Great Loochoo: A Study of Okinawan Village Life* by Clarence J. Glacken (Berkeley, 1955). *American Sociological Review, 21:* 404-405.

1957

REVIEWS: *Japan,* edited by D. Ogrizek, New York, 1957. *Far Eastern Survey, 26:* 111.

Japanese Politics, An Introductory Survey by Nobutaka Ike (New York, 1957). *American Anthropologist, 59:* 921-922.

1958

ARTICLES: "Folklore," *Encyclopedia Americana.*

"Malay," *Encyclopedia Americana.*

"Japan: General culture: family customs." Briefing paper for Institute of Intercultural Studies, Asian Seminar at Manila, 1959. Mimeo.

REVIEWS: *Three Geishas* by Kikou Yamata (N.Y., 1956). *Far Eastern Survey, 27:* 45-46.

Samurai by Saburo Sakai *et al.* (N.Y., 1957). *Far Eastern Survey, 27:* 110.

1959

ARTICLES: "Idolatry," *Encyclopedia Americana.*

"Cultural Patterns in the United States," in *American Foreign Policy, Principles and Problems,* ed. E. E. Palmer. Syracuse: Maxwell School, Syracuse University. (Misdated 1958.)

REVIEWS: *The Population of Japan* by Irene B. Taeuber (Princeton, 1958). *American Anthropologist, 61:* 324.

In Search of Identity: The Japanese Overseas Scholar in America and Japan by John W. Bennett, H. Passin, and R. McKnight (Minneapolis, 1958). *Far Eastern Survey, 28:* 174-175.

1960

ARTICLES: "Legend," *Encyclopedia Americana.*

"Migration, Human," *Encyclopedia Americana.*

"Comment" (On "Case Histories, I. Japan," by David P. McAllester . . . and Kei Hirano Howes, 1957). *Review and Newsletter, Transcultural Research in Mental Health Problems, Special Issue on Schizophrenia,* No. 9 (December 1960), Department of Psychiatry and Department of Sociology and Anthropology, McGill University, Montreal, Canada. Pp. 56-57.

TRANSLATION: (with T. Ishimitsu and K. Nakagawa) "Japanese Studies by American Anthropologists: Review and Evaluation" by Takao Sofue, in *American Anthropologist, 62:* 306-317. Original article, "Beikoku Jinruigakusha ni yoru Nihon Kenkyu, Tembo to Hyoka," appeared in *Minzokugaku Kenkyu (Japanese Journal of Ethnology),* Vol. 22, No. 3, 4: 141-148 (1959).

BIBLIOGRAPHY: Revised and expanded edition, *Books and Articles on Japan: A Reference List.* Syracuse University Bookstore. Dittoed. 92 pp. with more than 2600 entries.

1962

DRAFT BIBLIOGRAPHY: (with Momoyo Ise) *A List of Books and Articles on Ryukyu,* Syracuse, N.Y.: Maxwell Graduate School, Cross-Cultural Project (Part III of Publication No. 4). Bilingual. Mimeo, pp. 25, 46.

ARTICLES: *"Tsumugi,"* *Craft Horizons,* Vol. 22, No. 5: 34-37.

"Shinto," *Encyclopedia Americana,* 1962 edition.

1963

DRAFT BIBLIOGRAPHY: (with Momoyo Ise) *A List of Books and Articles on Ryukyu,* Syracuse, N.Y.: Maxwell Graduate School, Cross-Cultural

Project (Second Revision of Part III of Publication No. 4). Offset, 102 pp. Bilingual.

ARTICLE: "Selected Aspects of Chinese and Japanese Cultural Influences in the Northern Ryukyu Islands," *Sociologus* 13:56-67. (Read at Pacific Science Congress, Honolulu, 1961.)

REVIEW: *Japanese Character and Culture*, edited by Bernard S. Silberman (Tucson, 1962). *Journal of Asian Studies*, 22: 215-216.

OBITUARY: Daniel Clarence Holtom, 1884-1962. *American Anthropologist, 65*: 892-893.

IN PRESS

ARTICLES: "Chinese and Japanese Cultural Influences in Ryukyu: Aspects of Family and Kin Patterns," in *Ryukyuan Culture and Society—A Survey*, edited by Allan H. Smith. Honolulu: University of Hawaii Press.

"Asia via Japan: An Anthropologist's Attempts," in *Approaches to Asian Civilizations*, edited by W. T. deBary. N.Y.: Columbia University Press.

REVIEW: *Ryukyu: A Bibliographical Guide to Okinawan Studies* by Shunzo Sakamaki (Honolulu, 1963). To appear in *American Anthropologist*.

OBITUARY: Earl Hoyt Bell, 1903-1963. To appear in *American Anthropologist*.

UNPUBLISHED

TRANSLATION: (with W. Tsuneishi) Parts IV-V, *Nihon Shakaishi* (*Social History of Japan*) by M. Takikawa. Completed.

"Ethnography of Amami Oshima." Materials in hand (1,500 typed pages) still to be condensed, edited, organized.

Translation and editing of article by F. Yamashita, "Tattooing in Amami Oshima." Completed.

Translation and editing of article, "The Practice of Acupuncture and Moxacautery," by the Association of Doctors of Acupuncture and Moxacautery, Naze, Amami Oshima. Completed.

"A Study of Midwives in Amami Oshima." Completed.

"Kinship and Family Relations in Amami Oshima." Completed; needs some revision.

"Cultural Transformation, Individuals, and Administration." Paper delivered at symposium, Society for Applied Anthropology, 1963. Publication arrangements in process.

Part Two

Dimensions of Sociological Thought

WILLIAM C. LEHMANN

Chapter IV: Sociological and Cultural-Anthropological Elements
in the Writings of Johann Gottfried von Herder

THE STUDENT of the history of ideas and of the emergence of the social
sciences would profit from reexamining the work of Johann Gottfried
von Herder (1744-1803) from the point of view of the manner and
extent to which he anticipated ideas and findings of an empirical
sociology, social psychology, and cultural anthropology of a much
later date. It is the purpose of this study in historical analysis and
value-interpretation to point out some of the lines of his thinking and
exploration in this field.[1] In doing so we shall emphasize the essentially empirical and historical character of his investigations while at
the same time calling attention to the manner in which he was ever
intent upon relating his world of fact to a world of meaning and
values, upon discovering the significance of his historical *facta*—a
favorite expression of his—from the standpoint of some kind of end-
goal in human history.[2]

Herder did most of his writing in this field in the late 1770's and
in the 1780's, after having become fully conversant with the contemporary as well as the less recent philosophical and historical
literature of France, England and Scotland and, of course, of his
native Germany. A younger contemporary of Hume, Robertson,
Gibbon, Adam Smith, of Diderot and his fellow encyclopedists, and
of Lessing as well as Kant, by whom he was introduced to the natural
sciences and to philosophy—he was in many ways a child of the
Enlightenment in all its literary, philosophical, scientific and quasi-
historical reaches, while in other ways he looked forward toward the
romantic and other forms of the historical movement of the nineteenth century. We shall have to give at least passing attention to
these historical bearings of his thought.

First, we need to comment briefly on the seeming paradox in
Herder's thinking of a pretension to a severe empiricism and a
persistent quest for meanings, values, and ultimate ends, particularly
in their religious implications. Herder did pretend, at least, to be

35

severely empirical in his approach to the study of man, society and history, and on the whole he was remarkably successful in adhering to his ideal. His data for analysis were not ideas, values, moral preferences, speculative hypotheses, or "revealed knowledge," but the *facta* of history, of observation and experience, the historical records, things "known for a certainty or at least accepted on the best available authority as fact." (W.XIII, 15,290)

> On earth . . . I shall not be looking for angels of heaven, none of which my eyes have ever seen; rather, I shall be content to seek earth-dwellers, men brought forth, borne, nourished, tolerated and at last lovingly taken back into her bosom by our good mother-earth. (W.XIII, 15)

"Metaphysical speculation" he would shun as being but "flights into the blue yonder that will seldom lead to [one's] goal." (W.XIII, 9) A priori reasoning he strongly disapproved of; in fact, for any kind of philosophical abstraction he had so strong a dislike that he has been charged with lack of philosophical depth and hence ill-qualified to write a "philosophy" of history.

The metaphysician, he holds, has an easy task. He has merely to posit a certain conception of human nature and out of this to develop whatever can be developed, wherever and in whatever circumstances it may be found. But the philosopher of history cannot build on a mere abstraction. He must work with numberless facts, which he must, however, bring into some kind of order if he is to escape the danger of arriving at illusory results. (W.XIII, 290)

In his historical investigations he hopes to "ply close to the shore of the established or at least reasonably authenticated *facta* of history, keeping mere surmises in a separate compartment," as it were. And again, in his own picturesque language,

> God's course in Nature, the thoughts the Eternal One has actively revealed in his handiworks, these are the sacred books in the reading of which I may be but a poor apprentice, indeed, but the characters of which I have at least faithfully tried, and will continue to try, to spell out. (W.XIII, 9)

This figurative language—and in a sense it is more than merely a pungently ironic figure of speech—suggests the other side of the coin. Herder has a philosophy of history, and it is distinctly a religious one—in his own definition of that term, of course. It is religious in at least a fourfold sense: the pursuit of *ultimate* meaning in human history; belief in a divine purpose of overruling Providence in all the affairs of life and the universe; an identification of the laws of nature with the laws of God; and finally, a sense of the challenge that events and situations ever present to free men most fully to realize life's potentialities in the given situation. Not only does he accord religious beliefs, practices, institutions and leaders a prominent role in human society and in cultural history, as will be shown later, but his criteria of evaluation of socio-historic events and movements are, at bottom, religious ones, because his conception of *Humanity*,[3] which includes the ideas of enlightenment, rationality, human dignity, the sacredness of human personality, and the common good, are in his mind essentially religious conceptions. There is a strong teleological element in his thinking that offends the modern ear. Moreover, his very style of writing reveals a proneness to poetic and religious rapture, and to moralizing and often political criticism, where a later generation would wish he had held to calm description and analysis and had confined his conclusions to those following logically and of necessity from the facts in hand.

However, two observations are in place on this matter. First, this religious element, including his teleological conceptions, represents his evaluation of the facts, never their description of explanation, except as men's moral and religious beliefs, their personal convictions, loyalties and religious aspirations influence their conduct and in that sense, but only in that sense, themselves help to make history. Any kind of supernaturalistic intervention in history and in the affairs of men is completely ruled out. In the second place, Herder's very conception of religion itself is so thoroughly humanized—secularized if we will—that on the surface it would appear incompatible with his training in theology and with his lifelong connection with the Lutheran church, and in a high official capacity at that. In fact it would be hard to find anywhere in his day a mind more secularized and humanized—only Hume, Kant, and Goethe would be serious rivals; Voltaire or Diderot would be an unfair comparison.

That this combination of the religious and the secular is not a contradiction of terms can perhaps be best demonstrated by two examples. "Out of the dust of the four corners of the earth [meaning out of many races, adapted to many climates] was Adam formed, and the breath of the spirit of the wide earth [meaning, from the context, the contact of many cultures] was breathed into his nostrils." Herder freely interprets the Genesis account without any sense of violence to the Sacred Scriptures. (W.XIII, 261)

And again, not "in the fulness of time" nor "according to the prophets," but simply, "Seventy years before the fall of the Jewish state," he observes historical-mindedly,

> a man was born there who effected an unexpected revolution at once in the realm of human thought and in the customs and institutions of men: Jesus. . . . The few speeches of his that have been preserved bespeak a genuine *humanity*. . . . The revolution he effected was a spiritual one. (W.XIV, 290)

It rested not on a belief but on a faith and aimed at a community governed not by a secular arm of rulers and teachers but on "a spirit of brotherhood." (W.XIV, 297f.)

> What he demonstrated by his life and sealed by his death was pure *humanity*, even as he preferred the name "son of man" for himself to every other. . . . In reverence I bow before thy noble figure, thou head and founder of a kingdom so lofty . . . built on principles so vital . . . earth could barely contain it. (W.XIV, 290ff.)

If this is "humanization," "naturalization," "secularization" of religion, he was equally emphatic in his attack on that other element of the sacred, the sacred cow of tradition.

> Tradition is in itself an excellent thing, a device of Nature indispensable to the human race; but as soon as it puts shackles on our thinking—whether in practical political institutions or in education—stifles the progress of human reason and hinders all human improvements demanded by changed times and circumstances, it becomes the veritable opium of the spirit, for the whole society as well as for sects and individual men. (W.XIV, 89)

Man, Society and Culture

But to turn now to the substance of our thesis, three of Herder's basic tenets must first of all be clearly set forth: (1) Man is by nature and in historical fact a *social* being, living always and everywhere in society, his life being, even in its most individual aspects and in its highest spiritual reaches, still in society. (2) This life of men in society is in all of its aspects essentially cultural, deeply rooted in tradition transmitted from generation to generation by means of symbolic communication, never merely individual-psychological in character. (3) In all this, man is nonetheless an animal, ever subject to the laws of his biological as well as his spiritual being and ever in need of adapting to his earthly geographical as well as to his human, cultural, spiritual environment. A biological organism, yes; but with what a difference!

First, then, as to the fact itself of the social character of human experience. "The natural state of man is the state of society," he insists in opposition to Hobbes—he might have lifted this statement directly out of Montesquieu or Adam Ferguson.

> Conceived in the lap of love and nursed in her bosom, reared at the hand of fellow humans from whom he has received a thousand unearned benefits . . . he is formed in and for society; without it he could neither come into being at all, nor become genuinely human. (W.XIII, 320)
>
> Much as man may presume to create things out of himself, as it were, he is still completely dependent on others for the development of his capacities. (W.XII, 343)

What this means for Herder in detail can be only briefly illustrated here. He has, first of all, a very clear conception of the structure of the human community—of the nature and role of social, political and religious institutions, for example—and of group and functional differentiation within the community; this even though he does tend frequently to minimize institutional roles for fear, apparently, of their frequent tendency to dam and divert rather than channel and aid the free flow of the spirit. Particularly is this true of his treatment of the church and of government. Family, kin and folk groups, the *Volk* or nation, all come in for due consideration, as do also status groups or *Staende* such as the feudal hierarchy of nobility, freemen, serfs and slaves, and the clergy. So also do voluntary associations such as the guilds, which latter he views as particularly constructive forces in advancing the arts and sciences, in developing a spirit of solidarity, in promoting higher standards of integrity, in aiding political emancipation from feudal tyrannies, and in fostering a spirit of liberty. (W.XIV, 486ff.)

Only a few of these, central in Herder's thinking, can be slightly enlarged upon here. Most fundamental of all groups and governing institutions is for him clearly the family, conceived chiefly in terms of the small, intimate conjugal group but also in terms of the larger consanguine group, to use a modern terminology. (W.XIII, 375, 384, 387) Clearly recognizing but not greatly emphasizing varieties and continuous change in the form and to a lesser extent in the functions of the family in society, he makes its functions primary in every sense: reproductive, affectional, protective, educational, religious, "governmental" and traditional—this latter in giving a sense of genetic continuity and solidarity and in cementing the bonds of union with one's kin and ancestral group, which in turn leads naturally to the formation of the *Volk* or tribal-national group. This genetic or kin and ancestral-group solidarity, particularly in early society, is for him so fundamental as to take on an essentially religious character, religion becoming, therefore, a primary dynamic force in early society. Because of the close-rootedness of the family in man's biological nature and in the necessities of race-maintenance—in the sexual urge, bisexual reproduction, protracted and helpless infancy—and because of its universality and functional primacy, Herder attributes to the family a "natural" character which he denies to the state, for example—perhaps consciously giving the term "natural" at once a biological and a "rational" meaning. "Father and child relations were often the first government in the world, and with a shepherd people [like Israel] they long remained the strongest ties." (W.XII, 107) Perhaps this explains why he neglects somewhat variations in familial institutions.

Closely related, then, to the family role, he would undoubtedly place next in order among societal structures and functions the *Volk* or the tribal-national organization of society which of course represents not a functional division within the community but a form of organization of the total community, itself based on blood, soil, tradition, with a resulting common and yet distinctive culture. This "folk" (a really inadequate but convenient translation) is conceived, first of all, quite independently of the state as a political organization. It is much more than merely a population group attached to a particular territory, but rather is a genetic group, in the main, with a sense of solidarity based on the features mentioned and with a uniqueness of character considerably influenced by geographic factors. On all levels, consanguine-familial, tribal and national, it is a principal object of group loyalty and on the higher levels, at least, becomes a principal source of inspiration and a principal means of education toward *humanity*. In this function, only to a minor extent politically conceived, he sees it taking on an importance that almost rivals that of the family. (W.XIII, 375ff., 383f.)

Religion and religious institutions, the third among these basic elements, are viewed both structurally and functionally, and they are given a large place in his thinking, as already indicated. First of all, he distinguishes religion in its essence very sharply from both its doctrinal and its ceremonial and organizational expressions. Neither *Lehrmeinungen* nor the church as an institution is of that essence. Religion is a matter not of belief, primarily, but of attitude, of faith, of life-orientation, of the direction of the human will. It is

> a matter of conviction, that is our innermost consciousness of that which we are as a part of the universe, of what we are to be and have to do as human beings; dependent on no mathematical demonstration for its standing or its effectiveness. [And again] What have *Lehrmeiningen* to do with religion? Religion is . . . a matter of sentiment, of one's innermost consciousness . . . a matter of loyalty, reverence, obedience, confidence, faith. (W.XX, 133ff., 140, 159, *et passim.*)

Herder recognizes historically the existence and development of myths, creeds, *Lehrmeinungen*—the latter belonging for him really to philosophy—of rites, ceremonies, churches and other religious organizations; he grants their necessity if religion is to become effective in the lives of ordinary men and in the community; but he views them as mere *Didaskalia* (W.XX, 149), teaching devices, crutches for weak mortals, walking devices by which children learn to walk. And here as elsewhere he fears any institutionalization that threatens to confuse means with ends and to become a hindrance rather than an aid to the spirit. How meaningful, for example, were the "three innocent words, father, son and spirit" in the teachings of Jesus; but behold "what turmoil, what persecutions, what scandals" have resulted from men's attempt at their institutionalization! (W.XIV, 299. See also X, 117, 457-63)

But even so, creed-encased and institutionalized or not, religion remains for him most intimately tied up at once with the life of imagination, the rise of poetry and art, and, in early society at least, as we have seen, with family and blood ties, with ancestral solidarity and loyalty. Along with language it is among the oldest traditions of mankind, the mother of nearly all other traditions. (W.XIII, 463) In fact, he sees in it one of the deepest roots of culture and a principal bond of human society. (W.XIII, 387ff., 459ff.) He recognizes that through the church—particularly in the Middle Ages—positive charitable, educational, artistic, socializing, humanizing functions as well as more purely religious ones were performed in human society. (*Ideen*, Bk. IX, ch. v; Bk. XVII; Bk. XIX, chs. i and ii) All the more pity "that the course of religious worship has everywhere tended to become a matter of manipulation by priestcraft"; and even more that the reports on religion among primitive peoples "have so seldom been made by men of wisdom and a deeper understanding of human nature." (W.XXXII, 145ff.) Religious conceptions everywhere take on an essentially anthropomorphic character, reflecting the culture of which they are a part.

Herder is not completely neglectful of the structure and functional role of government and the state in the social order, though his almost violent antidespotism, antimilitarism, antiimperialism, and antistatism generally, as a political attitude, would seem to prevent his placing them in proper perspective, to blind him to the positive functions of government, and to give him a biased view of political institutions generally.[4] Moreover, his terminology is, to an American reader at least, confusing. The "state" may mean organized political authority, or it may mean society in its totality, especially in its advanced, complex stratified forms, regardless of political authority. "Government" (*Regierung*) likewise sometimes means political governance of the ruling, law-making body in the state, but often he makes it mean little more than what we today would call "social control," establishing orderly relations.

"The human race has never been without government," he is heard to say; "it is as natural to man as his very origin, as the bonds which unite individuals into kin and tribal groups." (W.IX, 313) "Government is everywhere a necessity," and its ideal functions are clear. "The chief purpose of all human communities and societies is mutual aid and security; the function of the state should be no other than this natural order, namely, to enable everyone to become and be that to which nature has destined him." (W.XIII, 385). In more primitive communities, as likewise under the Mosaic theocracy—in fact, wherever government remains relatively "invisible and silent," where the ties that bind men in societies appeal chiefly to "sentiment" as a motive of interaction, "with a free national law sitting, as it were, on an invisible throne,"—there this ideal is measurably realized. (W.XII, 117; XIII, 375f.) But where is this realized in modern societies? "Whoever expects enlightenment from the state as such, whoever expects 'the public' or even the rulers to guarantee him *Bildung* and happiness, (W.XIII, 453) speaks a language that is for me quite beyond understanding." (W.XIII, 433) "All our political institutions are aimed not at making men more virtuous and in themselves happier, but only at making them more useful to the state and at using them for its own not always virtuous ends." (W.XIII, 468) The most useless or dysfunctional of all political institutions he finds in hereditary monarchy or rather, in the hereditary principle applied to any form of government. He cannot see it as serving any useful purpose or having any historical justification. The hereditary monarch who claims to rule "by the grace of God" confesses by this very pretension that he can lay little claim to rule by any merits of his own! (W.XIII, 376f., 384ff.) That even despots have sometimes lent support to the arts and sciences does not change the principle, and it remains true, for Herder, that creative work in these fields has occurred chiefly in free republics. (W.IX, 375f., 383f., 327)

He does recognize great varieties in forms of government and finds them ever in flux but without much order in their sequence. He gives considerable attention to the feudal structure of society in the Middle Ages, politically as well as socially and economically, and finds its economy resting almost entirely on serfdom and slavery, its social structure on a status system that amounts practically to caste, and its political structure on despotism. And the church participates fully in all of these.

How Man Becomes Human

If a man is born into society and yet is not at birth a social being, in fact not in any significant sense human at all, how then does the human animal become a person, a member of a community, in fact a really *human* being at all? This question we shall let Herder answer himself without comment on our part.

This most helpless of all animals, with an infancy longer protracted but also more highly teachable than other animals,

> is born in the very bosom of society. . . . He learns language from his parents, and with language he receives knowledge, information, laws, rites. The concepts of his father, the teachings of his mother, he imbibes as with his mother's milk, just as he unconsciously imitates everyday customs, exercises, the youthful games of his playmates. (W.IX, 313)

And since his parents are to him ever the most wise, the most good, the most perfect, "their impressions are most deeply stamped upon the hearts of children," especially in the period of their "innocence and simplicity."

> All education must spring from imitation and exercise, by means of which the model passes into the copy; and how can this be more aptly expressed than by the term "tradition"? But the imitator must have the powers to receive what is communicated and communicable, and to convert it into his nature as the food by means of which he lives. . . . So that the education of our species is in a double sense genetic; genetic inasmuch as it is communicated; organic in that what is communicated is received

and applied. Whether we call this second genesis of man *culture,* from the cultivation of the soil, or *enlightenment,* from the action of light, is of little import; the chain of light and culture reaches to the ends of the earth. . . .

There is, therefore, an education of the human species; since everyone becomes human only by means of education, the whole species lives solely in this chain of individuals. True, should anyone maintain that the species is educated, not the individual, he would speak unintelligibly to my comprehension, for species and genus are only abstract ideas except so far as they exist in individuals. . . . [On the other hand] were I to confine everything to the individual and deny the existence of the chain that connects each to others and to the whole, I should run equally counter to the nature of man and his evident history. For no one of us becomes man by himself; the whole structure of his humanity is connected by a spiritual birth, by education, with his parents, teachers, friends, with all the circumstances of his life, and consequently with his countrymen and their forefathers, and finally with the whole chain of the human species, some link or other of which is continually acting on his mental faculties. (W.XIII, 345ff., Churchill translation)

This unity of the individual with his group, with the community of common habitat, culture and purpose, is, however, never such as completely to absorb the individual; individual initiative and responsibility remain. Nonexistent except in the community, he yet remains an individual; ever a child of tradition, he is yet ever, at least potentially, creative; "status as such merely makes puppets," only "personality makes for worth and merit [and leadership]" (W.XVI, 121) Leadership is not a fiction, a mere epiphenomenon, but is a historical and psychological reality. "God achieves his ends on earth only through chosen, elite men. . . ." (W.XIII, 351)

The Nature of Culture

From these and many other passages that might have been cited it becomes obvious that Herder had a clear conception of culture, a conception differing but little from that of the modern cultural anthropologist. Its elements are learned behavior on the basis of a distinctive biological equipment; symbolic communication by means of various kinds of meaningful signs; habits and customs that come to be combined and crystallized into institutions; and transmission of these from person to person, from generation to generation, from people to people, though never without some modification in the process, the whole becoming in time, if not disturbed by external influences, built into a more or less unified functional whole, unique in some measure for every folk or people.

BIOLOGICAL AND GEOGRAPHIC FOUNDATIONS

Once all this is clearly understood we can proceed without fear of misunderstanding to a brief consideration of the third of Herder's basic tenets laid down above; namely, that whatever else man may be he is and remains still an animal with animal drives and animal needs and ever under necessity of adapting to his geographic and organic as well as to his cultural and spiritual environment.

We need not review here the first three books of the *Ideen,* where he addresses himself most directly to this problem, except to remind the reader that Herder reveals a most remarkable familiarity with the latest findings and hypotheses in astronomy, geology, geography, biology, comparative anatomy and comparative psychology, and points out their significance for human adaptation and for any evaluation of man's place in nature—even such seemingly remote matters as the nonvertical position of the earth's axis, for its bearing on seasonal variation, length of days and nights at various latitudes to which man in turn must learn to adapt himself, (W.XIII, 27f.) or the difference in shape of hand, position of eyes, etc. between man and ape, or differences in skin texture between different races of men, as these affect adaptation to environment.

The two remaining books of Part I of the *Ideen* are still given to a study of the human animal, in its cultural capacities, to be sure, but still in biological and biopsychological terms. This is not a matter of biological analogy or biological preliminaries, merely. Discussed are such matters as the social implications of bisexual reproduction and of the sex urge; the nature of human infancy and man's greater learning capacity; (W.XII, 153f., 282f.) his struggles for existence as an animal in a generally hostile environment and his superior capacity to adapt to varieties of climate, food resources, etc.; and also such matters as man's capacity as an animal for rational reflection, language, art, freedom of choice, political organization, *humanity*, religion and the hope of immortality, such as are not found in any other animal.

> Even our rational powers are closely connected with the organization and health of the body, and all the passions and drives of the human heart are inseparable from our animal tempers. These

are all facts of nature that no hypothesis can upset nor scholastic argument destroy. . . . (W.XIII, 276)

A special point needs to be made here of the meaning and significance he attaches to *Klima* and to the geographic environment generally in relation to society and culture.

First of all, his grasp of the facts themselves of geography as the human habitat is most remarkable, and his understanding of the functional relations between land, topography, natural resources, bodies of water, seasonal variations and varieties of climate, on the one hand, and modes of subsistence, population density, migration and contacts of peoples, manner of life, symbolism of communication and even of human mentality and physical differentiations of the human type, on the other, represents for all the limitations of his position, perhaps his most distinctive contribution to the scientific study of this subject as further developed from Blumenbach, von Heeren, Humboldt, and Ritter down to Ratzel and Bruhnes. Next, the recurrence of this subject throughout his treatise and on all levels of cultural analysis deserves pointing out. Most of all, the manner in which he conceives the intricacy of interdependence and the complexity of cause and effect relations, both statically and dynamically and working forward and backward, of the geographic and the cultural factors is most remarkable indeed.

If, finally, he undoubtedly overdoes the direct influence of climate on physical man and his physiological functioning and would seem in fact to overstress the whole subject, three cautions at least need to be observed: (1) He insists that

> *Klima* does not compel; it inclines rather: it provides the intangible disposition that may indeed be observed in the total pattern of the customs and manner of life of peoples deeply rooted [in a given soil], but it is almost impossible to trace this in the isolated details of the picture. (W.XIII, 273)

(2) While he does indeed offer a careful definition of the concept *Klima,* he yet slips frequently into a very broad if not indeed vague use of the term to include, besides meteorological factors, not only the total geographic environment and its man-made modifications, but even the cultural environment, the general cultural milieu in which an individual or a people may find itself. (3) It can hardly be held against him that he still held to the notion of the inheritance of acquired characteristics in his evolutionary thinking. Under this conception any such environmental impact would become cumulative as it cannot in our present-day understanding of the matter.

DYNAMIC ASPECTS

No aspect of Herder's thought is more engaging than his dynamic approach to the study of human society and culture. Man and his institutions appear to interest him more in terms of their becoming than of their being. "The whole human race, even the inorganic world itself, is subject to one law of change" he assures us. "One and the same law of nature . . . reaches from the sun and the whole world of suns to the minutest activity of man . . . a balance of forces in periodic stability and order." (W.XIV, 233f.) "Nothing in nature is static; everything presses and moves ever forward." "Inventions never occur all of a sudden"; "they usually arise out of inconspicuous beginnings."

> The spirit of change is the very core of history; and whoever fails to single out and make this spirit the principal focus of his attention . . . is like a blind man who sees men as but trees and feeds not on the kernel but on the husks of history. (W.XXXII, 27)

Such change he sees and frequently attempts to trace in every aspect of culture and society: in the life of the individual himself, of course; in language, in the development of poetry and other forms of literature; in religious conceptions and practices; in modes of subsistence, in family life, in property, in all economic and political institutions; in art, science and technology; in tastes and modes of thought. In fact, change, orderly change, and continuity in change in every sphere of life, are a central theme in Herder's thinking.

The question at once arises whether or not his conception of change is an evolutionistic one. Not all change is, of course, evolutionistically conceived. Evolution implies orderly, gradual change with continuity in the process and by the operation of forces inherent in the process itself rather than extraneously imposed. It implies an "unfolding," as it were, or a development of structures or functions or potentialities already present in an embryonic or elementary form in an earlier stage and in a more or less consistent direction, usually in the direction of increasing differentiation and complexity, though not necessarily in the direction of ideal perfection. Does Herder's conception of change meet these tests? Let us see.

> Not revolutions but evolutions [*Evolutionen*] constitute the quiet course of our great mother Nature by which she awakens slumbering forces, develops embryos, rejuvenates premature age and often transforms even apparent death into new life. . . .

If we are to ascribe a single purpose to Nature on earth, this can be no other than a development of her potentialities in every form, genus and species. These evolutions proceed slowly, often unnoticed, and usually periodically. . . . (W.XVI, 117f.)

This sounds like the language of biology, but from the context it is clear that it is only in part so intended. He continues:

Man, a rational, moral and political creature, lives by means of his inherent powers and potentialities, in an almost unlimited environment. His rational development is so interdependent with that of his fellow men, his moral development with the conduct of others, his capacity to become a free being, by himself and in the company of others, is so closely interlinked with the modes of thought, with the approvals and the active undertakings of the many, that outside of such associations he is like a fish on dry land, like a bird trying to fly through space without the air to support it. . . . Individuals, classes [Staende], corporations, whole societies and peoples are irresistibly carried forward by the stream of change [and no powers on earth can] turn today into yesterday, or . . . permanently stem the tide of a progressive development of our common humanity. (W.XVI, 119f.)

On the more elementary—shall we say on the more anthropological—level, Herder makes these remarkable observations:

All creation is engaged in warfare and is under the sway of antagonistic forces. . . . Every kind is engaged in mutual struggle with each other, because it is itself under pressure. It must protect its own hide and provide for its own subsistence. (W.XIII, 60f.)

Man is not exempt from this struggle, but

has been able to achieve a place of dominance over other creatures only by the application of an almost godlike art of cunning and power [which his superior endowment made possible]. How he did this is the story of his culture, in which even the most primitive people have a part; and the most interesting part of the history of mankind it is. (W.XIII, 62)

In this development, no invention has ever come into being all at once or was in its inconspicuous beginnings what it is now. The inhabitants of Germany were but a few centuries ago Patagonians; but they are such no more. (W.XIII, 254)

Incidentally he remarks that most of these arts by which man achieved dominance he learned from the animals themselves; at least most of his education was acquired in outwitting the strength, fleetness and cunning of animals, be it in the chase or in their domestication, so much so that "the history of his culture becomes in large measure *zoological* and *geographical.*" (W.XIII, 62)

In applying these obviously evolutionary conceptions to the concreteness of history, Herder is always cautious. In his youthful writings he frequently spoke of cycles of development and used the biological analogy of childhood, youth, adulthood and senescence; but later these are largely discarded. The currently accepted stages of hunting, nomadic, agricultural and commercial economies he accepts only with considerable reservations. He is fascinated by the problem of origins but skeptical of our ability ever to arrive at the beginnings of social institutions. (W.XXXII, 94f.) The course of history seldom follows straight, uniform lines; rather we find "many a jutting," "rough-edged corner," like the sharp zigzags of a turbulent mountain stream, seldom "the gentle meandering of the brook through the meadow," much less a straight course. Yet "each step nevertheless leads us forward: such is the progress of culture among families, tribes and whole nations." (W.XIV, 233f., 236-38)

On the higher levels of civilization he gives increasing play to the rational factor, to man's capacity, individually and collectively, for self-direction toward a set goal. Never is this social evolution conceived in completely mechanistic terms, but evolution as above defined it still remains. (W.XIV, 235ff., 249)[5]

Like most of his contemporaries, Herder does not distinguish clearly between evolution and progress; that is, between a morally indifferent "natural history" and progressive change in the direction of ideal perfection or at least of some value goal, with the aid of human volition. He certainly does believe in the latter, but without denying the reality of the former.

History is irreversible; a return to a golden age of the past, as with the Greeks, or to the primitivism of a Rousseau, is a "poetic fiction, impossible in the very nature of the world and of time." The invention of agriculture, of houses, of cities, has put an end alike to "cannibalism and acorn diets," to "cave-dwelling," to "killing the poor stranger" merely because he is a stranger. "Trade has brought peoples closer together" and has tended to "minimize murder, oppression and deceit" as patterns of human interaction. "Every advance of the useful arts" has made for the "security of property," thereby "of necessity

laying the foundation for further advances of culture and *humanity*."
(W.XIV, 236-42, summarized)

If this might still be considered morally neutral, the following definitely is no longer so:

> In the meantime reason proceeds in its course in the race as a whole . . . and enlarges its domain on earth. It is no idle dream [Schwaermerei] to hope that rational, reasonable and happy men will one day dwell wherever men dwell at all: happy not only through their own individual effort, but through the cooperative reason of the whole fraternity of mankind. (W.XIV, 249)

The validity of this conception and of this his faith is not our present concern. How his view differs from those of most of his contemporaries, space does permit us to discuss. We do find further evidence here of Herder's effort to follow the *facta* of history as far as they will take him and beyond that to be guided by his faith in a world of values—the values of rationality, propriety [*Billigkeit*], human dignity, *humanity*—in the firm belief that the pursuit of this ideal will prove a principal factor in its own historical realization.

CULTURAL KINETICS

So much for what might be called Herder's social and cultural dynamics; his "kinetics," that is, his conception of causal factors in or "driving forces" behind such change, can be only summarily dealt with here. It is too intimately involved in his whole conception of history and society for separate treatment in any detail.

"Vital forces in man himself are the driving forces of history. . . . Necessity and circumstances have usually been the driving force that has made man what he is." (W.XIV, 69) Among human inventions to which he attaches particular importance in the further development of culture are language; the invention of writing and printing; the domestication of animals; the establishment of agriculture with resulting permanence of settlement and property in land; man-made alterations in the geographic environment; modes of warfare and military enterprise (usually viewed in an unfavorable light); religious beliefs, practices and organization (viewed both constructively and negatively); political institutions (their constructive influence generally minimized); migration, voluntary and enforced—most of these involve a rational factor in some measure.

On social causation more broadly viewed, these observations will be particularly pertinent: social causation is always multiple causation, never single-factor causation; the most important factors are very often intangible ones that are difficult to trace in any given situation; causal factors are never interventions in a "supernatural" sense and seldom extraneous in any sense. Rather the historian has but to attempt to

> grasp and judge the total situation in all its interrelationships and will never try to explain a real situation or event by a nonexistent one. . . . [One] has but to attempt to see what is there, and as soon as he has done this the causes usually become apparent, why the situation or event could not have been other than it actually was. (W.XIV, 145)

CULTURAL-ANTHROPOLOGICAL APPLICATIONS

Whatever was Herder's position among the founders of this branch of study, including human geography, certainly these things can with confidence be said about his contributions in this field. First, by his own testimony and from other evidence, he read literally almost everything in print, at least in German, English and French, and somewhat less, no doubt, in Italian and Spanish, in the large field of travel, ethnography, accounts of the customs, laws, institutions and culture in general of particular peoples—primitive, early historical and "civilized,"—and also almost everything of any consequence in the field of *Kulturgeschichte* and *Kulturphilosophie*. From Adair through Lafitau to Ulloa among the better known, from Cranz through Gumilla to Zimmermann among the less known—they all appear in his writings, as do also the classical historians, the folk-tales in Ossian, Percy's *Religues* and the Cid, Goguet, Robertson, Kames and Monboddo—and of course, in red letters, Montesquieu.

Next, he passes in review, however briefly of necessity in many cases, practically all the known "primitive" or otherwise "remote" peoples, attempting, so far as sources and space permitted, their physical, their mental or psychological and their cultural characterization, noting their material culture traits and modes of subsistence, their peculiar customs, family organization, religious beliefs and practices, in some cases the peculiarities of their language, often their contacts with other peoples, their inventions and cultural borrowing, and in the case of the more advanced ones their contributions to our own civilization—always viewing all of them in their regional or more local geographical setting, their *Klima* generally, and attempting to trace the influence of these on the physical being, the mentality and the material and nonmaterial culture of given peoples. Very few "primitive" peoples, from the Chuckchees and the Kamchadales to the Tahitians, the Iroquois, the Caribs, and the Fuegians are missing; nor those of the more advanced peoples from the Mongols to the Berbers, and the Sudanese, from China to India and Peru. Only the tribes of inner Africa, little known because "beyond the reach of European cannons,"[6] that is, the slave-traders and other exploiters (W.XIII, 232), are poorly represented.

That his characterizations are often crude from the standpoint of present-day knowledge, his explanations occasionally faulty in the light of modern science, is much less important than the fact that he attempted them at all, and attempted them from a definite viewpoint, geographical, anthropological, cultural-historical, *universalgeschichtlich*. And there is the further fact to be noted that he was keenly aware not only of the limitations of his sources but also of the danger of projecting one's own preconceptions and prejudices into his characterizations of little known peoples, easily mistaking his canvas for objective reality.

A few illustrative examples of his observations and characterizations must suffice here. On the matter of physical race he makes these interesting observations:

> Some students have, for example, thought fit to designate as "races" four or five divisions of mankind originally made on the basis of regions or even of color differentials. I see no reason for such designation. "Race" implies a distinctive line of descent, that either does not exist at all or that includes the most diverse "races" of every color in each of these regions. For every nation is a people with its own national character and its own language. To be sure environment has impressed upon each its distinctive character—sometimes clearcut, sometimes as but a faint veil— but without destroying the original ethnic character of the nation. This applies even down to families, and the transitions are as mutable as they are all but imperceptible. In short, we find on earth neither four nor five races nor any other number of exclusive varieties. Color differences shade into one another; structures serve the genetic character, and on the whole we have, in the last analysis, but shadings of one and the same painting, as it were, that extends over all regions and periods of time. Their study belongs, moreover, not so much to systematic *Naturgeschichte* as to the physical-geographic history of mankind. (W.XIII, 257f.)

On the material culture traits of primitive peoples, including the most backward, this characterization must suffice:

[South Sea Islanders, abundantly provided by nature, can live in rather idyllic comfort with but few inventions.]

> They were strangers to fire; the mildness of their climate rendered this unnecessary. . . . In his less temperate climate . . . the New Hollander pursues his kangaroo and his opossum, shoots birds, catches fish, eats yam-roots; he has combined as many modes of life as the range of his crude creature-comfort demands. So with the New Caledonians and New Zealanders. . . . They had . . . the rudiments of all the arts by which the most civilized peoples on earth have perfected their cultures. . . . (W.XIII, 311f.)

On inventions in the Near East, particularly in the Mesopotamian Valley, and their permanent contributions to our civilization, he lists no less than fifty-two items, some of them specific, such as bread-making, spinning, weaving, sewing; and some broader categories, such as agriculture, wine-culture, agricultural implements, or even so broad as "trade with the use of weights and measures" and "political arrangements." (W.XIV, 42f.)

In illustration of his nonmaterial cultural characterization, only this item:

> The Hindoos are the gentlest race of men. They are reluctant to injure any living thing; they honor whatever brings life, and their nurture is the most innocent of foods, such as milk, rice, fruits, and such healthy vegetables as their Mother Earth provides them with. Their body-form is most perfect and most beautiful . . . and so is the original cast of their mind and, discounting the pressures of superstition and slavery, their manner of life. Moderation and composure, gentleness of feeling and a quiet depth of soul characterize their work and their recreations, their ethics and their mythology, their arts and even their patience under the most extreme yoke ever imposed on men [by fellow-man]. (W.XIII, 222; cf. XIV, 27ff.)

The following are but a few examples of his observations, insights, and generalizations in this field:

Herder takes frequent cognizance of the role of migration and contact of peoples through conquest, trade, etc. in cultural characterization.

Peoples who have long lived in the same environment without

invasion from without manifest a more harmonious, integrated-culture than where there has been invasion, uprooting, etc. (W.XIV, 9f.)

He recognizes a similarity of processes of assimilation, acculturation and often demoralization resulting from modern trade and colonial contacts, on the one hand, and from comparable contacts of peoples that occurred in early times, on the other. (W.XIII, 284ff.)

He recognizes, specifically, the disruptive effects, morally and even physically—racially—of too sudden a transplanting of individuals or groups from one *Klima* to another; and similarly of the foisting of a dominant culture from outside upon a native culture without allowing time for a gradual assimilation.

On the other hand he recognizes the broadening humanizing effect, under favorable conditions, of contact between cultures, travel abroad, etc.

Backward peoples are usually found in secluded, mountainous, or otherwise remote, inaccessible regions—whether forced there by more progressive tribes, or remaining backward by reason of such isolation.

Many inventions are made in imitation of animal life or of natural processes: boat—fish; spears and arrows—long bills or powerful beaks of birds; poisoning of arrows—poisonous serpents or insects; human huts—beaver shelters. (W.XIII, 313)

Dreams play a powerful role in the life, culture and control systems of many primitive peoples.

Primitive mentality is seen as characterized by more pronounced sensory imagery than the mentality of *Kulturvoelker* and weaker in abstract imagery; the explanation being, however, a cultural, not a biological, one.

The deep psychological impact of shamanism is fully recognized: people who have courageously faced the fiercest tigers will still tremble in their whole being at a shamanistic representation of a tiger. (W.XIII, 303f.)

Of the many prevailing fallacies in ethnographic accounts and interpretations he attempts to correct, we can name but these: Reports of men with tails and like simian survivals he finds completely without confirmation. Authentic instances of such things as excessive hairiness, highly simian facial contours, etc., he explains as abortive freaks without genetic significance, just as likely to occur in the least simian as in the more nearly simian races, as he views them. Great cruelty, torturing, live scalping, etc., especially among the American Indians, are viewed as expressive not of native savagery, but of an understandable reaction against robbery of their ancestral soil, threats to their tribal existence, etc. Reports of anthropophagy are greatly exaggerated; and cannibalism where it does occur, shocking as it appears to us, is viewed as not an expression of gross brutality, but as a rite aimed at enhancing tribal spirit.

Mistaken conceptions, both of fact and interpretation, in the light of present knowledge, of course remain, but these are neither surprising nor in themselves significant.

Some of the implications of these observations for Herder's rating as a cultural anthropologist are obvious enough. Among the less obvious ones we may note particularly the following: (1) Herder is definitely interested in the material culture of the peoples he studies, but even more so in their mental and spiritual character and characterization. (2) His clear recognition of the material base of the culture of a given society, in adaptation to the conditions of its material environment, never leads him into an economic determinism in any absolute or exclusive sense. (3) The "folk" or national character of a particular people in its political and spiritual reaches is much more clearly recognized by him than by most later anthropologists who often concentrate on culture traits, trait complexes and overall patterns while losing sight of the "soul" of a people. (4) Herder brings to bear upon his study of culture an evolutionistic and an adaptation-to-the-total-environment point of view, without sacrificing historical objectivity, that would alone make him prophetic of many of the most significant developments in this field in the century that followed. (5) And finally, there is a quest for rationality, for an ever-increasing rationality in the culture of peoples, that lends a peculiar character to his work.

THE SOCIOCULTURAL BEARINGS OF LANGUAGE

An important subject of sociocultural inquiry and reflection on Herder's part was his concern with the nature, origin and development and cultural functions of language. Much of his discussion is of course of interest chiefly to the linguist; but much also is of vital concern to our present inquiry.

First of all, Herder here as elsewhere traces his subject back to its biological roots. He notes the rudimentary forms of vocal as well as other kinds of communication among animals, particularly among the apes, and the superficial similarities thereto of human vocalization; but he quickly proceeds to note the fundamental difference. In contrast with the purely instinctive and rationally meaningless vocal communication of animals—sometimes even their imitation of human vocalization—human language soon becomes symbolical, a matter of meaningful sounds and other gestures rationally derived, and therefore presuming a capacity for rational reflection totally absent even in the highest of the apes. The moment the ape should begin to reflect, he observes, the ape would cease to be an ape. No ape has ever been known to utter a single meaningful word that might have served as the foundation for human speech.

From this Herder proceeds to the observation that it is exactly language, that is, the use of meaningful symbols in conceptualization and communication, that first makes man truly human. It is not only the basis of all social life; it is the *sine qua non* of all rational development itself in man though the two, sociality and rationality, cannot be separated in time.

More than that, Herder finds language—not only language in the abstract, but languages in their particular forms and varieties, in their varying vocabularies, metaphorical and idiomatic expressions, even in their grammar and in their finer nuances of expression—most closely related to the life of imagination and feeling, to the origin and development of poetry and song, of religious adoration, invocation and supplication as, for example, in "the spirit of Hebrew poetry," in the ballads and folk-tales of early peoples.

This leads him to the further observation that the evolution of language and of languages is most intimately connected with the evolution of culture itself, from its most primitive to its most highly developed forms—oceanic, oriental, occidental, independently and in contact with one another. Vocabularies, metaphors, modes of expression, the predominance of nouns over verbs, or vice versa, come to reflect elements in the physical environment—"things" like sword or plow, beasts of burden or prey, warlike or peaceful habits, the prevailing social and cultural values of a people. Just how far Herder's observations rest on a sound empirical basis it would be hard to say. Certainly some of them remain speculative, "psychoanalytical;" some rest on secondary sources not necessarily always reliable. After all he was only twenty-six when his prize essay on *The Origin of Language* was written. But in the course of the further development of his ideas on the subject he came to know a number of languages intimately and a goodly number of others, including several oriental and other "out of the way" languages, at least to some extent.

Finally, he associates language and languages most intimately with the facts of human society as distinguished from culture merely—that is, with social differentiations, especially status differences; with tribal consciousness and nationhood; with the spirit of the *Volk*. Here, too, he attempts to trace a parallel and an interdependence between the age, the development, the contacts of given societies, on the one hand, and the development and characterization of their language, on the other, as the instrument at once of communication and of national self-expression.

It goes without saying that Herder here stands in diametric opposition to those who would see language as a divine, that is a supernatural creation. His theory is naturalistic, humanistic, cultural-historical. (W.V, 5ff.; *Ideen*, Bk. IX, chs. 1-3; *Ueber die neuere deutsche Literatur: Fragmente*)

WISSENSSOZIOLOGIE ANTICIPATED?

Intimately related to his realization of the essentially social bearings of language are his insights into the dependence of thought, thought-ways and knowledge upon the experience-world, the social situation, the historical circumstances in which men and peoples find themselves. Language itself is viewed as not only a necessary vehicle of communication but also as in many ways giving shape and character to the thought to be communicated. Prevailing occupation and life-habits relating thereto have a marked influence on mental imagery and patterns of thought. The rise and characterization of poetry and other forms of literary expression are intimately related to stages of culture, to military habits, to the spirit and customs of chivalry, etc. The urban dweller is more rationally conscious than the hunter, the shepherd or the tiller of soil. The necessity of meeting unfamiliar situations provokes reflection. Ecclesiastical dominance over the consciences of men tends strongly to affect not only men's freedom of conduct but also their freedom of thought, in fact to suppress all modes of thought not convenient to the ecclesiastical scheme of things. Even such historical accidents as his own early visit to France, and his casual meeting with the young Goethe, which soon of course resulted in the most intimate intellectual cooperation, do not go unnoticed in their influence upon their thinking—and, we might add, on German thought generally.

What Herder everywhere maintains as a general thesis—that the national character and present culture of any people are a product, though never in a rigidly deterministic way, of "original" ethnic character, geographic environment, mode of livelihood, tradition, the general stage of cultural development, the political constitution, etc.—he does not hesitate to apply also to the development of language, mythology, religious ideology, literature, art, science and philosophy. In the case of Egypt, for example, he sees the development of astronomy and geometry as an outgrowth of their climatic, geographic and peculiar economic situation—irrigation farming, for example. In the case of the Greeks he becomes even more explicit in attributing the rise of Greek philosophy, Greek moral and political conceptions, drama, historical writing, etc., to their political constitution, to events and tendencies of their socio-political experience world, to the presence of a public receptive to new ideas and of critical audiences to stimulate and otherwise to influence literary productions, and not a little to the genius of the Greek language itself. Particular ideas, moreover, and particular literary forms and other thought forms are seen as ever dependent upon previous formulations or inventions. (*Ideen*, Bk. XIII, ch. vii, par. 2)

Underlying Philosophy and Basic Method

It remains to attempt a summary statement of Herder's underlying philosophy and of his basic method, many elements of which have already found expression in the above analysis.

Herder was, by his own testimony and from other evidence, strongly influenced by Newton, Locke, Leibnitz, Spinoza and Shaftesbury. His near-identification of God and Nature, bordering at times on the pantheistic, and his identification of the laws of nature with the laws of God, denying all miracles and every other "supernaturalistic" intervention in human affairs, place him, for practical purposes, very nearly in the camp of the deists, though he would, perhaps, never have admitted as much. "The whole history of man is a purely natural history of human forces, actions and drives in time and place." (W.XIV, 145) "In the physical world we never count on miracles; we note laws that we find everywhere operative unchanging and orderly . . . should we except the kingdom of man with its forces, changes and passions from this chain of law?" (W.XIV, 144) "The God whom I seek in history must remain the same that he is in nature, of which man is but a small part." (W.XIV, 244) He is not a "ghost" or a "spook (*Poltergeist*) that every man may make the patron saint of his own petty follies" and he neither performs miracles to spare men the consequences of their own misdeeds (W.XIV, 244) nor does he "bind the hands of man other than by what he has made him to be in his essential nature." (W.XIV, 210) Such an identification of a religious and a naturalistic view of the universe would appear on the surface to be either a contradiction of terms or a kind of lip service merely to prevailing philosophical and theological orthodoxies. In reality the explanation probably lies chiefly in his very broad conception of the "laws of nature," in his view of human nature itself, and in his view of the Deity principally as an object of worship, reverence, devotion and love, rather than as the creator and upholder of the universe. Certainly he has absorbed much of the philosophy of the seventeenth and eighteenth centuries, but never to the point of conceiving the universe in terms merely of mechanism, much less in terms of materialism. His philosophy is a thoroughly humanistic one that brings him into opposition not with religion but with many of the dogmas of the church—in fact, with its whole underlying theology—and makes him a severe critic of its perversions and abuses of power. It opens into a conception of religion more pervasive, more deeply spiritual, and more challenging than the traditional one, with a deeper faith in life's possibilities and a stronger sense of the brotherhood of all men.

As to his method, we have already seen that Herder aimed, at least, always at being empirical in his approach to reality; while at the same time he was ever in pursuit of the significance of his *facta* under review, in terms either of their wider relationships or of ultimate values. Perhaps he best puts this matter himself when he says, "We generalize in order to particularize; but we cannot particularize without having some kind of whole in mind." (W.XXI, 252) The "particulars" are for him of course the concrete data of authentic history and of observation upon the contemporary scene; the "whole," without reference to which these *facta* must remain meaningless, is *Universalgeschichte*, the life, the progress, the destiny of the human race, humanistically conceived, naturalistically and we might say monistically interpreted, and finally evaluated from the standpoint of his idea of *humanity*, rationality and faith in an overruling purpose in history.

It should be remarked here that Herder is ever on guard—almost prophetically so in view of the frequent violation of this principle in later German thought—against the so-called "group-fallacy." All groups, from the smallest combinations of men all the way to the state itself, have no existence whatever and can wield no influence whatever except in and through the individuals who constitute them. Institutions of any kind are but names for a collectivity of men and for certain collective actions of a larger or smaller number of individuals. In themselves they can do nothing, they can wield no influence whatever. Herder repeats this caveat over and over again.

Herder was most widely read—astonishingly so—in the whole

field of literature, culture-history and *Kulturphilosophie*, in what was then known as *Universalgeschichte*, in the literature of travel and ethnography, as well as in the physical sciences. He was, as we have been well reminded[7] thoroughly at home in seven literatures: Hebrew, Greek, Roman, French, English, German and the international literature of the Middle Ages. He read critically, understandingly and with historical imagination and psychological insight, though not perhaps always without his own philosophical, political and religious biases; and he assimilated what he read to his own philosophy and to the particular purposes of his writing from time to time. He was not, of course, a man of intensive research in the modern sense of the word, nor was he in a position to do "field work" among the ethnic groups or in the culture areas about which he wrote; but he informed himself as best available resources permitted on the subjects on which he wrote, examined critically the findings and interpretations of other laborers in the field, imaginatively extended his observations from the known to the heretofore little explored, and ventured such explanations as seemed to him best in accord with the known facts and with reason. This done, he announced his findings with little regard to convention or to the prevailing orthodoxies.

And that is perhaps all that needs to be said concerning his underlying philosophy and his basic method.

It remains to observe, as we bring this survey to a close, that literally dozens of engaging questions still press in upon us—on the personal, historical, philosophical and circumstantial influences that entered into the shaping of Herder's thought; on his personal relations with his fellow-workers; on his educational, religious and other nonliterary activities; on his methods of work; on the consistency or sometimes, no doubt, inconsistency of his ideas; on the originality of his thought and on his place in the history of thought generally, to say nothing of his purely literary activities, his relation to the Enlightenment, on the one hand, and to the Romantic Movement on the other. With one exception all these questions will have to be passed up here except, again, as a few of them will be ever so lightly touched upon in our concluding paragraphs on "the cross-fertilization of culture."

We cannot refrain from a few observations on Herder's relations, both personal and intellectual, with two of his greatest living contemporaries. Mention has already been made of his having been a student of Kant's at Koenigsberg. Kant publicly recognized the promise of the young Herder, and Herder in turn had, at first, only words of the highest praise for his former master. Later though, in consequence chiefly, no doubt, of what seemed to be the needlessly severe tone of the Koenigsberg philosopher's review of Part I of Herder's *Ideen* on its appearance and an only slightly less caustic one on Part II, relations between the two became severely strained. Not only did Herder make repeated direct attacks upon Kant's *Critique of Pure Reason,* on his rationalist treatment of religion, and on his speculative tendencies generally; but the critical reader will find abundant evidence in many places, especially in his later writings, of only slightly veiled indirect attacks on his former teacher. Thus Clark, at least,[8] holds that the violence of Herder's attack on monarchical government, despotism and statism generally is intended chiefly as a backhanded slap at Kant's statism, and perhaps more accurately at Kant himself.

But this should not blind us to the fact that, at least in his earlier years, Herder was strongly influenced by his former teacher. The stimulus to his interest in the natural sciences—astronomy, physics, geography, comparative anatomy—is clearly traceable to Kant's lectures on *Naturgeschichte* and to some of his writings in this field. Herder himself makes repeated mention of Kant's *Natural History and Theory of the Heavens.* And his evolutionary theory— cosmic, biological and cultural—may well derive from this and other writings of Kant much more directly than from Leibnitz and other thinkers. Kant's various reflections on *Universalgeschichte* can hardly have been without influence on Herder, whatever their differences in point of view.[9]

Herder's relations with Goethe were in the main pleasant as well as constructive. Goethe early sought out Herder on the latter's return from France, and a friendly, helpful, cooperative relationship was soon established between them at Weimar. Goethe was greatly pleased with the earlier installments of the *Ideen* and frequently offered suggestions and constructive criticisms in the further progress of this, Herder's *magnum opus.* He was often helpful as well in his personal and family affairs. Herder in turn contributed not a little to Goethe's earlier labors in the field of natural science and to the development of his psychological understanding and interpretations. But he also harbored a measure of jealousy toward his obvious superior, and in the last decade or more of his life there was a "progressive deterioration of their friendship" that led finally to an all but complete break between the two. This no doubt resulted in part from differences in taste, temperament, political philosophy and general outlook on life. Goethe was a thoroughgoing Hellenist,

Herder much the Hebraist; Goethe had strong aristocratic leanings, while Herder was strongly democratic in feeling; Goethe sought expression most effectively in dramatic poetry, of which Herder had but little appreciation.[10] But it must not be forgotten that in personal and family matters Herder was always a rather "difficult" person.

A Study in Cultural Cross-Fertilization

Mention was made above of Herder's interest in cultural processes. May we observe in conclusion how perfectly he exemplifies in his own intellectual history the process of cultural cross-fertilization. Born of humble family in a remote parish in East Prussia, he had his roots both in the piety and in the orthodoxies of German Lutheranism and thus very deeply indeed in the German *Psyche*. The discipline of his Prussian schooling and the tutelage of Kant and others at Koenigsberg confirmed him in these tendencies on the spiritual side while yet arousing his skepticism of their doctrinal bearings. Deeply influenced by Leibnitz and Spinoza, he otherwise found little in the intellectual life of his own country, including the German Enlightenment, to satisfy his inquiring mind and instead eagerly turned to the West where he found both nourishment and inspiration. Newton, Locke, and Shaftesbury, as we have already seen, deeply influenced the philosophical bent of his mind. A passion for his beloved Ossian, to him a veritable Homer of the North, and an enthusiasm for the return to nature of a Rousseau, were his chief aesthetic inspiration, broadened and deepened on the more intellectual side by Shakespeare, Richardson, Lessing and Winckelmann. Hume, Robertson, Gibbon and Voltaire, and the author of "that noble monument," *The Spirit of Laws,* were his chief culture-philosophical and culture-historical inspiration. But a host of others—Young's *Night Thoughts,* Thomson's *Seasons,* Sterne and Fielding, Adam Smith, Ferguson, Kames and Millar, Fontenelle, Mably, Helvetius, D'Alembert and Diderot, to mention only the most outstanding—were almost as much at his fingertips as Klopstock, Winckelmann, Lessing, and later Schiller and Goethe. Above all there was his six months' sojourn in France (1769) at the youthful age of twenty-five, with personal contacts with most of the leading literary figures of the day—a revolutionary experience in his life and thought, reaching far beyond the impressions merely of the moment.

All of these he absorbed into his basically German being, and yet none of them did he accept wholly or uncritically. Rousseau was divine, but Herder refused to follow him into his primitivism as an escape from the realities of political and civilizational problems. Montesquieu—*"Spirit of Laws!"*, "Natural and civil history of law!", "Oh, that we had another Montesquieu!"—and yet in the same breath he finds the historical basis of his generalizations woefully lacking, his classification of forms of government naïvely oversimplified. Hume, that "fine man of learning," "worldly wise," "most philosophical of historians," he almost idealized; yet his *Natural History of Religion,* too, he finds not without shortcomings. The Encyclopedists he finds broadly illuminating and politically provocative, but he cannot accept their near-materialism nor, fully, their politics. Only Ossian passes completely unscathed, except for gnawing reservations about Macpherson's authenticity. Without destroying his basic idealism all these intellectual-cultural contacts gave his mind a historical cast and a fundamental realism that, joined with his native background and his environment at Weimar, including his intimate personal and intellectual association with Goethe, powerfully stimulated his imagination and deepened his insights into human nature and social and historical processes.

From an historical rather than a merely biographical standpoint, we find embodied in Herder's thought the most forward-looking elements of the Enlightenment, stripped yet of its most glaring defects, a development and a mighty forward surging of the idea of evolution as distinguished from the more conventional idea of progress that was to dominate much indeed of nineteenth century thinking, uncompromised yet with an unhistorical "comparative method;" a combination of moral and religious idealism with yet a strong historical realism that in a marked way enriched nineteenth century thought, including German historical and sociological thought, and might have done so even far more had his voice found a stronger echo there than it actually did.

Even so, we have the testimony some forty years after the appearance of his major work of perhaps the ablest mind of the time and of the man better in a position than any other living person to judge of such a matter, that this work had "an almost unbelievable impact [*unglaublich gewirkt*] on the national culture of Germany." He observes that the appearance of the *Ideen* in French translation in 1828, a work then "almost forgotten, its mission accomplished," evoked nostalgic memories in his own mind, and he expresses the hope that in this new dress it may in some measure continue that influence among so broadly cultured a people as the French nation.[11]

NOTES

1.   Major portions of this paper were previously published in slightly different form in *Sociologus* (Berlin: Duncker und Humblot), vol. x, pp. 17-33. All Herder citations are from the Suphan edition of his *Saemtliche Werke* (Berlin, 1877-89, with later supplements), abbreviated "W" for *Werke*, with volume indicated. The translations are my own except when followed by "Churchill translation" to indicate T. Churchill's translation of the *Ideen* as *Outlines of the Philosophy of the History of Man* (London, 1800), a volume that became accessible to me only late in the preparation of this paper. Of the many secondary sources consulted, space permits mention of only the following: J. M. Werner, *Herder's Voelker-psychologie unter besonderer Beruecksichtigung ihres religionsphiloso-phischen Blickpunktes* (Duesseldorf, 1934); Benno v. Wiese, *Herder: Grundzuege seines Weltbildes* (Leipzig, 1939); R. T. Clark, Jr., *Herder: His Life and Thought* (Berkeley and Los Angeles: Univ. of Calif. Press, 1955); Richart Noll, "Herders Verhaeltnis zur Naturwissenschaft und dem Entwicklungsgedanken" in *Archiv fuer Geschichte der Philosophie*, XXVI (1912-13), pp. 302-38); and Wolfgang Harich, "Herder und die buerger-liche Gesellschaft," prefaced to his *J. G. v. Herder, Zur Philosophie der Geschichte: eine Auswahl in zwei Baenden* (Berlin, 1952), vol. 1, pp. 7-82. While the last named essay is, as this author sees it, vitiated by an attempt to force Herder into an alien Marxist frame of reference, it is yet scholarly and offered many suggestions for this paper.

G. A. Wells' *Herder and After: A Study in the Development of Sociology* ('sGravenhage, Mouton, 1959) came to this author's attention only after this manuscript was ready for the press. It introduces much that is not touched upon here and makes a significant contribution in pointing to elements in the thought of his contemporaries, in Germany and else-where, that were hostile to a reception of Herder's ideas; but it calls for no changes in the present paper. The present author disagrees with Wells' interpretation of Herder's religious ideas as affecting his historical explana-tions.

2.   Critical analysis might well reveal deeper epistemological signifi-cance in Herder's appeal to the "facta" of history than appears on the surface. Certainly "facta" were for him more than merely tangible raw materials to be picked up like pebbles on the beach and run through a sieve of scientific or philosophic analysis. Even their perception involves a measure of generalization, and Herder clearly realized, in a kind of anticipation of modern *Wissenssoziologie,* that we see only what we have been conditioned by historical experience and the social situation in which we find ourselves to see. And historical "facta" were for him always processual rather than merely static entities. But since Herder was not interested in epistemological refinement, our purpose will be best served by seeing in his appeal to "facta" merely an insistence upon an empirical, historical approach to the problem under study and a protest against "metaphysical" abstractions, the confusion of religious doctrines and valuations with history, and a merely speculative approach.

3.   To indicate a distinctive meaning attached by Herder to the word *Humanitaet* while yet avoiding the clumsiness of retention of the German

form, we shall translate it as "humanity," but always in italics. For Herder's own definition of the term, see W.XVII, 137f.

4. Herder's political attitudes do not, of course, directly concern us in this paper, much as they may interest us in a personal way. Inasmuch, however, as his hatred of despotism, militarism and political chicanery of every form undoubtedly affected the objectivity of his analysis of political institutions and the role of government in society, a footnote illustrating the extremes of his position may be in place here. It is known that his section on government in the *Ideen* was cast and recast a number of times, but even the gently restraining hand of Goethe could not prevent the appearance of passages like the following:

> Who has given Germany, who has given cultivated Europe its governments? War . . . conquerors have ever been in possession of the land, and whatever changes have occurred [since the great barbarian conquests] have been decided by revolution, war, conspiracy of the mighty, always, that is, by the law of the stronger competitor. . . . Forceful conquests took the place of right, and only with the passing of the years, or as our politicians call it, "by a silent contract," did this become law: such a "silent contract" is, however, in this case nothing but an arbitrary assumption of power by the stronger and a giving of what he is unable to defend by the weaker, an enduring of what he is unable to avoid. . . .
>
> . . . Whether Nimrod is a killer of beasts or, later, a subjugator of men, he remains in either case a predatory hunter! . . . Thus has our old earth been subjugated by violence and her history becomes a canvas of manhunts and conquests; almost every local boundary, every new epoch, is delineated in the book of time, in the blood of human victims and with the tears of the oppressed. The most famous names in the world have been those of slaughterers [*Wuerger*] of the human race, crowned hangmen or seekers after a hangman's crown. (W.XIII, 377ff., 452ff.)
>
> In great states hundreds are made to go hungry in order that one may carouse and surfeit in luxury; ten thousand are pressed [into military service] and driven into the arms of death in order that a crowned fool—or even though he be a wise man—may indulge his personal fancies." (W.XIII, 340)

From the slavery and serfdom of the feudal despotism in medieval Europe "no relief was to be expected from Rome," that is, from the church. "Her own servants had joined with others in the rule of Europe, and Rome herself rested on the backs of a multitude of mental and spiritual [*geistliche*] slaves. . . ." Cultural possessions were used to enslave rather than to liberate the mind. Her rites and establishments were turned into "a magical despotism of souls to which the common herd [nevertheless] did homage on their knees, castigating themselves with rope and lash, doing penance [like beasts] with hay in their mouth. . . . The hierarchy had stifled freedom of thought with its fulminations and had crippled all noble enterprise with its yoke. The patient sufferers were promised their reward in another world, while oppressors were assured remission of their sins on their deathbed in return for their testamentary bestowals

upon the church. The kingdom of God on earth was placed in pawn."
(W.XIX, Ch. vi)

5.   Herder's contributions to, or more accurately anticipations of, nineteenth century theories of biological evolution, or what is generally known as Darwinism, have been both exaggerated and underestimated. He was not a biologist in a position to undertake first-hand investigations in this field. He was indeed greatly interested in, and possessed of a broad knowledge of botany, zoology, comparative anatomy, including such limited knowledge of "the record of the rocks" as was then available. In this he was stimulated first by Kant's lectures but followed chiefly the leads of Linnaeus, Buffon and the Swiss physiologist Haller. He also contributed not a little to Goethe's earlier biological and evolutionary studies. But he could have no knowledge of the actual mechanisms of genetic transmission, such as genetic cell structures or modifications therein which might produce variations that, surviving through successive generations, could bring about the actual transformation of species or the appearance of new kinds [of which Darwin also was ignorant—editor's note]. And while he made not a little of the principle of struggle, as we have seen, and of the survival of the better adapted in this struggle, he never, to our knowledge, made this a basis of favorable biological variation in a phylogenetic rather than merely in an ontogenetic evolutionary sequence; and this, of course, constitutes the very core of modern theories of biological evolution.

On the other hand, to call Herder's conception of biological evolution merely that of a general "metaphysical process," as does Clark (*Op. cit.*, pp. 304f. and 312)—a kind of speculative extension of Leibnitz's monadology applied, with a time element added, to living kinds—or to be misled by his occasional use of the term "creation" or by his general teleological frame of reference seems to this writer equally short of the mark. Herder did clearly hold to a naturalistic view of the emergence, *in some way*, of kind out of kind, usually of the higher out of the lower, in a biologically genetic sequence, however he may have conceived or failed to conceive the actual process itself of such emergence. (See, e.g., W.XIII, 23, 27f., 177f.)

6.   This is typical of Herder's injection of political barbs into otherwise nonpolitical discussion.

7.   Clark, *op. cit.*, p. 301.

8.   *Ibid.*, pp. 316ff. Also, ch. xii.

9.   See *ibid.*; see also, W. Harich, "Das Kantmotif im philosophischen Denken Herders," in his *Rudolf Haym und sein Herderbuch* (Berlin, 1955), pp. 163ff.

10.   Clark, *op. cit.*, pp. 184f., 414-22.

11.   Goethe, *Werke* (Weimar, 1903), Bd. 41(2), S.345, or any other edition of his *Rezensionen* for 1828-29, on the occasion of a French translation of the *Ideen*.

JOHN W. BENNETT

Chapter V: Myth, Theory, and Value in Cultural Anthropology:
Questions and Comments

THE ASSUMPTION underlying this informal essay is as follows: since
the social sciences have a reflexive character (subject is also object),
they will contain elements of perspective which can give meaning
and direction to research as well as distort research results when
used without awareness. Since the human reality is always in large
part a mental interpretation or construction of empirical existence,
social science must utilize such perspectives in order to provide an
understanding of the data. Social facts do not speak for themselves;
or only to a limited extent. This situation creates methodological and
epistemological problems for the social sciences which cannot be
solved, only continuously debated and explored. In light of the comprehensive objective of anthropology to reveal the variety and depth
of human existence, it should be clear that disciplined subjective
interpretation will be a most important methodological function
within this field.

I shall discuss the following aspects of this general situation: the
descriptive element in cultural anthropology which permits the ready
conversion of data into "stories" which in turn can become converted
into myths and images of man (hence suggesting some of the reasons
for anthropology's relative popularity with the general reader); the
relationship of these "mythic" qualities of anthropological research
to theory construction and the notion of "a culture;" and the role
of anthropology in the formation of values and social objectives, and
the effect of the rise of scientific method upon this function.

I.

When we compare sociology with cultural anthropology from the
standpoint of their public image, it is possible to say that of the two,
sociology has acquired greater acceptance as a source of means for
achieving social ends, while cultural anthropology has captured the
greater popular interest. The sociologist is sometimes painted as a

67

routine fact-gatherer or a jargoneer who obscures the familiar facts of everyday life with complicated and repetitive language. The anthropologist, deserving or not, seems to attract more glamor: he is seen as an intriguing, eccentric figure who is able to enjoy exotic experiences. His work, odd as it is, carries a special type of prestige not usually accorded the sociologist, based on the fact that the anthropologist has the unique authority of "he who was there," while the sociologist is merely in our midst.

However, it is the sociologist who is listened to more often than the anthropologist when specific problems or reforms of contemporary social life are concerned. Probably many more sociologists than anthropologists appear before congressional committees and are more frequently found in jobs in applied fields. The sociologist, though lacking in glamor and a certain prestige, nevertheless is "in;" he is well on his way to becoming an accepted functionary. Undoubtedly he will come to be at least as well accepted as the psychologist during the next decade.

For all we know the anthropologist *qua* anthropologist will never attain acceptance of this kind. If he works consistently with modern society he runs considerable risk of being assimilated into the sociologist's role. If he continues to work abroad, or in historical problems, he will retain his glamor but will probably not achieve much recognition as a formulator of answers to pressing social problems. He will be read, and probably ever more widely, but not for the specific advice he may have to offer. At the same time, the popularity of anthropology seems to grow if we may take as one index the fact that more and more paperbound books in the field flow from the presses (a recent count, made by the writer, of such books in anthropology and in peripheral fields such as Old World prehistory stopped at a conservative sixty-two; for sociology and its peripheries, twenty). Newspapers readily print accounts of anthropological discoveries and findings; magazines of mass circulation, like *Life*, feature "The Story of Man." Clearly anthropology has captured an important share of the popular interest—or at least it has found acceptance as a fascinating subject. The names of the great anthropologists seem more widely known than those of the sociologists, and most of those sociologists who have received popular recognition equal to that of certain anthropologists couch their knowledge in an evocative, discursive form more similar to anthropological writings than sociological.

On the whole, anthropologists themselves conceive of their field as a science while acknowledging an affinity to the humanities in the form of historical interests and in the creative activity of field work. In spite of this, criteria of evaluation of anthropological writings are scientific. That is, they concern the verification of factual data and the relationship of fact to theory or generalization. Of course, anthropologists seem less consciously preoccupied with methods than sociologists, who probably have made too much of methodology; but on the whole the anthropologist resembles the sociologist in his quest for scientific accuracy and reproducibility. In the face of this dominant concern for the rigor and dispassion of science, it is necessary to ask why anthropology has continued to retain a popular side. This is to be found, I believe, in the *narrative* quality of anthropology: its "story" or its ease of conversion into stories.

Of course, narrative is not the only factor; plain facts and even theories can become topics of general public interest. Certainly physical science has disseminated its factual and theoretical knowledge successfully in recent years. However, the public, as a general rule, is not interested in either the fact or theory of science, but rather in the "story." Among the human studies, only those theories which, like the Freudian, appear to provide large, resounding explanations of complex happenings have attracted much popular attention. Most theories of sociology and some fields of social anthropology are neither appealing nor comprehensible to the general public because they are not susceptible to narrative treatment.

The "story" of a scientific field consists of its knowledge put into the form of a dramatic narrative: the "romance of archeology;" the growth of the solar system; "disease detectives;" the adventures of Genghis Khan; life in the South Seas. A. J. Liebling's *The Jollity Building* is a good example of a straightforward piece of contemporary ethnography put in the form of a descriptive narrative. In such cases the emphasis is placed on a series of events or at least *probable* events considered either diachronically or synchronically and prepared mainly for impact on the reader's imagination. Such "stories" can be based on fact or completely imaginary, but if the latter, they must at least be in the realm of the possible. Immanuel Velikofsky's cosmological fantasies are not in the category; Fred Hoyle's imaginative but putative universes are.[1]

When we allow putative actuality in our category, according to contemporary thinking the work immediately escapes the classification of science and becomes literature—literature which is acknowledged to be close to science and scholarship but which is nevertheless not admitted into the inner circle. It is, in fact, regarded as popularization, more or less accurate, honest, or reputable. This is the essence of the media which attract public attention: while they are either based on fact or true to a set of possible facts, it is not the un-varnished factual element in them which is dominant in the public's interest, but rather the intrinsic narrative. Likewise for theory: the public is interested not in theory as such, but as the cement, the continuity, of the story. If theory can be presented as the *plot* of a scientific detective story, it will find acceptance. Theories do not interest the public unless they are already proven; that is, as a revelation of the relationships and meanings of facts and events, in which case they are no longer theories but simply the plot of a narrative.

Stories told over and over again sooner or later become a part of the imagination of the readers. In the process of retelling and of commentary the stories acquire embellishments or at least a con-stellation of meanings which begin to carry implications for many contexts of history and social life. These meanings will tend to revolve around the original intentions of the authors, but frequently they go beyond these into the realm of social mythology—which becomes as fundamental to interpretations made by intellectuals as to the everyday thinking and conversation of the average man. Myths are more than folklore; they help to define the meaning of life and the goals of a society, the ideals and the norms of a culture. In this way they begin to approach a definition of the human reality as opposed to mere existence.

Science, as one of the important activities of our age, has con-tributed its share to the making of social myths. Certainly evolution-ary science has done this. I am not certain whether social evolution is pure fancy, historical fact, or reasoned interpretation, but it most certainly has become a mythic account of the nature of modern society in the guise of "progress" and all this implies. The ideas of "lower" and "higher" culture are part of the everyday judgments of men in all walks of life; these judgments are constantly acted upon, used as rationalizations and explanations. Another example may be found in Marx's doctrine of class structure: the layer-cake image of three basic class divisions dominates the conceptions of society held in the civilized world, "free" and communist. These are true myths; that they also have a basis in social and historical fact only confirms their importance, their proximation to reality as the age defines it.

To illustrate the points of the preceding discussion I have included sociological materials as well as anthropological. However, while sociological knowledge has come to play a role in the making of social mythology, anthropology and its narrative still figures more importantly in the public imagination. I believe that the underlying reason for the narrative quality of anthropological knowledge lies in the character of its method. The anthropologist goes into the field, to exotic places, and *experiences* his data. The sociologist of course does field work in our own society, and insofar as he does, he is likely to capture some of the same kind of interest—witness David Riesman and W. H. White. But it is hard to equal the peculiar attraction of a field with a tradition of travel and exploration, and in this the anthropologist has the upper hand. The point is that the anthropologist writes ultimately about his personal experiences; the reader is there with him in imagination; the interest is vicarious, not purely intellectual or analytical. The anthropologist is not just a scientist in the public view but is a particular individual, a romantic hero. Note, for example, the character of the anthropologist in J. P. Marquand's novel, *Point of No Return:* a unique personality with uniquely disreputable dress different from and apart from all other characters in the book. The fact that the portrait is rather unfavorable and is based on a particular living anthropologist is beside the point. It is a matter of doubt as to whether any novelist would ever portray a sociologist with these distinctive symbolic characteristics.

The anthropologist's writings are predominantly descriptive. They represent compilations of information on something that was and is: the "ethnographic present," whatever its scientific disadvantages, has held a fascination not equalled by the detached, abstract, matter-of-fact anaylses of the sociologist or the sociological anthropologist. This is because it tells a concrete story about a concrete reality—or at least *seems* to. In this sense, the "ethnographic present" is openly mythic; at least partly fictional. The information offered in the purely scientific treatises of the anthropologist may not interest the public, but these same facts are readily translatable into "stories" about places, people and happenings, and it is these stories, as I have already remarked, that command popular interest.

Another way of putting this is to call it the anthropologist's *style*— his mode of presenting himself and his data. In the writings of the great anthropologists one may find a personal touch which is often lacking in the other social sciences. The anthropologist may not always use the personal pronoun, but it is implicit in all that he writes, since, as I have said, "he was there." There is a sense of drama in his work, whether he features it or not—a feeling of discovery, revelation, and uniqueness. The concrete case, in which the anthropologist specializes, can be offered on a platter, so to speak, as the experience and observations of a unique individual, a person who has done something no one else has been privileged to do.

This style of work has had its effect, in the most prominent instances, on the personalities, public and private, of the great anthropologists themselves. This is a two-way process; there seems little doubt that many anthropologists are themselves colorful and somewhat deviating individuals who seek out anthropology as a haven. At the same time, the field creates a role which can or must be lived out: the more conformist individual may find himself taking on some of the characteristics associated with the role in an effort to identify with the professional personality type. However, this pleasant deviance of the anthropologist should not be overstressed, since as the field comes of age a more sober professionalism is evident. Still, conventions of anthropologists are notoriously livelier than those of sociologists, and I am sure that a study of anthropological careers would reveal substantial differences in background and outlook from those of sociologists.

Those anthropologists who, because of their personal flair, their ability to tell stories or provide materials easily convertible into stories, or their ability to convey the sense of an important personal experience, a human reality, are the persons often regarded as the "great anthropologists"—Tylor, Frazer, Hooton, Malinowski, Linton, Mead, and Benedict come to mind immediately. These have not all had the same success in terms of purely popular interest, but most certainly their work has had a mythic significance in the culture of the modern world. They have contributed to what H. G. Wells, in *The Croquet Player,* called "breaking the frame of the present." Wells meant that anthropological knowledge, along with that of geology and paleontology, had destroyed the old Western image of man as recent, omnipotent, or divine and substituted a view of man as varied, ancient, and dependent upon a complex environment context. The discovery of human fossils meant that man must join the animal kingdom; the availability of prehistory required an understanding of present events as intimately dependent upon ancient prototypes; and the revelation of nonliterate cultures meant that history was not contained entirely in the experiences of the West and possibly China but must be written with the whole in view. Thus the old parochial myths of Western man had to be revised in the light of anthropological knowledge and new myths substituted. The groundwork for these had been laid in the democratic revolution, and anthropology and geology themselves were among the products of these revolutions.

II.

It is necessary to distinguish several phases in the creation of these myths. The phases are roughly equivalent to the theoretical development of anthropology as Goldenweiser saw it in numerous essays.[2] The doctrine of progress and evolutionary thought in general represented the first or optimistic stage in which the older myths of Western invincibility were retained but the newer knowledge contained within them. This was done via the familiar doctrine of progress which, of course, had nonanthropological origins. Man was presented as a conquering hero who had worked his way up out of slavery to the natural environment toward a high objective— the aristocratic industrial civilization of the nineteenth century. The existence of diverse brands of humanity was now recognized as was the historical depth of the adventure, but all non-Western and earlier stages were seen as somehow inferior, inadequate, or *unrealized* versions of man. These generalizations of the mythic content of nineteenth century anthropology are probably unrepresentative of the writings of their authors, but I am not talking about the scientific content per se; rather, the interpretations and popularizations made of the writings. At the same time, such interpretations are not entirely *ad hoc;* they represent a fair reading of the latent themes and central attitudes of these works. Fact, theory, and myth are inextricably interwoven in nineteenth century (and twentieth century?) science.

Thus, it is difficult to say, without careful investigation, precisely how much influence the anthropological writings had on the myths or to what extent the myths were larger creations which determined the course of anthropological theorizing. I cannot answer such questions here; I can only point to the fact that anthropological studies succeeded in combining the older parochial myths of Western uniqueness and superiority with the newer knowledge of human variability and history, and that insofar as they did, they played an important role in nineteenth century social ideology. As we look back upon this work, we are likely to see it as much in the context of social ideology as in the role of the foundation of anthropological science.

The second stage of anthropological myth-making or at least myth-joining was characterized by an interest in the details and variety of human phenomena, with little regard for large historical generalizations. The ideological content of this work was manifest in its relativistic emphasis on the autonomy or integrity of the unique culture. The peculiar relevance of this doctrine in American anthropology, and its lesser significance in Europe, testifies to its ideological character. Margaret Mead has recently noted Boas' preoccupation with the diginity and freedom of the individual which was transferred in some of his students to the notion of the integrity of cultures. In these ideas it is now relatively easy to trace the social issues of an industrializing, urbanizing America with its injustices, minority difficulties, and increasing problem of the role of the individual. These issues have by no means withered, and of course the myths abetted by the second stage of anthropological science survive. However, anthropology has its own scientific dynamic, and at this time interests are no longer concentrated upon depiction and relativism.

In the third and contemporary stage of anthropological thought there is a return to evolutionary approaches in that man is treated once more as a single species about which to generalize. At the same time the unique details of distinctive cultural adaptations are taken into account and built into the problem. It is too soon to predict the mythic significance of this, but perhaps certain outlines may be visible. Recall that the second-stage answer to the growing problem of the survival of the individual in the mass society was simply to reaffirm individualistic autonomy and independence. However, this answer is no longer relevant, since the simple assertion of individual freedom becomes a hollow slogan in the midst of great pressures and needs for channeling and directing the behavior of increasingly large numbers of people. Consequently the myths of the future, like sociologist William H. White's "social ethic," may come to stress the adjustment of groups of individuals to the demands of the environment, natural and social. This will be the case on a worldwide basis, on the ground of a common world culture; and the sense of the unique, individual culture may be lost. Self-fulfillment may be played down in favor of conformism. Such themes are visible in contemporary anthropological thought, and I believe it to be the general direction of social ideology as well.

It is important to note that whether anthropology is concerned with the sweep of human history, man as a species, or with the individual and the unique culture, the level at which generalizations are pitched is peculiarly susceptible to mythic construction. *Man* and *Culture* have a resonance largely absent in Group, Society, and other terms important to the sociologist. These latter suggest sociopolitical, contemporary phenomena; while the anthropological terms have a timeless connotation, a kind of grandeur. Of course, sociological and anthropological ideas have mingled often enough in the recent history of Western thought, but they also seem to speak to different intellectual and ideological traditions. The anthropologist talks to the philosophers of history and culture and the humanists in general; while the sociologist speaks more often to the administrator, planner, social engineer and statistician. It is noteworthy that the applied anthropologists, who frequently associate with administrators and planners, have created a good deal of unease in anthropological circles and have never been fully accepted by the profession. This division does not appear to be so marked for the applied wings of sociology and psychology, although some tension between theoretical and practical interests exists in all fields.

I have said that the mythic quality of anthropological materials lies in their strongly descriptive character, which makes them susceptible to conversion into "stories," which in turn become part of the belief system and reality definition of the times. Progress, stages of development, racial inequality, racial equality, cultural variability and integrity, and human social adjustment are all catchwords expressing these myths; the ethnological compilations and studies as well as paleontological and archeological research all contributed to their formation. The factual quality of the research materials was undeniable, but it should be apparent that the basic ideas were themselves difficult to prove. Developmental stages and cultural uniqueness were perhaps among the more obviously ideological, as subsequent critiques have claimed. In both cases we have ideas great in potency but extremely difficult to prove; in both cases these ideas were taken uncritically and for granted in their heyday. The evolutionists never conclusively demonstrated the existence of stages; the relativists never really demonstrated the uniqueness or autonomy of cultures.

III.

Within the profession the researches of the great anthropologists have played a role not entirely different from that of myths. These researches, in the first place, succeeded in pushing anthropological ideas in certain directions from which they rarely depart. Malinowski's attempted refutation or qualification of Freud's Oedipus situation is such a case: his finding that in the Trobriands the affective relationship supposed to exist between son and father was transferred to uncle and nephew has become validation of the principle of cultural variability and the relativity of generalization and social laws.[3] Spier's demonstration of pottery seriation became a basic postulate of the relationship between tine and the artifact; in larger terms, a proof of the *geological* aspect of the human adventure.[4] Benedict's *Patterns of Culture* lives on as an assertion of the reality of cultural uniqueness, even in the midst of the most strenuous revisions of her ideas. Redfield's Yucatecan continuum of change remains a basic postulate in the theory of change and development in spite of its situational specificity and conceptual ambiguities. Mead's studies of adolescence lie at the basis of our view of the individual and his milieu, even though many of her findings have been challenged and revised. Kluckhohn's interpretation of Navaho witchcraft as a form of socially approved redirection of hostility clinched an argument in the social and psychological sciences and exists today in dozens of versions.[5]

We may consider these theoretical perspectives as myths to the extent that they represent highly probable, meaningful, but nevertheless not entirely demonstrable generalizations about human experience. Each, or at least some, have been based upon unique researches—often studies of a single people; and it is hazardous in the extreme to generalize about a species as variable in behavior as man from a single case. A variety of defenses have been made of this anthropological propensity to generalize from very small numbers of cases, and many of the arguments are sound; but the fact remains that scientifically it is a tricky business. The plausibility of such generalizations cannot possibly derive from the representativeness of the case, since frequently this is totally unknown. Instead, it is based upon the comprehensive humanness of the case as a whole; that is, it has the comprehensiveness of a long novel but is told with the veracity of a competent witness. It is believable simply because of the large amount of detail presented by the anthropologist and the authority with which he presents it. Somehow this creates an atmosphere of conviction which tends to convert the particular existential case into a symbol or symptom of human reality, and it is this which begins to take on another characteristic of myth, in this case, the myth of "a culture."

The Trobriand Islanders have found their way into countless literary and scientific documents, in person and in disguise, as testimony of the human condition. What relationship these mythic Trobriand natives may bear to the living creatures observed by Malinowski, or, indeed, to the people of the contemporary archipelago, no one knows, although I understand that a restudy is under way. Malinowski in a sense *created* a culture or a people in the course of many volumes of reportage; they continue to be recreated by the reader and by those who mine the volumes for exemplary materials. The Trobrianders—small, insignificant pocket of humanity, doomed to eternal obscurity and anonymity until Bronislaw Malinowski happened to find them, now elevated to a major intellectual myth of the Western world—are a people no scholar will ever forget, no librarian ever pass over, no social science graduate student ever ignore. From time to time it will be necessary to review current interpretations of Trobriand culture and the causes it has been made to serve, by rereading Malinowski's volumes. I have little doubt that the Trobrianders painted in recent commentaries are not identical with Malinowski's originals.

The myth of Pueblo culture was built up in the years after the publication of Benedict's *Patterns,* reinforced by a number of American anthropologists. Fortunately for anthropological science this romantic myth was given an antidote beginning with Li An Che and continuing down through hardheaded ethnologists like Dorothy Eggan. Yet the original myth survives in some social science circles and in the arts-and-crafts tourist domain of Southwestern culture— the myth of those inscrutable, pacific, superhuman Pueblo Indians, mysteriously resisting contamination, efficiently socializing their young, and magnificently preserving the ancient arts and ceremonies.[6]

Wherever we find a major ethnological compilation on a particular people, there we shall also find the makings of myth and legend: the conversion of that people into a special Personage or Culture which lives in the "ethnographic present" and which becomes a type case of the human reality of variation and the inexhaustible novelty of man's behavior and relations with Nature. One curious aspect of this is that while anthropologists are known to the public as being responsible for our knowledge of these great primitive cultures and are viewed as eccentric romantics therefore, the emphasis *within* anthropology has shifted away from ethnological depiction toward a social science preoccupation with problems, not peoples. The authors of the contents of most anthropological journals strike a sharp contrast with the public image of the anthropologist as the romantic myth-maker and intrepid and tantalizingly eccentric explorer.

Aside from the conversion of ethnological writings into semi-mythological constructions of cultures by the readers, the ethnologist in the grand tradition engaged in something related to myth-making when he created his narrative. The literal rendering of tribal culture is an impossible task: even the most attenuated culture possesses a complexity far beyond the capacity or the patience of any ethnologist to record in detail. Such literal recording of the ongoing stuff of everyday existence was never the primary goal of ethnology; rather, the objective was the construction of a typical slice of life. The temporal ordering of events was telescoped in order to present this typical portrait in brief compass and within the attention span of the reader. Moreover, no ethnologist ever knew all there was to know about a tribal culture any more than any of us ever know all there is to know of any human situation, however, familiar it may be. The ethnologist was always required to fill in the gaps, to reconstruct situations with a disciplined use of the imagination. This technique is akin to that of the writer of responsible fiction, and numerous anthropologists, Redfield and Benedict in particular, have seen a humanities component in anthropology as a result. The meta-anthropological wing, as represented, say, by the work of Edmund Carpenter, is an established though not especially prominent contemporary development. David Bidney has written on some of its philosophical, that is, value-*creating*, implications.[7]

IV.

In earlier passages I have commented upon the role of anthropological knowledge vis-à-vis social ideology, remarking that as often as not, the major theories of anthropology have followed ideological currents of the age. In this concluding section I shall consider the question of the extent to which anthropology should explore or recommend desirable social objectives.

This is, of course, the most difficult issue of all, since in the development of Western thought, a clear, possibly irrevocable separation between science and philosophy has occurred. If science essays to recommend or discover social goals, it is accused of abandoning its objectivity; even more, the view is held sometimes that values have nothing to do with fact and therefore philosophers are better off if they remain ignorant of science. Who steps into the breach? Most often, it is the pragmatists—the politicians and social administrators who set objectives by fiat or piecemeal decision, while the scientists and philosophers sit on the sidelines, shackled by their own views on the negative relationship of truth to action.

But if, as I have suggested, a science creates myths willy-nilly, even if they are not visible until the second generation, then it is clearly in the business of creating values, and this should be explicitly recognized. The myths fostered by anthropology in the first three decades of this century—individual integrity and autonomy and cultural relativity—retain their nobility but are no longer completely serviceable in the face of new social problems and cultural forces. Needed now are new images and myths which, as Paul Goodman, a novelist, recently pointed out in a brilliant series of articles in *Commentary*, dignify work and give the individual a sense of accomplishment in the routine tasks of industrial civilization. Such images cannot be constructed *ad hoc;* man's rational control of society has not reached and probably never will reach the point where he is able to inject value vitamins at will. However, this does not absolve the anthropologist from the responsibility of thinking about the problem and studying it with all his skill and intelligence. Further diagnosis is needed—searching inquiry into the existence and reality of contemporary man—before the power of mass society destroys the ability to think and to feel strongly about those important issues.

In addition to dignifying work, contemporary civilization with its rapidly growing population requires thinking on the subject of interindividual responsibility. The growth of cities, the institutionalization of behavior brought about by crowding and by increasing rationalization of the economy and of choice, clashes with the individualistic striving for autonomy and license, creating vast moral problems of delinquency, conformism, and neurosis. Here again anthropology has work to do. Franz Boas once wrote a remarkable essay on the different meanings given freedom in various societies which suggests possibilities for an anthropological study of the basis of personal-social responsibility. I do not mean "study" in the literal sense of acquirement of a $200,000 grant from a foundation. There is too much of this monetary substitute for thinking in the social sciences. I mean a general effort toward the development of a social conscience among anthropologists. They might well consider their role a privilege, not a right, and one that carries definite obligations to serve society by doing a little critical thinking about its ends and means.

The point is that the problems of our time are poorly served by concepts like "cultural patterns," "interaction," "culture process," and "social structure." These concepts have their definite utility within the science, and I am not suggesting they be scrapped (as C. Wright Mills might do) simply because they have little relationship to the contemporary reality. However, they cannot interpret this reality because they are nonspecific, and the full meaning of contemporary human affairs will be found always in the specific situations. The mission of anthropology is not to write current history, of course, but its accumulated knowledge has much to say on the adaptive value of cultural traits and of course on the movements and directions of history, the major ideas and myths of the age. Above all, anthropology has research techniques which blend existential description with a search for reality—if you will, the "scientific" and the "spiritual" meaning of man.

Anthropologists at one time were voluble about these matters, pronouncing on the goals and meaning of civilization and the destiny and fulfillments of humanity. This was, in fact, the golden age of evolutionary ideology, and while it was shown to have made scientific errors, who is to say that the myth of social evolution was wrong from the standpoint of its general civilizational results? It sustained colonialism and its evils, to be sure, but it also helped produce nineteenth century European scholarship. It was, in fact, one of the great civilizing forces of our age, as Loren Eiseley has recently pointed out.

With some important exceptions, modern anthropologists rarely deliver themselves of interpretations of contemporary civilization—at least not at the level of the major myths. Possibly this is because anthropologists do not approve of the direction life has taken and refuse to justify it or explain it; after all, the nineteenth century anthropologists were apologists for the current order. This is not, however, very convincing. In the first place, the nineteenth century anthropologists rarely consciously justified or defended something; that is, they were not propagandists in the cynical modern sense, they were *participants* in the age. In the second place, I am not asking that anthropologists *defend* anything, only that they intellectually analyze, criticize, and possibly rebuild. In the third place, the loss of a public voice by the contemporary anthropologist has gone hand-in-hand with the rise of Scientific Objectivity. This is a most desirable attitude when it comes to methodology, but it is a curse when it is misapplied, as it has been so widely, to the role of the scientist, and his knowledge, in the public arena.

I believe that anthropologists have largely ceased to take an active role in the world of ideas because they are lost without their scientific orientation; secondly, because even with their science they are helpless, since it is highly generalized. It says little about the nature of contemporary historical reality, being mainly concerned with man in general, or with that ineffable substance, culture. In the mid-twentieth century, it is primarily physical scientists who speak out and (wholly justifiably, in my opinion) claim the authority of their profession in so speaking out. Surely anthropologists are aware of clear and present dangers in the drift of world society; yet there is no "Bulletin of Anthropological Scientists" to discuss these issues and their possible solutions. Anthropologists write about American culture patterns and values; but which anthropologists have made trenchant analyses of the current state of public morality, the citizen's role in politics, the influence of mass media, the problems of the automobile age, and the drift and inevitability, the hopelessness and powerlessness of the affluent society?

Only a few relatively independent thinkers and writers who are not academically hog-tied, or who use their academic and professional connections largely as a point of departure, seem to be able to make the analyses of contemporary civilization which the anthropologist has so signally failed to provide. Most of these men are to be found in the "policy sciences"—a *mélange* of sociology, administration, economics and related fields which seems to have escaped the curse of "objectivity" and professionalism for the time being. Of course there are exceptions within anthropological ranks: Redfield and Mead come to mind immediately. On the whole it has been those anthropologists who in their writings are willing to go beyond empirical factitiousness toward the construction of reality and meaning who have spoken out.

It is, in fact, the persistent confusion of existence with reality which lies at the root of the problem. The majority of anthropologists, although much less aggressive about this than many psychologists and sociologists, are nevertheless positivists who deny or do not care whether there is any reality beyond the scope of their measuring instruments, even while their own methods plainly imply the opposite, as I have said earlier. The utmost integrity and dispassion must be utilized at the data-collecting stage; no one questions this. But there are tools for data collection, and above all for interpretation, which permit a mental grasp and penetration far beyond the recording of visual and numerical observations. The intellectual, moral and even affective attempt to so penetrate is what I would regard as the search for the human reality, as over against existence. This reality can be constructed in various terms, but however it may be constructed, it is one route to an understanding of man in his moral as well as his naturalistic contexts. We should compliment anthropology on having made some recent attempts in this direction, but much remains to be done.

The effort called "applied anthropology" has sometimes been viewed as anthropology's contribution to the world of values and social action, but applied anthropologists are concerned with quite different matters. "Application" has come to refer mainly to *employment* by government and industry and the research periphery cultivated in such employment. "Applied anthropology" does not signify "engaged anthropology;" the role is that of the detached student or the loyal employee, and has very little in common with the role of the social analyst, critic, or idea-creator. Applied anthropologists have been eager to serve the organizations of society and to put their technical knowledge to use in the service of such organizations, but they have not shown much interest in diagnosing problems or, above all, suggesting new directions. "Application" is a vague term; surely within its meaning should be that of exploring the contemporary condition of man and the changes, actual and desirable, in that condition.

The implications of these arguments need to be summarized. The acquirement of a scientific orientation by anthropology in the twentieth century seems to have militated against anthropology's willingness to swim in or against the tide of social ideology, and to make statements on the direction and meaning of this tide. This, in my opinion, is a real loss. Secondly, while anthropology has lost its high ideological relevance, it has acquired popularity and a myth-making function which I suppose is a gain. However, this gain is also, perhaps, anthropology's loss, since it might well contribute to the feeling of detachment from great events and ideas. A sense of purpose is lost, and the emphasis comes to be placed on the *content* of the field, rather than on its meaning for man. The fascinating qualities of anthropological subject matter form the basis of popular interest, and the anthropologist makes no great effort to insist on the meaning these discoveries may hold for the nature of man, history and civilizational growth and decline. And while problems dealing with these matters sometimes occupy his *professional* attention, even there the emphasis is not on their ideological and human significance but on particular theories and concepts. Something has dropped out of anthropology: a middle ground of social awareness. Possibly this is the distinctive *American* element or contribution to the field. Most of the nineteenth century figures who did have this awareness were European.

There will be numerous objections to these conclusions. The most familiar will concern itself with the demand that anthropologists, as scientists, not engage in the formation of empirically undemonstrable positions. I have not recommended this in such flat terms. I have said that the very function of anthropological science inescapably involves "myth" even while investigating and painstakingly recording social existence. Existence is empirical; reality, however, is constructed and thought through. The great anthropologists have been those who have gone beyond mere existence and tried to create the sense of a human moral reality. In spite of the innumerable methodological faults of the configurationists, they have been more successful at this task than the factitious social anthropologists. This, too was Redfield's primary objective, and it was this that Oscar Lewis seems not to have grasped in his criticisms of Redfield's pioneer work on Tepoztlan.[8] Without this struggle to convey a sense of the human reality, anthropological knowledge is largely paper and ink, at least insofar as its relevance to contemporary issues of man and society are concerned—and it is these issues with which I am concerned here.

Thus, the mythic quality of anthropological knowledge, in its various dimensions, presents a challenge to the dominant scientific orientation of the professional discipline. There is no question that the growing prestige of the social sciences has influenced the outlook of anthropologists to the extent that there is a desire to join forces with the empiricists and systemic theorists among the sociologists and psychologists: the "behavior science" movement is the apotheosis of the trend. At the same time, the distinctive function of cultural anthropology remains the depictive and *interpretive* integration of masses of data upon real human situations; without this, the field will be indistinguishable from certain branches of sociology and social psychology. And this technique inevitably retains myth-making qualities and moral responsibilities which should be acknowledged and not disguised. My own predilections have always been in the social science direction; but as a professional anthropologist I have been of two minds on this score and have endeavored to keep alive in my work the anthropological quality of imagination, of descriptive impact.

At the same time, the mythic qualities of anthropological knowledge create problems of methodology, and hence of truth, which cannot be ignored. There must be a constant, never-ending search for better techniques of rendering the actuality of social life in order to guard against the unconscious propagation of romantic error. The anthropologist, to an extent greater than any other "social scientist," relies upon *words* as a device for the recording and presentation of data, and words are notoriously deceptive. It is a testimonial to Malinowski's greatness that he was constantly preoccupied with this problem and strove to overcome the shortcomings inherent within it as well as to realize its vast communicative potentialities. I am saying that the anthropologist must be, at least in part, a literary artist; and if he abandons this goal for abstract or enumerative modes of presentation (however valuable these are in dealing with data), he also abandons what is most unique in his professional heritage.

NOTES

1. *I.e., Worlds in Collision* (New York: Macmillan Co., 1950), *Ages in Chaos* (New York: Doubleday and Co., 1952), and *Earth in Upheaval* (New York: Doubleday and Co., 1955) by Immanuel Velikofsky; and *Frontiers of Astronomy* (New York: Harper and Bros., 1955), *Man and Materialism* (New York: Harper and Bros., 1956), and *The Black Cloud* (New York: Harper and Bros., 1957) by Fred Hoyle.

2. See especially A. A. Goldenweiser's *History, Psychology and Culture* (New York: A. A. Knopf, Inc., 1933), *An Introduction to Primitive Culture* (New York: F. S. Crofts, 1937), and *Robots and Gods* (New York: A. A. Knopf, 1931).

3. *Vide, Sex and Repression in Savage Society* (New York: Harcourt, Brace and Co., 1927) and *The Sexual Life of Savages* (New York: Halcyon House, 1929).

4. See Leslie Spier, *An Outline for a Chronology of Zuni Ruins*, Anthropological Papers, American Museum of Natural History, Vol. XVII, Part III, 1917.

5. Clyde Kluckhohn, *Navaho Witchcraft* (Cambridge, Mass.: Harvard University. Peabody Museum of American Archeology and Ethnology Papers, Vol. 22, 1944).

6. *Vide*, J. W. Bennett, "The Interpretation of Pueblo Culture: A Question of Values," *Southwestern Journal of Anthropology*, II (1946), 361-74; and Dorothy Eggan, "The General Problem of Hopi Adjustment," *American Anthropologist*, XLV: 357ff., and "The Significance of Dreams for Anthropological Research," *American Anthropologist*, LI: 177-98.

7. David Bidney, *Theoretical Anthropology* (New York: Columbia University Press, 1953).

8. See Robert Redfield, *Tepoztlan: A Mexican Village* (Chicago: University of Chicago Press, 1930), and Oscar Lewis, *Life in a Mexican Village: Tepoztlan Restudied* (Urbana: University of Illinois Press, 1951).

EARL W. COUNT

Chapter VI: Dimensions of Fact in Anthropology

"A FACT, in the scientific sense of the word, is the close agreement of many observations of the same phenomenon."[1]

"In scientific description of social life it is essential to restrict the term *significant fact* to those facts whose inclusion or exclusion alters the meaning of other facts."[2]

"An unplaced cultural phenomenon is not yet an anthropological fact."[3]

I. "FACT"

In the gallery of the world's cultures, a distinguishing feature of the Occidental is that latterly it has created an end-value out of the probing of phenomenal reality, has weighted this value heavily and pursued its goal with a commensurate energy and system, and has not been content with less than a comprehensive coverage of the reality. This feature the culture terms "science." There has resulted a battery of substantive disciplines which range, say, from "physics" to "linguistics."

Other cultures (and likewise this one) have developed disciplines which we term the "arts." Science and art are both domains of knowledge, and as such they treat "fact," which they are at liberty to define in their respective ways. Whatever else may distinguish them from each other, it seems that science emphasizes clarification of phenomenon, while art emphasizes experiencing reality. As a convenience, therefore, I would label the sciences "phenomenal" disciplines and the arts "experiential" disciplines.

And I would interject that, sheerly as a psychoecological proposition, a human organism is the less completely self-realizing, and by the same token so is a society or culture, in measure as it neglects one or the other domain. With this truth we shall find ourselves coming full circle at the close of our discussion.

II. "FACT" AS CODIFIED CULTURE

Gibraltar, according to Bartholomew's *Advanced Atlas of Modern Geography* (1950), had (has) a population of 21,233. This exact number may or may not ever have obtained; as births and deaths occurred, it may have occurred more than once, although always but for a negligible time; even while it was being totted up, it was not referring to the same aggregation of individuals. "Population," then, is a compromise with an unseizable reality. But the demographer would be distressed if he had to consider these actualities. He is, for instance, quite aware that the number has a spurious accuracy; that it actually does not mean what it says. But he could not care less; the number remains convenient under the contextual conditions which supply its meaning and which, in turn, it helps clarify. The number is a useful datum; it is not a "fact."

A photograph of the heavens registers no actual sidereal situation: light from Mars and from Alpha Centauri merely has struck a sensitive plate at exactly the same moment. The photograph registers in- differently bodies that have long ceased to exist and others that undoubtedly still exist. The mixture, once sorted over, is none the less informative.

Such considerations, almost too trivially obvious for mention, demonstrate that "facts"—whether those of common sense or of science—are symbolizations, encodifications, of experience; they are culture idioms. There are further considerations.

We have no reason to doubt that apprehending reality is an activity of all animal organisms. Man's closer relatives, furthermore, can "take in" a very great deal of a total situation, and can make appraisals, as far as they go, which resemble what a human co- observer makes. But symbolismal encodification is heavily character- istic of human apprehension of reality, and we shall reserve "fact" for what includes this specification.

It follows—although this is not so fully realized as it should be— that fact-identifications are culture-bound. To take an often-used example, "time" is a verbalism we use for a certain durativeness about the universe, which actually is untranslatable into any language that conceptualizes this durativeness in another way. When we encounter its homologue in another language, we commit an innocent ethno- centrism by "translating" it, which is merely to synonymize roughly.

Occidental culture treats time as though it were a rectilinear locus, an absolute constant, an irreversible vector ("time's arrow"), seg- mentable for scalar purposes, to the point where the segments become invested with a spurious reality. Consequently, science finds it feasible and resultful to treat it as one of an indefinite number of compatible parameters. Actually, time cannot be measured; we can only make believe it is measurable by substituting some spatial quantity that is measurable. Our sense of rhythm is innate physiology; we effect a conjunction with durative space by this indirect and artifactual device. Were our encodification of time cyclic, or recurving, or that of a pool having depth without flow yet capable of being rippled, or without a past-future dichotomy, we might have built an entirely different science. Such attitudes toward time do exist in other cultures. Over two decades ago Benjamin Whorf drew attention to the cultural relativity of the semantics of language, just as decades before that Franz Boas had demonstrated the cultural relativity of grammatical categories. To an Occidental, a ladder represents a verticality subdivided in a scalar fashion, with breadth an incidental structural requirement. To a southern Bantu, a ladder is a series of framed spaces. Both white and black learn with equal facility to climb it, and from their *ad hoc* behavior one would have no inkling about this contrast of view.

But we have begun to realize this point even without stepping beyond the confines of our own culture traditions. There have been consequences from the invasion of Riemannian and Lobatchevskian geometries; from the theory of relativity, which incorporated Newtonian motion as a limited case. Harold N. Lee has remarked: "Those sciences whose data are subject to quantitative measurement have been most successfully developed because we know little about order systems other than those exemplified in mathematics. We can say with certainty, however, that there are other kinds, for the advance of logic in the last half century has already indicated it. We may look for advances in many lines in science at present well founded if logic furnishes adequate knowledge of other types. We may also look for many subjects of inquiry whose methods are not strictly scientific at the present time to become so when new order systems are available."[4]

It should be increasingly clear that "fact" is an exercise of cultural idiom. There is, however, yet another aspect or dimension. The meaning of fact changes within a culture as time passes.

For several recent centuries the thought (in Theodore Merz' sense of the word) of Occidental culture has been disengaging itself from a mass of fixed-point propositions and conceptualizing one of fluid relationships. Fixed-point propositions are egocentric: the perspective originates from the beholder. But now flux is superseding fixity. Negatively, this started with the discovery of a universe wherein neither man nor earth nor sun is the center, and all the light received at one moment represents no actual simultaneity and so no objective reality. Positively, it starts with Leibnitz' and Newton's dissolving the fixity of number by inventing the calculus and with Napier's logarithms which stand behind all study of organic growth.

Now, these incipient achievements belong to an age of thought which convinced itself that there is a universal order which is seizable by reason. Linné's *Systema Naturae* represents a refinement upon the ancient and very rough classification of earth-forms stemming from the mixed Greco-Hebraic tradition. Animals, plants, minerals were respectively juxtaposed; reason not only saw differences and similarities but selectively and systematically weighted them, with the result that a hierarchical system of classifying them was "discovered" which was assumed to reflect a real universal orderliness—a process of collecting data and converting them into facts. And Linné's system has survived even though its metaphysical postulates have not.

Between Linné and Darwin is a century which accumulated a vast deal of the same *sort* of information; yet to Darwin it means something more than to Linné, as well as something less. There exists no sort of law of mass action which compels an evolutionary connotation out of data. We often shorthand the account of the nineteenth century transformation with the cliché that there was a change of "intellectual climate" or "Zeitgeist." But Zeitgeists have no spontaneous generation. What happened was that the authority of some institutions waxed while that of others waned. Events occurred that were beyond the control of any particular human agency. By comparison with the universe of eighteenth century thought, that of the nineteenth century was untidy—not unlike the sooty paleotechnics of a burgeoning industrialism which settled itself upon the cities, emphasizing the preexistent slums and jeopardizing the condition of the peasantry. Mass-made screws put an adequate musketry into the hands of mass-levied armies. Arcadian shepherdesses ceased to be interesting: sheepherding in reality is dirty and dull. Folksong was elevated to orchestration, and Orpheus and Eurydice became quaint. The essential difference between Linné and Darwin lies in the fact that to the eighteenth century a natural phenomenon was so because it fitted a universal clockwork; to the nineteenth century, it was so by virtue of having *become* that out of what was previously *otherwise*. This is a difference of definition of fact. What proves a fact or alters the meaning of other facts for one "Zeitgeist" would carry no such message for the other.

And it was the becoming that challenged analysis. The Great Chain of Being of the eighteenth century was never refuted; it obsolesced. It was by virtue of this remodeled definition of what is fact that Darwin brought stockbreeding and population pressure to bear upon *systema naturae*. *Systema* there continued to be, but its definition was different. And it might or might not reflect a Primal Creator: the matter pulled no oar in the exploration of process.

Psychologically, I believe the difference between the eighteenth and nineteenth century attitudes toward what is fact might be described thus: If Linné's fellow-thinkers had been in possession of the mass of natural data which Darwin's fellows accumulated, they would have derived satisfaction and confirmation of their philosophy. But to nineteenth century naturalists, the accumulation brought unease: as data accumulated, the unexplained "becomingness" mounted like a log jam, so that *The Origin of Species* broke upon them bringing relief; here at last was an operable clue to fact-as-process or process-in-fact.

Fact, then, is culture-in-history-bound. The binding is a ceiling cast over the space of thought, so that every age is limited in its interpreting of data. A modern, from the superior vantage of his hindsight, may read the anthropological treatises of Kant or Blumenbach with admiration and a frustrate pity that these authors failed to rise higher than they did, with such promising information in their hands. He will read Sir William Lawrence, who could join a modern conversation, in the same domain and feel exasperated that Sir William's contemporaries did not see the meaning of his facts which today seem so unneedful of proof.

III. The "Facts" of Social Science

All scientific disciplines have started with descriptions of their phenomena; they then proceed to devise techniques—idioms—by which they analyze and express their data; then they restate their phenomena in terms of the results.

The "physical" sciences have found in experiment and the grammar of number their effective idioms. Now, it is partly their successes —their phenomena having proven amenable to this treatment—and partly the fortunes of culture-history, which have brought them farther and faster than other disciplines along this route, and therefore have made them convenient models for other disciplines which have sought incorporation within the thought of science.

Lord Kelvin's dictum that knowledge is less than satisfactory until measurement has been applied was spoken with respect to the kind of data with which he was familiar. It is not hard to see how quantification has been generalized into an ideal by many social scientists, and that they should see in this the way for keeping their systems open and an avenue for eventual reductions which will rest those systems in more "primary" sciences.

Now, of course, as a semantic proposition, nothing "happens" in nature but "events," and every event is somehow unique. Further, that science would not exist if it did not explain event, is a statement of *petitio principi*. But the focus of all science, from physical to social, is the elucidation of process, and event is treated as but the symptomatology of process. By contrast, the disciplines whose focus is event are historical. The contrast has been debated for a century under the entry nomothetic-idiographic; all we need recognize here is that these concepts, taken as absolute principles, stand at the poles of a continuous disciplinary spectrum. But we cannot merely arrange the intellectual disciplines in some linear order along this spectrum; for although in proportion as the uniqueness of an event demands attention, the idiographic tint becomes heavier and vice versa, there exists a series of sciences which *ex hypothesi* are processual—physics, chemistry, biology, perhaps psychology may be included—and another, roughly parallel, series which *ex hypothesi* constitutes "object" sciences: astronomy, geology, anthropology. Thus—our particular solar system has occurred but once; between Silurian and Mississippian rocks and organisms lie the Devonian; Neanderthal man was Paleolithic and late-glacial. The idiography of the "object" sciences does not render them the less scientific. Nevertheless, they have an approach to their idiography that derives no guidebook from historiography. The historiographer might comment that historical geology and paleontology are eventless sequences, not history.

That every electron is "erratic" and every photograph of subatomic particles is unique—"perfectly" improbable—surely need not keep us from accepting the fact that the idiographic weighs far more in social phenomena than it does in physical. Now, frequently the test prescribed for the maturity of a science is its capacity to predict. This deemphasizes the philosophical aspect—that of science as a particular and precise strategy for making phenomenal reality intelligible—and emphasizes a pragmatic aspect. It is true that Neptune was predicted from mathematical analysis of astronomical data, and the prediction led to discovery. But prediction of what will finally happen to the solar system must wait quite awhile for verification. We accept on the faith behind reason what the predicters tell us about this only by inferential transfer: in other and utterly different events they have proven so very right. The predictive test works well as long as indeterminacy may be discounted. But it cannot be discounted where the idiosyncratic ingredient is relatively large. In a human group of N individuals, each unit is compounded of an indefinite number of variables, and the variables themselves identify under a large number of incommensurate classes. As John Ciardi has aptly remarked, "no electric brain could be set up that would write a poem or win a hand at poker."[5] It is not a matter of some unseizable *tertium quid* intruded into the human formula from some extranatural source; it only indicates that indeterminacy has a very low threshold at the organic level and emphatically at that of human sociality. Certainly this does not invalidate all sociologic quantifications; it does indicate that here quantification cannot be transferred from sciences whose threshold of indeterminacy is high merely because physical sciences have been spectacularly successful, that to indulge in it without a serious reconsideration of its metascientific undergirding renders its validity suspect, and that the "naturalistic" social scientists either may be promising themselves far more than they can deliver or else they have undersurveyed the scope of the domain they have chosen for analyzing.

There will be more to say about this in course; but first we need a closer characterization of social phenomena as these are framed by social science, and this has been set forth nowhere better than in Douglas Haring's "Science and Social Phenomena" in which he makes the following points: (1) *"All significantly related events of social phenomena are dynamically inequivalent."* The "exact sciences," on the other hand, "continue to rely upon the principle of dynamic equivalence in all study of macroscopic phenomena." (2) *"All social phenomena are sequential."* They occur, that is, in irreversible order; whereas physical phenomena are "coexistent"—that is, "they are observed repeatedly and in any order." (This acute appraisal goes back to Herbert Spencer.) (3) *"Every human community, grouping, or social situation is unique."* This inheres in the very fact that individuals are constantly being replaced by births, migrations, and deaths; and cultural innovations alter the field irreversibly. (4) *"A central problem in social science is description of the circumstances that attend relative social stability."* It is change rather than stasis that inheres in social phenomena, so that it is "semblance of stability" that calls for a special accounting. And, from all the foregoing, the surmise of uniformity may be illusive. But this problem is commonly ignored. (5) *"Cultural behavior is observable and scientifically definable; 'culture' is not."* "Culture and culture traits never act and never provide a valid subject of an active verb." (6) *"Differing patterns of cultural behavior are incommensurable."* "No measurements based on explicitly denotable, quantitatively fixed units reduce cultural activities that differ in pattern to common terms." (7) *"Cultural behavior involves purposeful selection of patterns of response in terms of subjective criteria."* "Rarely if ever does social behavior occur according to mathematical probability or so-called statistical chance." (8) *"Human beings never behave socially in ways whose patterns they have not learned."* (9) *"In any locality individuals manifest patterns of cultural behavior that are current among their associations."* (10) *"The objective unit of observation is a human being behaving."* Not a "group," a "culture trait," etc., which "can be reduced to judgments passed upon something human individuals do or have done together."[6]

It would be surprising indeed if social scientists were to find much to disagree about in this "manifesto" when the statements are taken in their context. They clear the atmosphere considerably. A fair share of what is to follow will be a paraphrasing set to further background. Nonetheless, the points do not dispose of the issues involving quantifications and reductions and the issue of positivism as an adequate epistemology for anthropology.[7]

IV. The "Natural Science" Approach to Social Phenomena

In a forthright apologia for neopositivism (he prefers "natural science") in sociology, G. A. Lundberg states: "Whatever exists at all exists in some quantity and to the extent that this aspect is relevant in any scientific problem we find it convenient or necessary to express our observations in quantitative terms. . . . Quantification is only a way of expressing degrees of qualities and relationships. . . . We have never thought of either quantification or operationism as entirely supplanting or preventing other forms of thinking, including the most vague and heuristic speculation imaginable."[8]

It is impossible, from this statement, to tell whether or how far Dr. Lundberg would subscribe to Lord Kelvin's dictum as applicable to sociology. At any rate, he appears to be saying, "I am not opposed to poetry; but don't call it science." But the issue he raises is not as simple as he states it. There is a great deal that "exists" about which "quantity" cannot be asserted or only trivially so at best. Before his first quoted sentence could become intelligible, the meaning of "exist" would need to be clarified. If it means that all that "exists" is quantifiable material, his assertion becomes a tautology. Next, "quantity" is scientifically clear if we are dealing with physics and chemistry; when used in social science, at least frequently it is a matter of analogic borrowing. Genuine scientific quantification rests upon definable units with tangible referents, and they are standard-ized—for instance, grams, calories, mols. If there exist such quantities in social science, I have yet to encounter them. It does not follow that because relative intensities in physical phenomena can be reduced to scalar quantities, greater and lesser intensities of attitudes represent comparable quantities. Positive, comparative, superlative are linguistic code terms no matter how they are masked by statistical numerology. Still, we will allow readily that there is plenty of reality to which more, most, less, least apply. But this done, it remains undemonstrated that the "degrees of qualities and relationships" are their most im-portant or interesting, to say nothing of their basic, attributes. Further, it is hard to see how quantification can be the path by which con-figurations are arrived at. As with anything else, quantifications in social science serve at times to sharpen and clarify; but thus far their record for heuristic insight has been unimpressive. And finally, Harold Lee's remarks quoted earlier reenter the stage.

A scientific discipline receives its primary definition not from the techniques it develops but from the domain it investigates; recipro-cally, of course, the discipline defines the domain, and technique is inseparable from discipline. Still, every thoughtful scientist realizes the dangers of letting technique dictate the definition of the domain in which his discipline shall operate. The "exact" sciences have gone the farthest in covering domain with discipline; a physical phe-nomenon is one which can be investigated by physics and vice versa. (If preferred, substitute "physics-chemistry" in the sentence.) The reason why this excludes ghostly apparitions from physical investi-gation (apart from the marginal reason that the technical awkward-ness is insurmountable) is the logical contradiction of "material" light emanating from an "immaterial" body. The principle behind the definition is that the domain obligates the discipline; if a factor is effective in the situation, that factor may not be ruled out of con-sideration by the discipline because it is technically inconvenient to include it.

This does not appear to be the principle under which all "behavior-science" investigators operate. But here we must not digress too far; our topic is anthropology, and the critiques must remain pertinent.

To begin with, anthropology as science is still largely in the "descriptive stage." It is often assumed for science in general that such a stage is the mark of infancy; that with ensuing maturation it is transcended and left behind. The notion has an unrelieved linearity about it; however, if we pursue an organic analogy a little farther, we realize that maturation is not a matter of eliminating infancy but an evolute of something that is never really discarded—to narrow the analogy, the child is ever within the man. The point to our analogy is simply this: whatever be the matter with regard to the physical sciences, at the level of social phenomena a full maturity of its disciplines may never slough off the "descriptive stage," no matter what further they develop into. This is a point not covered by Dr. Haring's listing, although it comes as a corollary to several of the points, particularly the second and third. For as long as there shall be social change there will be an inexhaustible need for description. Here, maturation of a science does not consist in transcending the descriptive stage but in developing more sophisticated descriptive powers. Beside this, ethnography is living in a state of emergency: the "primitive" cultures are doomed irretrievably, and time is running short. Either the people themselves are becoming extinct, or their life-ways are being transmuted. Both conditions feed problems. Anthropologists are not free to indulge in the luxury of choosing only those things to investigate which are convenient to a limited set of techniques. Gideon Sjoberg's comments about sociology have a wider pertinence:

". . . The rigid operationalists, as strict empiricists, devote little attention to the whys and wherefores of selecting problems for study. From the contention that a set of operations defines the concept they leap to the conclusion that a problem to be significant must be treated operationally (and perhaps even that a problem be treated operationally is therefore significant). . . . The tendency of physical operationalists to select problems for study simply on the basis of research-ability is illustrated by a conversation I witnessed between two colleagues of mine. X was propounding a sociological problem, primarily theoretical in nature, which he was pursuing in the field of social control. Y listened attentively and after some reflection insisted the question should be put to the test in a small group laboratory. It was evident from Y's observations that he equated a problem's significance with its amenability to experimental and operational treatment. As X walked away he turned to me and remarked: 'Just how does Y propose to test theories on the spread of communism in Asia, or measure its effect, in a small group laboratory?' "[9]

Reduction is a process by which the sciences attempt to achieve consistency and integrity in a common world-view. The assumption that a common metaphysic can subsume all phenomenal reality is an act of faith; it leads scientists to band together in Associations for the Advancement of Science.

Genuine reductions simplify the concepts of a "secondary" science by restating them in the more analytic categories of a "primary" science. Spurious reductions borrow terms analogically from a science which the perpetrator takes as more "primary" and uses as a model. Thus, "force" and "pressure" are perfectly definable in physics; "social force" has no relation to $F = ma$, and "population pressure" is not formulable under the Boyle-Charles law. The social science usage is analogical borrowing; the model is mechanical. Choice of model is arbitrary. There is, of course, no objection to this—provided the borrower is sharply aware of what he is doing—and of what he may not do.

Among anthropologists, spurious reduction is likely to take a somewhat different form from that of the examples just given. For instance, the obvious fact that humans learn, and that learning processes of rats and men are to a significant extent demonstrably similar, even homologous, prompts definitions of culture to the effect that it is a special—the human—case of learned behavior. This seems a deduction from Haring's point five; presumably, "culture" is a philosophical abstraction which the reductive definition converts into operable science.

Plausible as this may seem, there are serious strictures. First— operationally, reduction is meaningful if it enables further refinements of analysis and dissolves the hitherto special into the more general. Unhappily in our illustrative case, "culture" is *ex hypothesi* that about human behavior which has no substantive equivalent among rats or even monkeys. Man's peculiarly high symbolopoetic capacity—what has generated culture—undoubtedly is a function of brain; indeed, neurosurgery is now supplying luminous comments upon this, and it cannot be safely ignored (it is, however, now being ignored by students of symbolopoea). But, if A stands for the learning process and C for symbolopoea (however this be related to A), then setting A (human) equivalent to or homologous somehow with A (rat, monkey, other)—and admittedly the homology exists—still yields no significant statement about C.

Second—that "cultural behavior is observable and scientifically definable; 'culture' is not," is good positivism. It is "safe" only insofar as positivism itself is "safe" or an adequate philosophy for science. In the nineteenth century it may have been so; in the twentieth century, this is being gravely doubted. But again we must limit ourselves to recording the fact of the matter—the literary conversation about it is copious already. Suffice it here that, while a totem pole, an Australian kinship system, a Central Asiatic conception of a sky god would not exist but for the "cultural behavior" that produced them, they are bodies of discourse in their own right, they have been so studied fruitfully, and they are more identifiable than whatever "behavior" quanta produced them. We have not had to wait, that is, until "learned behavior" came along before realizing that these artifacts are products of skills and attitudes learned. How humans learn their culture is an important domain of study. But so far, "learned behavior" as a comprehensive reference-frame gives no clue as to how we might have recognized and analyzed the art-motifs of the totem pole or the thought-content of the sky-god concept with its help. "There are more things under heaven and earth, Horatio, than are dreamed of your philosophy," and "learned behavior" seems a sterile matrix in which to grow cultural analysis. As one of the nutrient chemicals, it can indeed help, but it is not a meal.

Third—reduction to a "behaviorism" assigns culturology to a particular operational camp within the domain of psychology whose title to the entire domain is far from probated. Reduction in any science can afford to invest permanently only in gilt-edged securities.

This point has an important corollary. No piece of "behavior" ever is purely a matter of "learning"—any more than there is behavior that is purely genetic. Cultural conditioning has a wide range of freedom and such potential for compounding, but failure to recognize the innate basis of all psychoneurological externalizations has its real dangers. In fact, illiteracy among cultural anthropologists with respect to human biology in general and neurology in particular is one of the weakest spots in the discipline.

Reductions, I believe, are easiest where atomistic procedures are indicated; which accounts for their success in the nineteenth century. They have yet to prove their value where a configurational approach is adopted.

In the nature of the case, reduction from a secondary to a primary science can occur only after establishment of the propositions in the primary science; or, they should—else the reduction is premature. Meanwhile, the primary science does not stand still; and there results a cultural lag of the secondary. Such seems to be the case where social sciences have leaned heavily on mechanistic models: mechanics no longer is the universal for physics. Laura Thompson offers this overview: "Certain disciplines—such as nuclear physics, the non-Euclidean geometries, modern architecture, abstract painting and sculpture, general semantics, developmental psychology, perception psychology, psychiatry, and psychoanalysis—express the modern direction of conceptual development to a considerable degree. By contrast, other disciplines—such as classical physics and chemistry, classical sociology and political science, behavioristic psychology, classical economics, documentary history, and law—illustrate, in varying degrees, a cultural lag. Still others—like cultural and social anthropology, comparative sociology, comparative economics, social psychology, city and regional planning, much of biology, including ecology, psychosomatic medicine, and nutrition—are in a transition period from old ways of thinking to new. This process of change toward new working hypotheses, more in keeping with the findings of modern science, generates much discussion, even a certain amount of name-calling."[10] Scientists who read this will have mixed reactions, but no matter. Dr. Thompson's point is well enough taken.

All the foregoing hints broadly that there is a season for reductions and "a closed season." The shopper for models may be purchasing yesteryear's; *caveat emptor*. At all events, I doubt if there are many social scientists who believe that reduction and modeling procedures are now stabilized and promising withal. Perhaps the trouble roots deeper than the social sciences. We shall try to bring this out by returning to Dr. Sjoberg's anecdote.

Ostensibly, small group experimentation, like other experimentation, holds constant as many factors as possible, permitting variation to no more than can be handled for the occasion. What makes the procedure inapplicable to analyzing the spread of communism in Asia is that elimination of relevant dimensions has been equated with holding some variables constant, with no provision for their reinstatement. To explain. A common and useful technique for studying social behavior has been to take isolated paired units: place two macaques together at a time and study their interactions (see Haring's point ten). So we obtain dossiers on male-male, female-female, male-female, and so on. But nothing about this gives a hint as to what will happen when *three* macaques are placed together. Or four. Or five. It cannot handle phenomena of crowd psychology. And a very simple mathematics suffices to show that the piecemeal procedure is headed for astronomical unwieldiness.

Perhaps the impasse lies in an unsuspected quarter: the calculus we are using may not be built for the demands made upon it.

In "Science and Complexity,"[11] Warren Weaver finds that over the range of scientific problems there are three amplitudes,[12] namely, those of "simplicity," of "disorganized complexity," and of "organized complexity." The first covers problems that break down into a few, usually two, variables; of the few, all but one are held constant while the latter is free to vary. Physics in the seventeenth through nineteenth centuries was immensely successful within this range of ampli-

tude. The second amplitude covers problems containing an indetermi-
nately large number of variables—but all having simplex class-identity,
no matter how "erratic" or even unknown they may be as individuals.
Here statistical techniques take over.

But in the matter of the third amplitude, "the importance of this
middle region does not depend primarily on the fact that the number
of variables is moderate—large compared to two, but small compared
to the number of atoms in a pinch of salt. The problems in this middle
region, in fact, will often involve a considerable number of variables.
The really important characteristics of this middle region, which
science has as yet little explored and conquered, lies in the fact that
these problems, as compared with the disorganized situations with
which statistics can cope, show the essential feature of *organization*.
In fact, one can refer to this group of problems as those of *organized
complexity*.

"What makes an evening primrose open when it does? . . . Why is
one chemical substance a poison when another, whose molecules have
just the same atoms but assembled in mirror-image pattern, is
completely harmless? . . . What is a gene, and how does the original
genetic constitution of a living organism express itself in the developed characteristics of the adult? . . . On what does the price of
wheat depend? . . . To what extent is it safe to depend on the free
interplay of such economic forces as supply and demand? . . . How
can one explain the behavior pattern of an organized group of persons
such as a labor union, or a group of manufacturers, or a racial minority?
There are clearly many factors involved here, but it is equally obvious
that here also something more is needed than the mathematics of
averages. . . . These problems . . . are just too complicated to yield to
the old nineteenth-century techniques which were so dramatically
successful on two-, three-, or four-variable problems of simplicity.
These problems, morever, cannot be handled with the statistical
techniques so effective in describing average behavior in problems of
disorganized complexity."[13] Here Haring's first three points are
relevant.

This suggests, I believe, a principle of model limitation that is
usually overlooked in the social sciences. Modeling and reduction
work best if they remain within the region of amplitude where the
situation itself lies. Since models are simplifications, and the regions
of "simplicity" and "disorganized complexity" are themselves abstractions of convenience, modeling is a ready device. The dangers from
overabstraction are minimal.

Real phenomena, on the other hand, take place in the middle

region; at least this is unexceptionally true of sociocultural phenomena. Also, by Haring's point two, we cannot devise a model which makes the experiment or observation repeatable; yet this is what models are meant to do. We can, of course, arrive at a model by overabstraction; but this begs the present question.

In a small group laboratory, the subjects cannot be halted in mid-reaction and instructed to repeat. That also begs the question. Such instruction itself would constitute an injection of another and very radical factor in a dynamic situation that is continuing, not repeating. The repetitive feature of a physical experiment is replicated approximately only in stage-play rehearsals.

I hardly need interrupt to say that this critique is not saying that small group laboratories are wasted effort; I am only suggesting that small group experimentation is ancillary and *ad hoc*, not the key method to analyzing sociocultural phenomena.

Up to now, we have been paying rather more attention to the inadequacy of transferring problems of "organized complexity" to the region of "simplicity" than to the inadequacy of transferring them to the region of "disorganized complexity."[14] A further note about the latter—however interesting a statistic may be, it remains but a kind of preliminary to an explanation; it does not itself explain.

We have already noted that applying statistical techniques respectively to a sampling of simplex units and to a sampling of complex units is two different things. The parallelism is analogic; to lose sight of this is to obscure essential information. Let us reinforce this stricture.

A correlation coefficient is a confession of ignorance. The magnitudes of two statistical quantities are found to vary somewhat regularly and concomitantly. This is interesting, but it yields no clue as to why it is so. It suggests quantitatively a putative relationship; the explanation still lies ahead, unprobed. In the social sciences, too often such quantifications abet the illusion of more result than actually is there. A statistical agnosticism is no valid substitute for hypothesis and theorem.

It is indeed interesting if the frequency with which a sampling of suburbanites visits the metropolis should vary inversely as the square of the distance to be covered. But the parallel with the law of attraction between physical masses is either accidental or epiphenomenal; it may indeed prove meaningful in some as yet recondite way; nonetheless the factors behind the social statistic are not those behind the physical formulation, and the social factors fall in the range of "organized complexity"; the physical do not.

Much of what has been said may now be paraphrased and summarized in a commentary by W. H. Werkmeister: "The basic framework of the physical sciences includes the assumption that reality is a matter-energy pattern in space-time which is determined in its structure and governed in its functioning by the principle of the conservation of matter-energy (etc.). . . . It must be noted, however, that the principles pertain, and can pertain, only to *physical* reality. If this limitation is disregarded, and if the principles are set forth as determining or governing the whole of reality, serious difficulties (the difficulties inherent in naturalistic reductionism) arise, for there are aspects of human existence—such as consciousness, perception, insight, and logical reasoning as well as valuations and esthetic appreciations and the normal *ought*—which are hardly amenable to an interpretation in terms of physics and chemistry. . . . To refuse to admit in the light of such facts that there are aspects of reality which lie outside the framework of the broad principles of the physical sciences is but to reveal a prejudice in favor of the physical sciences and to betray a lack of objectivity in the most profound sense possible.

"What is true in the case of the physical sciences is equally true, of course, in the case of all partial approaches to reality which masquerade as the whole. They lack that objectivity which is synonymous with 'being detached, impersonal, unprejudiced.' If it now be argued that to insist upon the whole of reality as the ultimate criterion of objectivity is itself but a prejudice, then it can readily be shown that the argument misses the point; for we do not prejudge an approach or attitude or belief by insisting that it remain within its own framework of principles and valuations, limited though they may be. . . . The difficulty is to find a framework of principles broad enough to include the whole of reality. . . ."[15]

It seems that "naturalistic" social scientists fail to realize that the reason they can make their circumscribed inquiries within a total situation is that the humanists have long been there before them and have done the spadework which furnishes the insight into Occidental society without which the social scientists could not even conceive their questions, let alone produce any answers. Neopositivists, in other words, have been furnished with a prefabricated value-frame: their test-batteries and questionnaires are self-revelatory. A testimonial in reverse English is the fact that there is nothing duller or more dispensable than a naive researcher operating upon the sophistications of the culture that shaped him.

The anthropologists are faced with a far more difficult and perplexing task than that of the "naturalists." With few exceptions—

where the "applied anthropologist" borrows leaves from the laboratory manuals of experimental sociologists and social psychologists—
they deal with problems in the region of "organized complexity."
Themselves preconditioned by their Occidental culture, they nevertheless must seek to escape from the consequent ethnocentrism and,
on contact with an exotic culture and its uncomprehended world-
view, attempt to do for themselves—and quickly—the spadework
that in the homeland devolved for centuries upon the humanists;
that is, they must try to understand the exotic culture first in its own
terms before transposing its sense into Occidental semantic. And
to achieve this, they must convert their equipment from an ethnocentric liability into a catholic asset. It now becomes apparent why a
cultivated disciplined capacity for empathy is a *sine qua non* for an
intelligent investigation. Understandably, the colleague from another
social science questions the feasibility of such a *pium desiderium*.
The anthropologist can answer only that he tries; that the incidence
of failure perhaps is high; that it is enormously important nevertheless
that it be tried; and that often he has his reward when the natives
among whom he moves not only volunteer that he is actually getting
somewhere but even discover spontaneously—and amazedly—things
about themselves they never before had been aware of.

And the anthropologist can snub the criticism that there is a
logical contradiction between empathy and scientific objectivity—
even while admitting that empathy is an insidious beverage. He
would also admit readily that he seldom can, or tries to, quantify.
As for scientific objectivity—"the moment we accept scientific rather
than nonscientific procedures of investigation," says Werkmeister,
"we are caught up in that pattern of valuations summarized in the
term 'standards of research.' Exactitude and meticulous care in the
compilation of data, integrity and intellectual honesty, sound reasoning, objectivity in the evaluation of facts, imagination in seeing alternative possibilities of interpretation, courage to follow an argument
to its logical conclusion and willingness to abandon cherished ideas
in the light of new evidence—these are but some of the qualifications
and valuations indispensable to the enterprise of science as such."[16]
If to do this be to practice science, then the anthropologist qualifies.

The question whether or not empathy is incompatible with science
(it is granted that it is incompatible with positivism) goes back
to the mid-nineteenth century—to the *verstehende Soziologie* and the
neo-Kantians. To rehearse the debate (it died down rather than
reached a resolution) would carry us too far afield. There are those
who would frankly judge empathy to belong to the art side of their

science, and claim that its justification is not to be looked for by asking whether it leads directly to formulable, scientifically objective problems. Robert Redfield says forthrightly: "The artist may reveal something of universal human or social nature. So too may the social scientist. No one has ever applied, as a key to a lock, Sumner's *Folkways*, or Tawney's *Religion and the Rise of Capitalism*, or James' *The Varieties of Religious Experience*. These are not the works of social science that can be directly consulted and applied when a government or a business concern has an immediate problem. But they are the books of lasting reference."[17]

There is art in all science, and the great books from any domain are art, because insight is art. Has "naturalistic" social science produced some great books?

V. HISTORY-SCIENCE

We have seen already that to speak of the "descriptive stage" in a science as its infancy is not yet meaningful until "description" has been characterized. It is also granted that social analysis with a historical orientation only is history rather than science; that the aim of science on the other hand is to discover law.

But this does not dispose of the question of the historical dimension in sociocultural fact. The period of the *verstehende Soziologie* included the debate over the diagnostics of nomothetic science and idiographic history; there developed an impasse which to this day has not been satisfactorily resolved, despite the work of thinkers such as A. L. Kroeber—one of the richest and most seminal minds ever to grace anthropological discipline.

As the latter pointed out on more than one occasion, social scientists who are not history-minded will tend to dispense with the dimension of history when shaping their problems. And again there is plausibility. "History" is an abstraction, and so understood certainly cannot exert "force" upon a current situation; the "past" indeed has no "existence;" only "forces" obtaining at the moment of action are operant; if we could take their census, we should have an inventory of content.

Ahistorical anthropology is congenial to American anthropologists not only because of the way their culture has shaped them but by virtue of the tradition stemming from it.

Kroeber once remarked that Americans feel the past "not as a receding stereoscopic continuum but as a uniform non-present."[18] We shall not dally over protests that the generalization is too sweeping; Kroeber's remark penetrates. Americans find the pursuit of ahistorical culturology far more congenial than historical. A great deal of American current anthropology attempts to capture the situation-as-it-now-is; it seems to treat change itself (it is very alert to this) as a feature of that kind of situation. This writer, at any rate, has failed to find a sense of historical perspective in these very treatments of change. And of course—understandably—the sense of urgency about capturing vanishing cultures as well as the changes affecting them all whether or not they are actually being extinguished, abets what is congenial to the American temper. Anthropologists inherit in addition a tradition from Franz Boas, whilom physicist whose precise versatility was mainly responsible for drawing operable concepts out of descriptive reports; and the whilom physicist did not choose to wrestle with the dimension of history in sociocultural fact. At this point his pupil Kroeber parted company with him.

The attitude in American anthropology was all to the good, in its day; for in its day it challenged anthropology to move into the concert that was attempting a *science* of man; and the thinking of scientists was not the thinking of historians. Eventually, a "functionalism" emerged which considered historical reconstruction of cultures idle and nonscientific speculation, and that how a culture (*sive* culture participants) behaves here-and-now is scientifically the only valid and feasible exploration.

There is more than a casual parallel to the eighteenth-century assertion—which rested in Newton's laws of motion—that, were there a mind which could know at some instant the position of all the particles in the universe, it could account for all the past and predict all the future. The fact that operationally this is the *ne plus ultra* of idle statement is the least interesting thing about it. . . . It is more interesting as a symptom of the differentiation of scientific thinking out of a more undifferentiated matrix which contained also theology and history.

The resemblance of the two cases lies in an attitude toward what constitutes fact. The underlying assumption is that the only thing I can investigate is the here-and-now, but that if I know all factors in the here-and-now—more accurately, in measure as I approach complete knowledge of them—this *instanter* cognizance will enable reliable prediction. But I doubt if this attitude—it is too well documented to need further elaboration here—has been thought through to the realization that the locus of a point cannot be established from a knowledge of one instantaneous position and that, even granted we know two positions, they may be too close for the caliber of our tools of vector analysis and curve-fitting.

And what that omniscient mind of the eighteenth century was ignorant of is the principle of indeterminacy; and here enters Ciardi's poker player. Moreover, while the nineteenth century had moved away from fact as static point to process-in-fact, it had not moved so far but that it could still remark that one or more monkeys punching typewriters over endless time would in due course have lettered out all of Shakespeare. (For that matter, we might have added— all that mankind has ever said or will say.) What is infinitely more significant is that Shakespeare took infinitely less time to do it.

Here Haring's first, second, and third points are in full operation. When, therefore, we are confronted with a human culture, we are not in the presence of a situation where the phenomena are coexistent: they are irreversibly sequential. This is sufficient to intrude history as a configurative dimension.

However, to some degree this applies to nonhuman societies also. The human condition adds the effective agency of symbolopoea which has made tradition an actuality; whereupon tradition has been injected into the dynamics of every situation. So symbolopoea rides time's arrow. The small-group laboratory confronting the spread of communism in Asia is a quaintly inapplicable procedure, because to measure tradition in terms of a social momentum is a tour de force of reduction it never bargained for. But social science cannot dodge its obligation of discovering, if and insofar as it denies having done so hitherto, how to include the dimension of history in its configurations. This realization, I think, is what lay behind much of Kroeber's "meta-anthropology."[19]

It may help here to spell this out a little further, in terms of theory models. Let us return for a moment to what was said earlier about fact as static, process-in-fact, and fact-as-process, because "fact" altered after the eighteenth century.

Where fact is conceived as a static matter, it may be likened to the final right-hand expression in a solved equation. "Fact" emerges as the end product of an investigation, with the emphasis upon "end." Or again, "fact" is like a point in a space-field. Here "change" is merely a matter of adding and subtracting fact-points, and this without regard to time.

A mathematical parable for process-in-fact would be the equations of the differential calculus or a graph of such an equation. When the equation has been solved, we may substitute numerical quantities for the algebraic ones in the final right-hand expression and so obtain the value of a special case or instant; but the special case or instant derives its meaning from the regularity that harbors it—the differential equation.

It seems to me that the twentieth-century attitude toward fact has been elaborating upon this motional treatment of fact, that twentieth-century process-in-fact is proving to be the *aditus* to a twentieth-century attitude describable, for want of something better, as fact-as-process. At risk of distorting by oversimplifying, we might say that to the eighteenth century fact was a point, to the nineteenth century it often came to be a vector, and to the twentieth century it is becoming some kind of vector-and-mutant which is to be seized only in terms of its relationships. The several disciplines—experiential as well as phenomenal—seem to be in various stages of developing this new attitude. This, I think, is what lies behind Dr. Thompson's acute observation quoted earlier.

There is a derivative yet important consideration. The history-as-it-actually-occurred of a culture is not the same thing as the "history" its cultural heirs believe it to have been. The former fits a principle which also makes a physician's diagnosis the surer if he knows his patient's biological past. In the second case, a myth has evolved because a value system has been applied to past event: tradition has generated "social dynamic." But in both cases, it is the history of their development which alone makes them intelligible. In both cases, a history-less social analysis is less than adequate analysis. If the history is as unrecoverable as the flesh, voices, and love affairs of the dinosaurs, that is so much loss; and we are quite within role as scientists to regret it, even though regret be vain. But we should be unforgivable if we viewed as irrelevant to treatment of cervical fistula the patient's embryologic gill slits, or, when confronted with an infant's obstinate thumb-sucking, we gave no weight at all to the fact that monkey infants too suck their thumbs. To England's Charles I it probably made no difference that the ruler of Babylonia was reinvested with his kingship every year by Marduk; but if that had not happened, English dynastic history would lack a certain capital casualty and Scottish border warface in the eighteenth century would have had to find some other rationalizations. Briefly—when we can have history in social analysis, we must have it.

And a final consideration. Eventually, the social sciences stand to be appraised not so much in terms of what problems they formulated in scientific idiom but in terms of how accessible they made their fact to the experiential domain of thought. (There is a reverse to this observation: the experiential disciplines have much to say to the phenomenal; how well they can say it, and how carefully the phenomenal will heed them—all this is crucial, but outside our present topic.)

At this juncture, culture history catches up with us. For, upon the resolution of this problem rests the issue of whether Occidentalism shall be "two cultures" or one; and in the incipient cosmopolitanism of man's new world, it is a rather important question.

NOTES

1. F. N. Giddings, *Inductive Sociology*, p. 13; quoted by D. G. Haring and M. E. Johnson in *Order and Possibility in Social Life* (New York: R. R. Smith, 1940), p. 446.

2. Haring and Johnson, *op. cit.*, p. 452.

3. A. L. Kroeber, *Anthropology* (New York: Harcourt, Brace and Co., 1948), p. 542, paraphrasing R. H. Lowie.

4. H. N. Lee, "Modern Logic and the Task of the Natural Sciences," *American Scientist*, XXVIII, No. 3 (1940), 25.

5. "Poetry as Knowledge," *Saturday Review*, XLIV (July 22, 1961), 9-10.

6. D. G. Haring, "Science and Social Phenomena," *American Scientist*, XXXV (July 1947), 351-63. Condensed and partly paraphrased.

7. I must expect to be summoned to show hand. Gordon W. Allport, in *Becoming*, pushes back the metascientific issue in psychology to the opposing views of Locke and Leibnitz. Here, what obtains for psychology obtains for anthropology and sociology, and I admit to getting along better with Leibnitz than with Locke.

8. G. A. Lundberg, "The Natural Science Trend in Sociology," *The American Journal of Sociology*, LXI, No. 3 (Nov. 1955), 191-202. Copyright 1955 by The University of Chicago.

9. G. Sjoberg, "Operationalism and Research," in *Symposium on Sociological Theory* (Llewellyn Gross, ed.) (Evanston, Ill.: Row, Peterson, 1959), pp. 608ff. Quoted by permission of Harper & Row, Publishers, Inc.

10. Laura Thompson, *Toward A Science of Mankind* (New York: McGraw-Hill, 1961), p. 75.

11. W. Weaver, "Science and Complexity," *American Scientist*, XXXVI, No. 4 (Oct. 1948), 536-44.

12. The term is ours.

13. Weaver, *op. cit.*, pp. 539-40.

14. Parenthetically, "unorganized" would seem preferable to "disorganized;" the latter prefix connotes privative alteration from a contrary state.

15. W. H. Werkmeister, "Theory Construction and the Problem of Objectivity," in *Symposium on Sociological Theory* (L. Gross, ed.) (Evanston, Ill.: Row, Peterson, 1959), pp. 506-07. Quoted by permission of Harper & Row, Publishers, Inc.

16. *Ibid.*, p. 501.

17. R. Redfield, "The Art of Social Science," *The American Journal of Sociology*, LIV, No. 3 (1948), 181-90. Copyright 1948 by The University of Chicago.

18. "The History and Present Orientation of Cultural Anthropology," in *The Nature of Culture* (A. L. Kroeber, ed.) (Chicago: University of Chicago Press, 1952), pp. 144-51.

19. The term is David Bidney's.

ROBERT E. L. FARIS

Chapter VII: Some Issues of Relevance of Data for Behavioral Science

I.

ONCE UPON A TIME we scholars held in our minds an image of a bearded astronomer who pointed his instrument at a speck of light and stopped a clock at the exact instant he perceived it to cross the spider strand that bisected the telescopic field. He had a precise observation and knew what he was observing—a star, in a specified direction, at a particular moment in time.

Or we saw a paleontologist cracking a rock with his hammer and finding a fossil shell, which he readily identified and placed in its proper time sequence and relation to other species.

Here was science par excellence. A fact is a fact is a fact. Many a philosopher, professional and amateur, has pondered the comparison of this sort of activity with the investigative task of the student of human behavior and has pronounced that the latter can never hope to build a science.

Perhaps to the general public the matter would appear otherwise and the social scientist would seem to have the easier task of observation—he deals with people, and these can be seen without instruments. Even the social scientist felt this way in an earlier time, until he learned better through decades of painful labor.

The childlike trust in simple observation in the early period of direct investigation is powerfully illustrated in the field notes of the worker who made the observations on the mentality of the subjects of the famous and influential study of the Kallikaks. Here were no mental tests, no techniques, no cultivated objectivity, and it should be clearly stated however obvious it now may be, no trustworthy knowledge. Here is the specimen, quoted directly from the field notes of the worker:

It was a bitter cold day in February and about eleven in the morning when the field worker knocked at the door. Used as she was to sights of misery and degradation, she was hardly prepared for the spectacle within. The father, a strong, healthy,

107

broad-shouldered man, was sitting helplessly in a corner. The mother, a pretty woman still, with remnants of ragged garments drawn about her, sat in a chair, the picture of despondency. Three children, scantily clad and with shoes that would barely hold together, stood about with drooping jaws and *the unmistakable look of the feeble-minded.* Another child, neither more intelligent nor better clad, was attempting to wash a few greasy dishes in cold water. The deaf boy was nowhere to be seen. On being urgently requested, his mother went out of the room to get him, for he was not yet out of bed. In a few moments she returned. The boy with her wore an old suit that evidently was made to do service by night as well as by day. *A glance sufficed to establish his mentality, which was low.* The whole family was a living demonstration of the futility of trying to make desirable citizens of defective stock through making and enforcing compulsory education laws. Here were children who seldom went to school because they seldom had shoes, but when they went, had neither will nor power to learn anything out of books. The father, himself though strong and vigorous, showed by his face that *he had only a child's mentality.* The mother in her filth and rags *was also a child.* In this house of abject poverty, only one sure prospect was ahead, that it would produce more feeble-minded children with which to clog the wheels of human progress.[1]

Of course nothing as crude and destructively passionate as this example can be found in the operations of recent social science research. Still, it may seem to an inexperienced inquirer that such staple social science grist as the basic facts on personal items, activities, attitudes, and beliefs may be adequately obtained simply by asking for such information from a number of relevant persons. Experience in the social science fields, however, has shown an almost limitless purgatory of pitfalls in the questionnaire and interview processes. Not everyone even gives a true statement of his age. Income is often reluctantly and inaccurately given. Behavior and attitudes may be misreported because of embarrassment or other emotional reactions.

Volumes could be, and in fact are, filled with examples of characteristic errors in the responses of persons on questionnaires and in interviews. Some result from unwillingness of the respondent to admit that he does not understand the question. During the run of a popular man-on-the-street interviewing program, for example, an announcer asked, "Do you think it is fair to call President Roosevelt a philatelist?" The respondent answered firmly, though incorrectly, "No!" in preference to revealing ignorance of the meaning of the strange word.

The dress and manner of the interviewer has been repeatedly shown to be a factor influencing answers on certain subjects. Any visible racial identity of an interviewer, for example, has effects on the pattern of answers in a study of race relations. Manner of dress, revealing class level of the interviewer, may influence the responses in a labor relations study.

Items on a questionnaire may influence one another, thereby affecting results to an important degree. A wartime study of worker absenteeism contained a series of items asking the men why they thought workers stayed away from the plant for reasons other than illness. Responses included a number of reasons tending to connote selfishness and other unworthy motives. Then the question was asked about the respondent's own absences, and this elicited a denial of any absences, for reasons other than illness, from a large majority of workers known to the investigators to have had such absences.

When agencies of mass communication saturate a population with statements concerning a product or concept there may be a reflection of these, in responses of consumers, with no correspondence with the original meanings. It has been reported that several years of warnings in dentifrice advertisements against bleeding gums—referring to "pink toothbrush" as the danger signal—resulted in a considerable number of attempts to buy pink toothbrushes. Repetition of emotional statements against the Taft-Hartley labor law in political campaigns apparently caused a considerable number of persons to hold a negative attitude toward the symbol even when they favored each of the principal provisions of the law—a fact demonstrated by a national opinion poll indicating a clear majority against the act and a clear majority for every one of its principal features.

A not infrequent consequence of extensive frustration in finding the true meaning behind the words of respondents is to seek a quick and easy evasion of the problem by simply holding the statements of the persons to be in themselves data for study. This is legitimate, of course, as long as it is acknowledged that the original study has been abandoned and the investigator has turned to other matters. He has not solved a problem but has only abandoned it and taken up a different one.

Five persons may respond with the monosyllable "No" to the same question and with five different meanings, and among these meanings some may be actually affirmative. We can readily understand an investigator's decision, on recognizing this state of affairs, to quit science and turn to poetry where ambiguity of meaning is the heart of the game. If only slightly less discouraged he may draw on the seemingly legitimate device of "operationally defining" a response in such a fashion that its validity may be ignored as irrelevant.

A commercial polling agency asked a sample of the public which of two leading refrigerators it planned to buy next. Brand A consistently won the popularity vote, and if validity of the item could be assumed, should have outsold Brand B. The result, however, was opposite. The question, "What do you intend to do?" is of imperfect validity, possibly because as the time approaches to make an important purchase a new inquiry and process of comparison by the cautious consumer introduces elements not present at the time the question was merely hypothetical.

Some persons who find themselves weary of seeking accuracy from words turn to instruments for greater certainty. The camera is not supposed to lie, and a Chinese photographer presumably outperforms hosts of words. It is easy, however, to expect too much of a photograph. Some of our literature on the mythical Wolf Children of India contained blurry snapshots of a pair of human children, nearly naked, kneeling on the ground. This impressed readers and in effect contributed authenticity to a fantastic account, although the picture could have been of any children anywhere in Asia or even elsewhere, and there was nothing in the scene having any relation to a history of association with wolves.

An author of a text on research methods recommends the use of photographs in the following words: "Photographs tend to present accurately a mass of detail which is apt to escape the human reporter. The photographic 'eye' views with authenticity and impartiality. It has no preconceived notions and selective interests."[2] It is no quibble to add, however, that the human eye and brain never see the photograph without interpreting, and so the "authenticity and impartiality" of the camera cannot guarantee freedom from the problems of interpretation. Long ago Stuart Rice demonstrated the point in his experiment on student reactions to photographs of faces taken from newspaper accounts.[3] The students perceived intelligence in the faces according to the status attributed to each subject, so that the gangster, falsely identified as an ambassador, was perceived as more intelligent than the senator, falsely labeled a bootlegger.

Cameras can and often do overdramatize. Historians of contemporary events would do well to ponder a unique study made of the celebration of MacArthur Day in Chicago on the occasion of the

General's triumphant homecoming.[4] A carefully organized check by independent observers stationed along the processional route provided a measurement of the degree of distortion produced by camera selectivity and by the announcers' calculated overdramatization. The mass media of radio and television gave viewers an impression of great excited crowds along the way and at the place of the main address. The independent sociological observers described people going about their business along the route of procession, turning toward the curbs as the General's car passed, sometimes following him with a little wave of hand clapping. The cameras were generally limited to a view of the particular segment of crowd that was temporarily attentive to the celebration and left viewers with the impression of a much larger crowd and higher pitch of excitement. The television viewer is in danger of experiencing such a moment of history with the illusion that he was *present at the event.* We may properly wonder if professional historians of contemporary events are free of the same kind of error.

It was once common in research manuals to present the process of investigation in clearly defined temporal stages. This has never been a realistic description of how knowledge is gained, however. Most issues of general interest are actually nibbled at by a variety of researchers, using a range of methods. The activity spreads over a period of years, during which the nature of the question is continuously restated, the conceptualization of what constitutes revelant data revised, the hypotheses refined again and again. It is not necessary or even desirable to attempt to perfect each stage before undertaking the next. An experienced sociological researcher testifies on this point in connection with a large-scale study extending over three years:

> In the first year of Project Concord we seemed almost compulsive about repeatedly pretesting a questionnaire devised to test certain hypotheses formulated prior to gathering any data. In retrospect it seems regrettable that we thus delayed for so long the collection of our first empirical evidence, for when we finally did have data in hand, it afforded us an additional and invaluable basis for the formulation of more incisive hypotheses. These new hypotheses in turn guided subsequent construction of instruments and collection of further data.[5]

This assertion that we do not really begin research by taking hold of hard facts can be elaborated by the history of inquiry into the nature of social classes in the United States and related investigations of changes in the amount of vertical mobility from one generation to another.

Here the obvious beginning would seem to be easy—to list the social classes existing in this country. This would not have been too difficult in eighteenth-century France or Germany, where the concept of class was clearly embodied in the law. In order to know the class to which any persons belonged, it was necessary only to consult the law. The law specified which occupations were open to which classes, and what legal rights, privileges, and duties belonged to each category. Research on social class at such a time and place would have had the convenience of clearly relevant basic data.

The problem of grasping the beginning facts on social class in the contemporary United States is an entirely different matter. Our laws do not recognize classes except to deny them. Nor are customs explicit, clear, or uniform on any aspect of the subject. To be sure, when national polls ask persons to which class they belong, specifying a few categories within which the choices must be made, most respondents do give answers and some readers may draw conclusions.

Much attention, for example, was paid by scholars and by the public to a famous inquiry published in *Fortune* magazine in February 1940. Of those responding, 7.3 per cent of the persons in the sample stated that they belonged to the upper class, 70.4 to the middle class, and only 22.3 to the lower class. A separate poll, conducted in the same year, was based on the question, "To what social class in this country do you think you belong—the middle class, the upper, or the lower?"[6] Here the middle class almost swamped the other two, claiming 88 per cent of the sample, compared to 6 per cent each for the other two classes. Could we conclude from these results that there is little variation of class level in the country? Many have done so but should not from data of this sort which seem on the surface so hard and definite but turn out to have a fatal semantic bias.

The worm in the apple was, of course, clearly revealed in a subsequent publication of Centers, who offered the additional choice of the concept of "working class" to the respondents.[7] Fifty-one per cent now claimed membership in this "working class," leaving only 1 per cent admitting inclusion in the lower class, reducing the middle class size to 43 per cent, and leaving a trivial 3 per cent in the upper class.

The minor change in the kind of question asked here made the difference between a picture of a largely middle-class society in the

United States versus a two-class society virtually lacking in upper and lower classes. Obviously "facts" here are not self-evident, and data-gathering on such a subject as this is a major research problem, not merely a simple first step.

What does a careful investigator have to do to obtain the proper basis for enumerating the social classes in United States society? The more than twenty-year record of modern study of this question furnishes a clear account of the complexity of the data-gathering task.

This turns out to require a great deal more than merely asking selected persons how many classes exist in their community and to what class they belong. To be sure, such a method will get a result, and has done so. A. B. Hollingshead, for example, found five clear-cut classes in Elmtown, a midwestern town of about six thousand population.[8] His procedure will be summarized to indicate how the selection of informants may yield an unrepresentative image of the structure of a community.

The first step of Hollingshead and his helpers was to interview a number of town residents until there began to emerge a list of family names mentioned by various informants, whose status in the community appeared to be a matter of consensus—"the Sweitzers are tops here" "Joe Emerson is plain middle class," "the Soper tribe is on the bottom." Fifty interviews produced a list of thirty families which were placed in similar status positions by different respondents.

The names of the husbands and wives in these thirty families were then typed on separate cards, and twenty-five persons who had been previously interviewed were asked to order these families according to standing in the community, without specification of criteria for standing. Nineteen of the persons arranged the cards into five class categories, two into four categories, three into three categories, and one into two. The fact that 76 per cent of these judges, then, believed that there were five strata in Elmtown society, with a "high order of agreement on which families belonged in each group," is the initial basis for the assertion that the community had a five-class stratification system.

The "high order of agreement," however, was not perfect agreement on which family belonged in each level. "Consistent disagreement occurred on 9 families and some on a tenth one." The investigators concluded that in general these cases represented instability of status or disparity between status of husbands and wives and dropped these ten names from the list before making further use of it. The remaining twenty families then constituted a "control list" which could be arranged into five social classes.

This "control list" was then rerated by a new list of twelve adults who had been previously interviewed but were not on the first panel that rated the names. This fresh panel consisted of persons who "appeared to be representative of the five strata" and who were *long-time residents* of the town. Their ratings of the families correlated highly, though not perfectly, with the first set of ratings. This result gave the investigators their basis for believing that "the 20 names on the control list were diagnostic of the five major classes or strata in the Elmtown social structure as it was conceived by 29 out of 35 raters, or 83 per cent."

Here the comment can properly be made that the consensus of 83 per cent of 35 *selected raters* cannot at all be properly held to be representative of the Elmtown population in general. A sophisticated researcher should hesitate to claim anything more than that among the over six thousand residents of this community it is possible to find, by selecting persons who seem to be interested in the question, a small number who can sort another small number of families consistently into five levels of status.

The final step in the classification of the Elmtown families into five levels was made by having a special panel of raters judge the status of each family by comparing it with the control list. Thirty-one raters were used—these being chosen from adults who had resided in the community twenty years or more, and who themselves appeared to be stable in their station. Again these constitute not a representative group, but a set of persons most likely to be sensitive to class distinctions. The arrangement of the population into five classes was made by this panel, with disagreements in their judgments settled by "clinical judgment" of the investigators.

The research issue under discussion here is this: Do the results cited show that "the Elmtown social structure was found to be stratified into five classes" (p. 439) or merely that it was possible to find a very small and stable panel of long-time residents who could agree on classifying families known to them into five levels of status previously defined for them by consensus among an even smaller highly selected group?

Such a question was asked and tested by Thomas Lasswell, who selected a small California town in the orange belt for study.[9] To discover whether the population of Citrus City in general, rather than a small selected set of old residents, could arrange themselves into a clear-cut class system, Lasswell drew a probability sample of the town population, and without loading the answers by previous discussion of social classes, as was done in the Elmtown study, merely asked the respondents to describe the "social classes" in the community, to nominate persons whom they believed to be representative of each "class," and to tell how they thought persons became identified with each of the "classes." The results were in sharp contrast with those obtained in Elmtown. Citrus City respondents named from no class to seven classes, no one number of classes being named by more than 17 per cent of the sample. As many as twenty-five criteria were given as bases of class identification. Almost a third of the families rated (29 per cent) were of such indeterminate status as to be rated in every level from the highest to the lowest used by the respondents.

To be sure, Citrus City is not Elmtown, but the results of the Lasswell study raise a legitimate question as to how much "class system" consensus would have been found in Elmtown if the raters had been chosen in a fashion representative of the population, rather than in a manner having maximum likelihood of coming to consensus on the subject of class levels.

Nobody could seriously deny that population differentiation in some vertical sense affects human life and behavior in important ways. Incomes, for example, vary over an enormous range and in a way that is loosely interconnected with life chances, prestige, style of life, power, and other aspects of experience. But this continuum is not necessarily best represented as a set of layers such as appears to be implied in the concept of a "class system."

The concept of class we inherited from earlier centuries in Europe is no such simple matter as a scale of income difference. It is rather a set of close, institutionalized interrelations among occupation, prestige, style of life, and legal privileges which were never characteristic of United States society. If the old system of Europe had the shape of a sort of conical layer cake, the contemporary condition of stratification in this country is more confused than a marbleized fruit cake having lighter elements in the top levels but no objectively distinguishable layers. The concept of "class system" clearly connotes layers and is therefore inappropriate. It remains desirable and proper, however, to press sociological investigation into gradations of any variables in the population, and into their interrelations and their consequences to human behavior and welfare.

A related question, long considered important by historians and social scientists, is the matter of changes in freedom of movement among occupations of varying degrees of attractiveness. A reasonable freedom of upward vertical mobility is often suggested as a necessary condition in a healthy civilization, and a decline in the relative amount of such mobility has been considered to be an indication of development of a pathological condition in the society.

Investigations bearing on this issue require the kind of data-gathering that identifies occupations clearly and provides measurement of their positions on some kind of vertical scale. Neither of these tasks is automatically easy—the recorded experience of some decades of work on the question is full of instances of errors resulting from overconfidence.

How does an investigator discover the occupation of a particular person? An obvious but naive approach, frequently used, is to ask the person, "What is your occupation?" In some cases this yields a usable answer—for example, "Superior Court judge," "principal of a small-town grade school," "city bus driver," are all clear enough for most purposes, although it has been found advisable to ascertain that the named occupation is the actual and *principal occupation,* rather than a temporary or hoped-for job. College professors have been known to drive taxis in their summer vacation period, for example, and their correct answer to the above occupational question would be misleading if asked in July.

What if the response is "engineer"? Does it designate such a highly paid and honored occupation as the designing of suspension bridges or the less favored job of mechanic on a tugboat? It may even mean janitor of a public school, since in some large cities the members of the custodial craft have successfully organized to have this occupational designation applied to them.

In a general discussion of the problem of ascertaining occupations, Edward Gross has provided a number of illuminating observations.[10] We are accustomed to thinking of a man's occupation as a stable and determining aspect of his style of life, as it so often has been. Questionnaires have generally had a place for only one reply on the item for "occupation." This may often mislead by forcing into an oversimplified reply the response from a person who is occupationally unstable or who has more than one occupation.

Do most persons in fact have a stable occupation? If stability is defined as generously as "three years on a job," then, according to a recent study, 88 per cent of professionals are stable, but only 24 per cent of unskilled workers are stable.[11] But if stability means "remaining in major occupational groups for the whole of their careers," only a third of the professionals, a fourth of the managers and officials, a fifth of operatives and kindred workers, and even fewer service workers and urban laborers qualify. Thus the response to a schedule item "occupation," clear and definite as it may appear, should actually be conceived as a *sample of one case* from the range of occupations the particular respondent may have in his working lifetime.[12] From a study of 935 principal wage-earners in Oakland, California, it has been found that in the occupational categories of unskilled labor, sales, white collar, and ownership of business, the sample of one case is more likely to be wrong than right—that is, that more than 50 per cent of the work life of persons in these categories is spent in other than the specified occupational group.[13]

Gross presents several additional illuminating examples of ambiguities in occupational data.[14] There is the question of whether a person actually has an occupation at all. League of Nations statistical practice, using the *gainful worker concept,* takes the person's word for it thus: "*If he conceives of himself as having an occupation, whether he happens to be at work or not,* he reports himself as gainfully occupied." The concept of *labor force,* as used in the U.S. Census, refers to the matter of whether the person is actually at work at present ("Last week what was this person's activity?") or actively looking for work.

Among the dangers in taking the person's word regarding his occupational category when he reports that he seeks work of a particular kind is that of the bias of wishful responding. During the brief life of the Works Progress Administration which sought to keep persons active in their regular occupational tasks, a number of applicants declared themselves to be writers, artists, and educators and so were set to writing, painting, and educating. A considerable proportion were soon found to be incapable of qualifying at a reasonable level at these forms of work; they had simply decided that it might be pleasant to be supported by such high-status activity, even though lacking in training and experience.

Decisions on the occupations of women present further ambiguities. Gross points out that "if it is considered appropriate for a woman of a particular class to be working at all she may report an occupation, but if her social class frowns on such employment she may report herself as a housewife." Is being a farmer's wife an occupation? In France it is considered so; in Sweden it is not. Some countries consider being a housewife an occupation if she actually does the housework; others do not.

Gross properly concludes that in gathering data on occupations a single blank space to enter "occupation" will not do. What is needed is a series of items calling for a description of the nature of the work over a specified period and the amount of time spent at different types of work. What the inexperienced investigator takes as a simple matter is found to be technical and complex.

Suppose these difficulties to be overcome by means of a proper series of questions so that it becomes possible to say that a person's occupation is, say, "physician." Is this datum now in the refined state needed for investigations of changes in occupational mobility? A final affirmative answer should not yet be given, since there remains a large range of variation in income, prestige, power, and life chances among physicians—there may be greater differences than similarities in the way of life of a small-town general practitioner and a noted surgeon in a great city. Each occupation has, to its own degree, such a range of life-patterns; and to express their measures as averages without stating some indication of dispersion involves risks of serious misuse of the information in drawing conclusions on vertical mobility.

II.

Having amply made the point that "social class" and "occupation" are far from simple observable data, it may be fitting to indicate that such is the case for a considerable number of other familiar concepts needed in sociological research, and further, to cement the thought that there may be more problems than immediately meet the eye in all data-gathering activity.

A city, for example, appears to be a thing and a unit, and city size is a relevant dimension in a variety of useful studies. Size in terms of area and population is given in readily available figures for cities in the United States, at various periods in our history.

Some of the statistics on city size refer to the unit enclosed by the political boundaries—the city limits. This may be the most appropriate unit for some kinds of administrative and political studies. But the city as a sociological and economic unit is not confined to these boundaries. The inhabitants of many a suburb are, in every other respect but the political, inhabitants of the city, deriving their incomes from it, spending most of their money there, participating in its life in a variety of ways, and conceiving of themselves as members of it. The same can be said even more of such enclaves as Hamtramck, the separate municipality inside of Detroit, and of patches of Los Angeles County surrounded by but not politically a part of the city of Los Angeles.

Such concepts as *metropolitan area* and *metropolitan region* have been devised and used by census experts to deal with such considerations, but these have the disadvantage as well as the advantage of being defined uniformly for each city, as they necessarily must be. They are also composed of a number of arbitrary decisions for the sake of standardization. For some legitimate research purposes it would be desirable to define each city in special terms for the purposes of that particular research question, laborious as this might be. For example, an inquiry into the relation between certain forms of disorganization and rate of city growth might require both a special delimitation of the sociological boundaries of the city and a definition of growth in terms of migration only, excluding both natural increase and annexation. Those cities which have grown rapidly principally through annexation of suburbs with high birth rates have not necessarily experienced the same sociological growth pains and consequent disorganization that afflict cities in which new industries have attracted large and sudden population increases. A study of the relation between rate of city growth and disorganization which fails to separate these different kinds of growth may fail because of the unlike effects of the different kinds of growth.

Our data-gathering difficulties are furthur illustrated by the search for instances of committed crimes. Once again, to the inexperienced seeker for knowledge, the question may appear to be simple. A criminal is a person who has committed a crime. A crime is the violation of a law. But of course as soon as we ask "*Any* violation of *any* law?" we begin to perceive the difficulties and realize that to conceive of crime in such broad terms would be to make practically everyone a criminal. We have already learned, however, the undesirability of taking the other extreme and defining as criminal only those who are imprisoned for a crime—this approach leaves out of the definition a considerable number of prominent gangsters who constitute important forces in the world of organized crime. Also, as Sutherland long ago pointed out, it would omit almost an entire class of white-collar criminals.[15] Sutherland proposed supplementation of the above conception by its extension in four respects: (1) Action by agencies other than the criminal court should be counted. A number of administrative boards, bureaus, and commissions deal with cases which are in violation of criminal law. For example, the Federal Trade Commission has issued orders to companies requiring the latter to cease certain representations which, in Sutherland's view, might well have been tried in criminal courts as fraud. (2) Behavior should be counted as criminal if there is a reasonable expectation of conviction if tried in a criminal court or substitute agency. Here the concept is extended from conviction to convictability. Sutherland mentions cases in which an injured party seeks restitution rather than the punishment of the guilty persons, and mentions that a high proportion of embezzlements may escape prosecution because this measure might interfere with restitution or salvage. (3) Behavior should be considered to be criminal if the reason for lack of conviction is pressure brought to bear on the court or agency. (4) The definition of criminal should include persons who are accessories to a crime. In bribery cases, for example, the persons taking a bribe may be convicted but the persons unlawfully giving it often are not even prosecuted.

Sutherland's arguments are well taken and contribute to accuracy in the delimitation of the concept of crime. It is obvious, however, that the task of deciding whether a particular act is a crime, or a particular person a criminal, becomes more rather than less complicated as a result of these suggestions. It is particularly hard to make clear decisions on such matters as what is "a *reasonable expectation* of conviction" if a case were to be tried in a court. The difficulty of meeting a problem, however, is not adequate grounds for ignoring it. We have gained in knowledge by knowing how large is the task of isolating the necessary data for criminological study. This gain may protect us from the temptation to close our eyes to complexity and return to the crude and inefficient definition of crime as behavior which in fact results in convictions.

We may reflect that a society which pays for the costs of its crime in billions of dollars each year could in time be persuaded to make available the relatively modest fraction of its expenditures for protection that would be required to *create* the data needed for satisfactory research in criminology. Instead of using convicted persons as objects of study, we might create *research courts* to retry hypothetically a specified proportion of cases that have come to the attention of enforcement authorities, using not the prevailing court procedures strongly biased in favor of finding persons innocent but procedures expressly designed to get the *most probably correct* decision in each case, accepting an equal risk of error in either direction— of innocents found guilty and of guilty pronounced innocent. It is possible that such a slow and expensive means of deciding on each single item for research could, by making a science of criminology efficient, eventually pay for itself many times over.

Definitions of data involve questions of borderlines such as, at what point does scantiness of costume become indecent exposure, or, at what point does use of another person's property without permission become larceny? A student roommate may get away with borrowing a necktie for overnight use, but to take a neighbor's car intending to return it two years later gets well into the area of criminality. Somewhere between there is a borderline at which the separation between crime and non-crime is arbitrary. Society has a mechanism for making this decision—the jury—but this is known to be a highly unsatisfactory mechanism for scientific purposes.

This borderline problem is also well illustrated by research difficulties in the field of alcoholism. Alcoholism is an important problem, and there is a clear need to study alcoholics. But persons appear to become alcoholics by degrees in a process that usually extends over many years. At what point in the progress can a scientific decision be justifiably made that here a man becomes an alcoholic? Whatever the answer, we have a sense that arbitrary judgment may have to be involved.

It may not be the best policy, however, to transform arbitrarily every continuum to a dichotomy. We speak of tall men and short men but never debate the matter of the precise stature which separates the two height classes. Where height is a matter of scientific interest it is much more satisfactory to correlate heights with other continuous variables, rather than to make comparisons involving two categories of height. The same approach could be made with alcoholism if it could be established that degrees of the phenomenon could be measured by a scale. In fact, the beginnings of such a device have been made.[16] With sufficient refinement, this instrument may in time make possible the statistical treatment of alcoholism in terms of degree of a continuous variable, making unnecessary a decision concerning a borderline.

If and when we reach the point of clearly defining all objects of study, we will still need all of our data-identifying skills. Time flows, and the organization of matter and life never stand still, and the clearly identified *things* we study change their nature before our eyes, until we feel frustrated by the difficulty of recognizing whether the entity we first observed is after awhile the same thing. In the law a corporation may be forced to honor a contract fifty years and more after it is signed, although all officials on both sides of the agreement may be dead. They are linked by continuity with the present officials, and that is sufficient for legal purposes. But law is not science, and it remains a necessary question whether it is useful to hold that Du Pont in 1960 is the same as Du Pont in 1910, or whether Brown University today should be thought of in the same way as Brown University of ninety years ago, even though already a century old. It is unlikely that anyone has made a sociological pronouncement on the continuity of identity of these particular organizations, but there do exist studies of social movements which pass through a set of stages, sometimes evolving into stable and complex organizations which have no resemblance at all sociologically to the fanatical little band in its early stages.

A useful example is furnished by a sociological study of the Townsend Movement.[17] This organization began as a scheme in the mind of an elderly physician who supposed that the great depression might be relieved or cured by a device to get a large quantity of money into circulation. This was to be done by a pension plan for the aged, who would be required to spend all the pension allotment within thirty days after each payment. An organization was formed under the leadership of the inventor of the scheme, Dr. Francis E. Townsend, and was first called Old Age Revolving Pensions, Ltd. The name was changed in 1936 to Townsend National Recovery Plan, Inc. The purpose of the organization was made clear in its pronouncements—to press for national legislation putting the pension scheme into effect. Townsend clubs were formed around the nation to influence state governments as well as the Congress, and during the middle and late Thirties their influence was great enough to concern responsible statesmen. The 1936 membership was estimated to be two and a quarter million in size.

The passage of Social Security legislation plus the emerging prosperity in the prewar and war periods so altered the conditions that the forces supporting the organization were greatly reduced. Organizations usually tend to die hard, however, in spite of these difficulties, and there is inevitably a high turnover of membership in a society of old persons; the Townsend Movement has continued up to the present period. The contemporary organization is linked with the old through continuity, but their resemblance is small, so that they offer material for a thorough study of the very question of identity.

The early Townsend Club meetings in communities about the country centered their activities on matters of indoctrination, political strategy, and morale. Some recreational activity inevitably developed at the regular meetings until in time the business meeting dwindled to a mere vestige and the card tables became the principal reason for the attendance of members. The national leadership early learned to raise money partly through selling to its members propaganda materials and small items such as stickers, buttons, and license-plate holders carrying the organization's emblem. By 1939 consumable items such as a Townsend candy bar, a Townsend Club toilet soap, and a Townsend granulated soap were profitably sold to members; later coffee was added, and in 1943 there appeared a series of health foods, including Dr. Townsend's vitamins and minerals. Eventually, in the judgment of the investigating sociologist, the movement evolved into a combined merchandising and recreational organization for idle and lonely retired persons. Sociologically it appears to have become a different thing.[18]

It may be some comfort to the behavior scientist to know that things change in a disconcerting way in other sciences. An amoeba, *Dictyostelium discoideum*, has been of much interest to zoology because of the contrast between two phases of its life. A part of the time it lives as any other amoeba, moving, feeding, and dividing in the characteristic way. But on occasions a number of these individual blobs will gather toward a center, arrange themselves into a sausage-shaped mass, and crawl in a wormlike fashion for a short distance; then this mass forms an upright stalk in which the cells differentiate into two types, the cells in the bulbous top of the stalk becoming spores and eventually dispersing to form new amoebae. This example does not necessarily provide us with a rule on what is a thing, but it may help us realize that there are times when this particular question may be set aside so that we can investigate processes occurring before our eyes.

III.

It can be a disheartening experience to spend a concentrated period in contemplation of the barriers between our senses and the basic facts which would appear to be the first steps in the process of building organized knowledge. But even this much knowledge is better than the fool's blissful ignorance. There is hope of progress only when we know what the task is. The data-gathering problems cannot be bypassed; they must be solved. Nothing is hopeless, however, and the best of the research literature of the 1950's appears to show results which are convergent and cumulative, even with imperfect data. Many of the defects of observations are now avoidable by the use of sufficient effort and expense. There is reason to be optimistic in view of the coming gains in supply of research talent guaranteed by recent surges in colleges and graduate schools, and by the reasonable expectation that a nation which now spends over 8.1 billions of federal government funds a year for research will before long perceive the value of putting considerably more than the present 4 per cent of these funds into the pursuit of knowledge of humans.

NOTES

1. H. H. Goddard, *The Kallikak Family* (New York: Macmillan, 1912), p. 77. Italics added by the present author.

2. Pauline V. Young, *Scientific Social Surveys and Research* (2nd ed.; Englewood Cliffs, N. J., McGraw-Hill Book Co., 1949), p. 211.

3. Stuart A. Rice, " 'Stereotypes': A Source of Error in Judging Human Character," *Journal of Personnel Research*, V (1926), 268-76.

4. Kurt Lang and Gladys E. Lang, "The Unique Perspective of Television and Its Effect: A Pilot Study," *American Sociological Review*, XVIII, No. 1 (February 1953), 3-12.

5. William R. Catton, Jr., personal communication to the author.

6. George Gallup and S. F. Rae, *The Pulse of Democracy* (New York: Simon and Schuster, 1940), p. 169.

7. Richard Centers, "The American Class Structure: A Psychological Analysis," in Theodore Newcomb and E. L. Hartley (eds.), *Readings in Social Psychology* (New York: Henry Holt, 1947), p. 483.

8. August B. Hollingshead, *Elmtown's Youth: The Impact of Social Classes on Adolescents* (New York: John Wiley and Sons, Inc., 1949).

9. Thomas E. Lasswell, "A Study of Social Stratification Using an Area Sample of Voters," *American Sociological Review*, XIX, No. 2 (June 1954), 205-15.

10. Edward Gross, "The Occupational Variable as a Research Category," *American Sociological Review*, XXV, No. 4 (October 1959), 640-49.

11. Delbert C. Miller and William H. Form, "Measuring Patterns of Occupational Security," *Sociometry*, X (November 1947), 362-75.

12. From a study by A. J. Jaffe and R. O. Carleton, *Occupational Mobility in the United States, 1930–1960* (New York: King's Crown Press, 1954), 53-57.

13. Seymour M. Lipset and Reinhard Bendix, "Social Mobility and Occupational Career Patterns. I. Stability of Jobholding," *American Journal of Sociology*, LVII (January 1952), 366-74.

14. Gross, *op. cit.*, pp. 643ff.

15. Edwin H. Sutherland, "White-Collar Criminality," *American Sociological Review*, V, No. 1 (February 1940), 1-12.

16. E. M. Jellinek, *Phases in the Drinking History of Alcoholics*, New Haven, 1946.

17. Sheldon L. Messinger, "Organizational Transformation: A Case Study of a Declining Social Movement," *American Sociological Review*, XX, No. 1 (February 1955), 3-10.

18. Law does not have to rest on sociological principles, and such changes as described above would not affect the legal entity. In a famous contemporary parole hearing, however, a man who had served nearly a half-century on a life sentence for murder based a part of his plea on the contention that in the life process all the material of the body is replaced in less than twenty years, and that therefore he, the prisoner, was not the same creature who was sentenced for the crime. The parole was granted, but not for this particular reason.

Part Three

Developments in Social Theory

CARL J. FRIEDRICH

Chapter VIII: The Uses of Anthropological Materials in Political
Theory

ANY broadly comparative theory of politics needs to make all possible
use of the kind of data concerning "primitive" societies which anthropology is able to furnish. Often these data fit in well with what
historical studies have shown to have been the forms of, for example,
early Greek, Roman and Germanic political orders; they are well able
to illumine each other as we have shown in dealing with a number
of topics. Yet, these data are often made rather inaccessible by the
way in which they are presented as well as by their prolixity.

The great body of material which the Human Relations Area Files
have brought together about so-called "primitive" cultures might
help to dispel the difficulty. It may be recalled that the "ultimate
objective" of these files, according to their authors, was "to organize
in readily accessible form the available data on a statistically representative sample of all known cultures—primitive, historical and
contemporary—for the purpose of testing cross-cultural generalizations, revealing deficiencies in the descriptive literature, and directing
corrective field work."[1] It is evident that political theory constitutes,
or rather consists of, "cross-cultural generalizations." In aspiration at
least it seeks to state propositions that are of general validity and
to qualify these general principles or propositions by suitable secondary propositions which assist in making them applicable to particular
cultures or subdivisions thereof. The materials of HRAF ought therefore to be of primary value to the political theorist. In fact, however,
they are found to have been used very little; even a detailed
inspection of writings in the field since the establishment of HRAF in
1937 does not reveal any significant impact upon even that strand of
theory which is empirical in intention and in its cast of reasoning. I
have myself only very recently and with the help of competent
anthropological assistance made a determined effort to use these
materials for the primitive societies, and while I have derived some
useful evidence, the results of these inquiries have on the whole not
been as helpful as might have been hoped and expected. The political

127

theory I have presented elsewhere will bear witness to these materials; it has not been changed in many important respects by this evidence, though there are some significant exceptions.[2]

My experience apparently is not an isolated one. For we are told by the HRAF that the staff "have frequently been asked to elucidate the theoretical principles underlying the system of classification." Other theorists than political ones have, presumably, had difficulties similar to those which I encountered. HRAF has defended itself in terms of pragmatism. They tell us that they admit only "that they have attempted to group inherently related categories in the same section and that they have arranged the sections in an order that is not wholly without logic." But how is one to determine that categories are related if one does not first determine what the substantive content of these categories is? My experience would suggest that it is precisely the substantive content which creates the greatest difficulty. Yet, HRAF claims that beyond what has just been cited as their attempt of grouping coherently the categories involved, "the classification is wholly pragmatic." By this term they evidently mean to refer to "categories in general use," for they contrast such "categories in general use" with "classificatory innovations." They tell us that they in several instances undertook to substitute such innovations for the categories in general use, and that "in practically every such case, they were compelled to abandon the innovation because the attempt *to press the data into a new mold* invariably necessitated splitting up passages in the sources and distributing the parts so widely that the context for each individual item evaporated." Looked at from a methodological standpoint, it is difficult to follow this line of reasoning. Admittedly, the material which mostly consists of integral studies of tribes, kinship groups and other cultural groupings has to be "split up" in any case. If it should appear that from a theoretical standpoint category A now in use is less sound than category B, it is hard to see how its substitution could disrupt the material unduly. The only basis on which the argument could presumably hold would be the suggestion that the materials themselves are arranged according to the "categories in general use." Even a casual inspection of the writings involved shows this to be incorrect, at least as far as politics is concerned. Anthropologists have been divided over the meaning and significance of such terms as "state," "authority" and so forth,[3] as have been others. If Lowie uses the term "state" in the sense Vinogradoff expounded it—and he says so explicitly[4]—then he will inevitably be running afoul of all those who would reject this particular conception.

HRAF seems to think, though, that there is a kind of *communis opinio doctorum*. For they write that "through trial and error, the categories have come to represent a sort of common denominator of the ways in which anthropologists, geographers, sociologists, historians, and nonprofessional recorders of cultural data habitually organize their materials." Can it really be shown that there exists any such habitual use? Or are we not likely to find on closer inspection that the significant variations in use are obliterated by *treating* these categories *as if* they stood for the same referent when as a matter of fact they do so only very partially. Even though HRAF uses its own categories, rather than the particular author's, in codifying the material, the author's outlook and categorial scheme will impinge upon his treatment. Does it make no difference whether the particular historian or anthropologist was an idealist, a pragmatist, or a follower of Spencer, Pareto or Max Weber? Does not the very term "culture" have in spite of some common ground a different connotation in each of these philosophical and theoretical contexts? It would seem that when due care is taken what we learn is that writers habitually use the basic terms in different ways, assigning different referents to common terms.[5]

We are told that perhaps the chief theoretical assumption affecting the organization of the *Outline* is the recognition that "any element of culture may have as many as seven major facets, any one of which can be taken as a primary basis of classification." These seven major facets are described as follows: "Every element of culture involves, in the first place, a patterned activity, that is, a customary norm of motor, verbal, or implicit (covert or ideational) behavior.

"Second, an activity is normally considered appropriate only under certain *circumstances*, for example, of time or place.

"In the third place, customary activities are frequently associated with a particular *subject*, that is, a culturally defined class of persons, the occupants of a particular status, or the members of a specified social group. Fourth, an activity is commonly directed toward some *object*, which may be an inanimate thing, an animal, or a person. In the fifth place, many activities are accomplished by the use of some *means* external to both the subject and the object, for example, an artifact or a human assistant. Sixth, activities are normally performed with a *purpose* or goal in mind. Finally, an activity commonly has some concrete *result*, affecting either the subject, the object, or both. The result often corresponds closely to the purpose, especially in technological activities. The two, however, may bear no relationship to each other.

"To give full and separate expression to each of the above seven principles, though theoretically possible, would produce an intolerably cumbersome system of classification and would seriously fragment the descriptive materials. The authors have consequently chosen in most instances to follow the sources in which commonsense categories predominate. These reflect now one principle of classification, now another, oftentimes two or more in combination. When alternative principles are in widespread use these are recognized, even though they sometimes lead to assigning similar data to different categories." It would seem that so varied a possibility as these facets suggest would suffice to make the material theoretically unmanageable for validation purposes.

These "elements" of culture are seen as a *patterned activity.* By patterned activity is meant that it occurs in accordance with a customary "norm of behavior." It should be evident that such a conception leads right into the heart of one of the most difficult theoretical issues, and that is the problem of the relation of "norm" to "fact" or "actual behavior." We are told that what is meant is that "an activity is normally considered appropriate only under certain *circumstances"*—circumstances, that is, of time and place. While such an approach happens to fit in very well with my own theoretical predilections, because it suggests a situational analysis, there are a good many other theorists who would take exception.[6] In keeping with the situational approach which denies a sharp division between norm and fact, we find further that HRAF identifies *persons* as a vital focus: ". . . activities are frequently associated with a particular *subject,* that is culturally defined class of persons, the occupants of a particular status, or the members of a specified group." One could hardly quarrel with the statement, but the theoretical difficulties arise in connection with the definition of "status" and related matters, such as the categories of leadership.

Similar perplexities arise in connection with such statements as that "an activity is commonly directed toward some object," that "activities are accomplished by means of some external means . . . some artifact," or that activity commonly has some concrete result. At least within my own theoretical framework there is no ground for disputing these statements, but I find myself obliged to point out that they do not eliminate the difficulties which a political theorist encounters with these materials. If one examines them, for example, with the question in mind of determining whether the basic object of warfare is defense of the community, he finds that it is hard to arrive at an answer because of the way in which the problem has been approached.[7] Similarly, the artifacts which are of primary significance in politics are such matters as symbols, myths, and various institutional devices which raise again the kind of theoretical problem we have been suggesting. The same is true when one turns to "results." What are the "results" of political activities?

Nonetheless, and after all is said, those who developed the HRAF have been reasonably successful in organizing their data. Unfortunately for the nonanthropological theorist, these data are assembled under the heading of the many tribal units contained in the files, rather than under the analytical categories themselves. Thus the theorist has to go through the entire corpus of tribal units for each proposition that he might wish to test. What this suggests is that an analytical duplicate be prepared.

One further question deserves mention. Besides the controversies over theoretical positions and concepts among Western theorists, there is the problem raised by the "culture-bound" limits of all these Western notions. There are clear indications that in regard to some problems not only the data but their theoretical grasp are much distorted by this kind of onesidedness. Two different responses to this issue are possible. One is to adopt the position that all theoretical and analytical views are culture-bound and that you therefore have to accept a strictly relativistic outlook and to seek to understand the phenomena studied in terms of the several theoretical possibilities contained in these cultures.[8] The other is to continue the search for universally valid propositions, transcending the older and admittedly culture-bound theories of the West. Much research will be needed to elucidate either of these possible approaches.

If we now turn to the categories which constitute the political realm within the totality of HRAF's classifications scheme, we find the following list:

62 COMMUNITY
- 621 Community Structure
- 622 Headmen
- 623 Councils
- 624 Local Officials
- 625 Police
- 626 Social Control
- 627 Informal Ingroup Justice
- 628 Inter-community Relations

63 TERRITORIAL ORGANIZATION
- 631 Territorial Hierarchy
- 632 Towns
- 633 Cities
- 634 Districts
- 635 Provinces
- 636 Dependencies

64 STATE

   641 Citizenship
   642 Constitution
   643 Chief Executive
   644 Executive Household
   645 Cabinet
   646 Parliament
   647 Administrative Agencies
   648 International Relations

65 GOVERNMENT ACTIVITIES

   651 Taxation and Public Income
   652 Public Finance
   653 Public Works
   654 Research and Development
   655 Government Enterprises
   656 Government Regulation
   657 Public Welfare
   658 Public Education
   659 Miscellaneous Governmental
   Activities

66 POLITICAL BEHAVIOR

   661 Exploitation
   662 Political Intrigue
   663 Public Service
   664 Pressure Politics
   665 Political Parties
   666 Elections
   667 Political Machines
   668 Political Movements
   669 Revolution

69 JUSTICE

   691 Litigation
   692 Judicial Authority
   693 Legal and Judicial Personnel
   694 Initiation of Judicial Proceedings
   695 Trial Procedure
   696 Execution and Justice
   697 Prisons and Jails
   698 Special Courts

72 WAR

   721 Instigation of War
   722 Wartime Adjustments
   723 Strategy
   724 Logistics
   725 Tactics
   726 Warfare
   727 Aftermath of Combat
   728 Peacemaking
   729 War Veterans

79 ECCLESIASTICAL ORGANI-
ZATION

   791 Magicians and Diviners
   792 Holy Men
   793 Priesthood
   794 Congregations
   795 Sects
   796 Organized Ceremonial
   797 Mission
   798 Religious Intolerance

It will be seen that this list is heavily loaded on the "structural" and "institutional" side, even though implemented by a section called "political behavior." This section might have turned to "processes," but it does so only in a few cases such as "political intrigue." The broad categories are missing, even the much discussed "decision making," let alone such more esoteric ones as "negotiating," "founding" or "persuading." Analysis of politics in terms of process can, of course, be carried much further than these specific processes suggest. Yet, precisely the broad and general categories are those which would be most useful, because only if categories are sufficiently general can many different researchers make effective use of them. Such broad and general categories are also more likely to be valid for a considerable period of time. This is, of course, also a matter of expediency;

obviously so large an operation as HRAF cannot be revamped continually in terms of new categories, though some flexibility may be attainable.

The analysis here developed nonetheless suggests that a different conceptual scheme than the one employed in the making of Human Relations Area Files is needed. But how could the existing "pragmatic" scheme be successfully revised? After all, the position here outlined is a somewhat novel one, and therefore not shared by many. How, in any case, could one arbitrate between different theorists? Views of leading theorists differ widely, not only on the subject of authority, but on such other basic concepts as power and influence. Where does the "pragmatic" conceptualist come out in such situations? How is he to mediate between the rival claims? Ecclecticism has usually been a poor way of going about theoretical inquiries; it tends to produce never-ending confusion as incompatible thought elements are combined. Is there any way in which a conceptual scheme could continually be redevised? In many ways the problem confronting us is comparable to that of the lexicographer, and it is therefore not surprising that a "pragmatic" approach suggests dependence upon the makers of dictionaries and encyclopedias. These, however, are slow in picking up new thought, though supplementary volumes and similar devices, even movable pages, have been employed in efforts at coping with the problem. Actually, only a singularly self-centered man will expect all researchers to adopt his own conceptual scheme, especially where it deviates markedly from customary use.

All in all, the technical problems involved in the use of available anthropological material are great; but these difficulties should not allow one to be deterred from making such use of them as can be worked out. To give one indication, there follow some anthropological data tables which were devised in connection with some recent theory work, on the basis of the HRAF files.

Mrs. Marion Kilson designed these tables showing the frequency distribution of certain factors which our analysis calls for. I am presenting these tables here because they provide the schematized empirical evidence for the statements in the text. They are based upon the writings which the Human Relations Area Files contain. They show the value of these files for systematic theoretical analysis, while limited by the adequacy of the conceptual framework which was used in their compilation, to be considerable. Further systematic use of these materials and extension of the research suggested by various lacunae is indicated.

TABLE 1
DEFENSE OF THE COMMUNITY

SOCIETY	Territorial Defense	Booty	Territorial Expansion	Reduction of Power of Others	Expul-sion, Excess Population	Revenge
Trobriand Is.						X
Alor						X
Samoa						X
Tikopia					X	
Murngin						X
Ganda			X	X		
Kikuyu		X				
Nuer		X	X			
Hottentot			X			
Bushmen			X			
Ashanti			X			
Nupe			X	X		
Nansa			X			
Rwala Bedouin		X	X			X
Rif	X					X
Iroquois	X		X			
Creek						X
Crow		X				X
Siriono	X					
Jivaro						X
Tlingit		X				X
Zuni						X

TABLE 2
SUCCESSION IN PRIMITIVE SOCIETY

SOCIETY	Personal Inspiration	Heredity Wealth, etc.	Election/ Selection	Force
Shilluk	X	X	X	possible
Bergdama	X	X	X	
Nupe	X	X	X	
Yoruba		X	X	
Ashanti		X	X	
Nyakusa		X		
Ganda		X	X	
Bemba	X	X		
Hottentot	X	X	X	
Lovedu		X	X	X
Hausa		X		
Trobriand		X		
Zuni			X	
Rwala Bedouin	X	X		
Ifaluk		X		
Tikopia		X		
Samoa		X		
Ojibwa	X	X	X	
Comanche	X			
Siriono		X		
Nambicuara	X			
Jivaro	X	X	X	

TABLE 3
DELIBERATE DECISION MAKING

A. Extent of Data

SOCIETY	No Data	Limited Data	Adequate Data
Nuer	X		
Kikuyu			X
Nambicuara	X		
Siriono	X		
Comanche			X
Samoa			X
Tallensi	X		
Rwala	X		
Murngin		X	
Tlingit			X
Naskapi		X	
Iroquois			X
Zuni		X	
Yahgan	X		
Jivaro	X		
Ojibwa			X
Trobriand		X	
Marquesas		X	
Alor	X		

B. Persons Making the Decisions

SOCIETY	Council of Elder Men	Council of Adult Men	Council of Limited Membership
Marquesas	X		
Murngin	X		
Naskapi	X		
Aranda	X		
Kikuyu	X		
Trobriand		X	
Ojibwa		X	
Zuni			X
Comanche			X
Iroquois			X
Samoa			X
Tlingit			X

TABLE 4
TYPES OF FORMATION (EDUCATION)

						INFORMAL INSTRUCTION	
	FORMAL INSTRUCTION						Parents
			Age				and
	Initiation	Koranic	Grade	Evening	Peer	Elder	Older
SOCIETY	Ceremony	School	System	School	Group	Siblings	People
Yahgan	X						
Hausa		X					
Rif		X					
Amhara					X		
Ifaluk						X	
Fanti							X
Nupe		X					
Tiv							X
Bembo	X						
Mende	X						
Ganda				X			
Kikuyu	X			X			
Nuer						X	X
Tikopia							X
Samoa						X	
Alor							X
Ojibwa				X			
Iroquois							X

This table is not intended to imply that informal education does not occur in the societies with one or more forms of formal education, but merely to show that although informal education is probably a universal of all societies in all times and places, formal education need not be but it is not a prerogative of "civilized" societies.

These data tables show underlying uniformities as well as wide variety. They help to make persuasive the case for closer cooperation between anthropologists and political and other social theorists. Political theory, in spite of its central role in the understanding of man, has not so far coped with the problems anthropological research has raised, through beginnings are to be noted.[9] There can be little doubt that the gain for both disciplines would be considerable. That the political ways of men are a part of their general culture and that hence a political segment of each "culture" is worth distinguishing seems patent. Whether that segment ought to be holistically separated from the rest, as the term "political culture" suggests, may be doubtful and certainly calls for further inquiry and research. But until political theory utilizes to the full the findings of anthropological researchers (and stimulates researchers to extend them in accordance with the questions political theory asks), we can hardly expect political theory to be "general" in any justifiable sense of a systematic set of generalizations concerning established matters of political experience.[10]

NOTES

1. See *Outline of Cultural Materials*, ed. G. P. Murdock (4th rev. ed.; Taplinger Publishing Co., Human Relations Area Files Press, 1961).

2. The following observations were in part presented to a research seminar held under the auspices of the Social Science Research Council, chaired by Gabriel Almond and James Coleman, in 1962. They are intended to explain the use made of anthropological data in my book, *Man and His Government—A Theory of Politics*, 1963.

3. R. H. Lowie, *The Origin of the State*, 1927, 1948; L. P. Mair, *Primitive Government*, 1962; I. Schapera, *Government and Politics in Tribal Societies*, 1956 (for discussion of meaning of government, see pp. 38-39); M. G. Smith, "On Segmentary Lineage Systems," *Journal of the Royal Anthropological Institute*, LXXXVI (1956), pp. 39-80 (for discussion of political action, government, etc., see pp. 43ff.).

4. Lowie, *op. cit.*, p. 43. Vinogradoff is in the general tradition represented by Austin, Esmein, Jellinek, and others.

5. For a careful review of the complexities of anthropological writings on culture compare F. M. Keesing, *Culture Change*, 1953.

6. See Chapter 2 of my *Man and His Government*, 1963.

7. L. P. Mair, *An African People in the Twentieth Century*, 1934; M. Fortes and E. E. Evans-Pritchard, *African Political Systems*, 1940; K. A. Busia, *The Position of the Chief in the Modern Political System of Ashanti: a Study of the Influence of Contemporary Social Changes in Ashanti Political Institutions*, 1951; S. F. Nadel, *A Black Byzantium: The Kingdom of Nupe in Nigeria*, 1942; M. G. Smith, *The Economy of Hausa Commu-*

nities in Zaria, 1955 and A. Musil, *The Manners and Customs of the Rwala Bedouins,* 1928.

8. Many anthropologists lean in this direction, as do writers like Spengler. Cf. Mair, *op. cit.,* 1962, p. 198 echoing Ruth Benedict, *Patterns of Culture,* 1934; *contra,* Clyde Kluckhohn, *Mirror for Man,* 1949.

9. Gabriel Almond and James Coleman, *The Politics of Developing Areas,* 1961, and the literature cited there. Is it quite accidental that an anthropologist seeking to cope with the politics of a Mexican village should feel obliged to go back to the originator of "modern" political theory, Machiavelli? Cf. Paul W. Friedrich, "A Tarascan Cacicazgo—Structure and Function" in *Systems of Political Control and Bureaucracy in Human Societies,* 1958.

10. See for example, Bertrand de Jouvenel, *Pure Theory of Politics,* 1963, or A. P. d'Entreves, *Dottrina dello Stato,* 1962; Charles E. Merriam, *Political Power,* 1934, already called attention to this problem.

TALCOTT PARSONS

Chapter IX: Recent Trends in Structural-Functional Theory

THE CATEGORY of structural-functional theory should probably be regarded not so much as a school or type of theory in the usual sense as a stage in the more general development of theory in the social sciences.[1] It seems to me to be the stage characterized above all by the emergence into importance of the concept of system. At the same time it embodies a concern with systems which wishes to retain as close touch as possible with significant empirical generalizations and problems but at the same time realizes that these two aims are, in the current state of knowledge, incompatible with the requirement for an *ideal* theoretical system—that it should be a deductive propositional system in which all propositions of empirical relevance should be strictly deductible from a small number of basic assumptions.[2]

Within this broad conception there are, I think, two principal special features of such theory in sociology, as distinguished, for example, from biology from which the model has to an important degree been drawn. These may be said to be the two central categories of content which must be utilized for the interpretation of social action (*Handeln*), as this problem was above all formulated by Max Weber in his methodological studies. One of these is the reference to cultural content with its complexes of symbolically meaningful patterns (*Sinnzusammenhänge*) which have normative significance for the actor—*i.e.*, in many different ways define what he ought to do and discriminate between more and less valued modes of action. The other is the concern for the psychological motivation of the actor in terms of the gratifications and deprivations of interests which are at stake in his relations to others and in relation both to the normative cultural components of the system and to the external, *i.e.* nonaction, environment.

This type of theory can perhaps be said to have come to some kind of crystallization in the United States in the 1930's. It has resulted mainly from a synthesis between three traditions, namely those of British social anthropology in which, with all their differences, Malinowski and Radcliffe-Brown were the most important influences, of Emile Durkheim, and of Max Weber. Perhaps the Durkheim—Radcliffe-Brown influence was most important for the concepts of function and system and that of Weber for analytical method within that framework. It may be noted that the two elements emphasized by Weber, as noted above, have formed the starting points for the attempt to define the relations between social systems and, on the one hand, cultural systems, and on the other hand, psychological or personality systems.

I shall divide this paper into two approximately equal parts. In the first part I shall review what I feel to be the main features of the structural-functional tradition of sociological theory and a few developments from this tradition which I have personally felt to be particularly important for its future trends. In the second part I shall then take up a very schematic review of a few major trends in American sociological thought, including not only theory as such but types of empirical research. My intention is to show that these main trends fit into a meaningful pattern of development of the broad mode of theoretical analysis, one by which the stage of structural-functional theory is beginning to give way to a more advanced type of analysis.

I

One of the most difficult problems of sociological theory has been, among the many kinds of description of social phenomena which have been current on a common-sense basis—in a very broad meaning of common sense which would from this point of view include law—to select and order these descriptions in terms of a technical interest of its own. It is perhaps as providing criteria of relevance and importance for this process of selection and ordering that the conception of function in and for a social system has performed its greatest services to sociological science. It has forced, within a systematic framework, posing of the question of the place in a wider system of any given descriptive item. The basic assumption of course has been the presumption that items stand in some kind of systematic interdependence with each other, though just what kind has been highly problematical.

It is here that the most important relevance of the concept of structure becomes evident. Structure, a concept common, of course, to all the empirical sciences, designates an aspect of a system which has relative stability—particularly familiar in the case of anatomical structure. The simplest use of the concept is to describe aspects of the system which for a particular purpose may be assumed to be given in such a way that problems concern only the ascertaining of their properties and their relations to other related elements.

Carrying out structural analysis in this sense may seem to be so elementary a matter that it would not be legitimate to call it theoretical analysis in any sense. With such a view I emphatically disagree. In the first place, selection among an infinite variety of properties possibly considered to be important cannot be a matter of common sense but requires theoretical criteria. Thus in the early history of mechanics it was by no means obvious that the mass rather than the density of a body had special theoretical significance. Similarly in recent social science careful discrimination between the *role*—participation of an individual in social interaction—and the characteristics of his personality which are independent of this role structure has become commonplace, but the history of social thought testifies eloquently to the fact that consistently making this discrimination has been much more than a matter of simple common sense.

The same reasoning applies to the establishment of relations among components of a social system at the purely structural level. Such distinctions as that, importantly used in slightly different terminology by Max Weber, between universalistic and particularistic modes of ordering the relations among structural units in a social system will illustrate this point. Thus the structure of kinship is overwhelmingly ordered in particularistic terms, whereas that of allocation of status by achievement, e.g., in a school system, is universalistic.

It has been remarked that it is the concept of function, including of course the systematic classification of different types of function, which constitutes the primary set of theoretical reference points for structural analysis even at this elementary level. The question of the functional contribution of a structural component to the operation of a system is always, implicitly if not explicitly, the question of the probable consequences of specifiable alterations in this operation which would result from specifiable changes in the structure. Theoretically, of course, the specification of the relations between these two sets of changes implies on the one hand a systematically ordered classification of structural types with reference to each kind of component and to each category of relations among them. On the other hand the establishment of relations between changes and their consequences requires empirical evidence of the relationship over a sufficient range of variability among cases.

This "simple" level of theoretical analysis thus carries with it a structure of problems which can lead very far indeed. There are at least three limiting fields of structural generalization which are implicit in this way. The first is generalization about the interrelations of structural components in particular types of social systems, the degrees of rigidity and flexibility of such relations, and the limits of compatibility of different components in the same system. The second is the problem of the comparative typology of social systems and hence of the range of variability of systems as such rather than of their component parts. Again, as Weber showed, the logic of proof of causal relationship in social process depends on a systematic comparative typology. Finally, there is the problem of genetic relationships among structural types. Structural change is an inherent potentiality of all social systems. Hence the question of what structures under what conditions are likely to change into what others is an inherent question of structural analysis. It is my contention that without the functional reference points, there is no possibility of orderly conceptual analysis of the problems in any or all of these three directions. It is furthermore my contention that, once embarked on the task of functional analysis, there is no stopping place short of the attainment of satisfactory structural generalization with respect to all three of the above problem areas.

This brings me to the central question of the relation between structure and process. Provided one adheres to the *same level* of structural conceptualization, which in turn implies a consistent set of references to system and function, the only type of empirical generalization which can be validated by purely structural analysis is correlational and probabilistic. The value of this is not to be underestimated, but most sciences operate analytically, not on one but on two levels—for example in mechanics, the level involving properties and locations of units on the one hand and that involving motion on the other; in biology, the levels of anatomy and physiology.

The two corresponding levels in the sciences of action, including sociology, are, I think, the structure which consists in the framework of institutionalized and internalized cultural patterns which, to use a famous phrase derived from W. I. Thomas, "define the situation" for action and, on the other hand, the "intentional" or goal-oriented or motivated actions of persons—including on occasion collective persons. To use Weber's terms, the "physiology" of social systems consists in the motivated action of their members, in goal-setting, choice of means, expressive symbolization and the like. To be accessible to analysis in terms of the theory we are discussing, such action must be "meaningful" in the *double* references of cultural symbolization and of psychological motivation. But to be sociologically significant it must also have reference to a structural scheme analyzed in functional terms for one or more social systems. This is to say the consequences for the system itself of alternative types of meaningful action of units of the system must be explicitly considered.

The relations among these theoretically essential elements in the analysis of process must be established by a specifically sociological articulation between the cultural categories of meaning and the psychological categories of motivation, an articulation which has been taking shape in the conception of institutionalized values and norms on the one hand, of roles and collectivities on the other, as the primary structural components of social systems within which meaningful motivated action can be analyzed.

In one sense systematic attention to this type of analysis of motivated action is no longer a matter of "structural-functional" theory in the simpler meaning of that concept. It establishes a new level on which I think it safe to say that the parallel terms are not structure and function but structure and *process*. The concept of function then becomes the common point of reference for the formulation of problems, which is common to both the others and which binds them together in terms of their relevance to the master concept of system.

By these criteria Max Weber was not in a strict sense a structural-functional theorist—not as strict as Durkheim or Radcliffe-Brown. He did, however, think in very similar terms, but without such strict reference to the concept of a social system. His greater emphasis on motivated action and the cognate conceptions of process, however, has made his work a very important bridge to a more process-oriented sociology. The firm foundation in a systematic conception of a functionally ordered and differentiated system outlined above has, however, made it possible to make the Weberian type of analysis more rigorous and hence fruitful than it originally was.

Let us now approach another exceedingly important aspect of this body of theory which relates to but goes beyond these main traditions. The emphasis on the importance of normative references as defining the situation for motivated and meaningful action has been noted. On the one hand, Weber, with reference to the cultural level, and Durkheim to the social, then came to the important conception of *common* normative elements, especially beliefs and values for Weber and the *conscience collective* for Durkheim. From these starting points it has gradually come to be understood that what I have called institutionalization and internalization (with reference to personality of the individual) of these normative elements constitute the primary focus of the *control* of action in social systems, through processes whose general nature has come to be much better understood in recent years than previously.

The first aspect of this better understanding has come mainly from outside the behavioral sciences, namely from the biological analysis of self-regulating systems and from the engineering analysis and design of information-processing and automatically regulated systems. The biological model goes back at least to the conception of the constancy of the internal environment of the organism as self-regulating by Claude Bernard, especially as further developed by W. B. Cannon in his concept of homeostasis. It has, however, received an enormous recent impetus by the extension of such conceptions to the field of cellular biology and biochemistry in the new knowledge about the mechanisms of heredity, both of species and of individual cells, through the complex molecules of DNA and RNA. The developments from engineering have of course involved the analysis of communications systems, computers and automation.

All of these developments have introduced a new perspective. It is that of the importance of the mechanisms responsible for the implementation of patterns for "plans" which, operating with low energy, can control systems of much higher energy. It has become clear that the outputs of such systems are closely analogous to symbols having meanings, and indeed there has been established a direct bridge between information theory and linguistics. It is above all across this bridge that contact has been made by these natural science conceptions with the historic problem areas of the disciplines dealing with human social behavior.

The key proposition, one might say, is that social interaction operates overwhelmingly through linguistic communication and that language and other symbolic media constitute the primary mechanisms of its control articulating as they must with the motivational mechanisms, internal to the personality, which are involved in intentional linguistic expression and in turn those involved with stimulus, through reception of meanings, to overt action.

The bearing of this development on the ancient controversy over the relative significance of *Idealfaktoren* and *Realfaktoren* in the social process should be evident. This very old problem presents quite clearly a false dilemma in the sense that the nineteenth century argument over hereditary versus environment in the biological sense involved a false dilemma. Quite clearly both sets of factors are essential to any adequate analysis of processes in social systems, including those by which concrete structures come to be changed from one form into another. This bald statement is not, however, taken alone, very helpful. It is necessary to be in a position to be much more specific about just *what* the changes are and just *how* (*i.e.*, by what processes) they occur.

The answers to the questions of *what* must, as I have suggested, be couched in terms of categorizing structures which are organized in specifically theoretical terms. These constitute for social systems, the roles of individuals, the collectivities constituted by their organization and association with each, the norms to which both are subject which are differentiated by the functional contributions of roles and collective contributions to the system, and the overall values in terms of which differential legitimation of different functions is defined.

These categories of structural components of social systems are arranged in terms of a reverse order of hierarchy of control in the normative sense, which at the same time is a positive order of necessary conditions. This means that formulation of the interests of persons at the level of roles is a statement of the conditions necessary for the formation of effective collectivities at the next higher level. Certain levels of satisfaction of the interests of collectivities then become necessary—but not sufficient—conditions of the maintenance of a set of norms which cuts across the difference between types of collectivities, e.g. in such fields as the institutionalization of authority or of the inheritance and alienation of property rights. Interests in the maintenance of norms then in turn condition the possibility of implementing certain categories of value such as that of equality of opportunity.

What I have called control is the obverse perspective of this hierarchy from that of interests treated as conditions. Thus the basic immediate limitation on the realization of the primarily economic interests of units at the role level lies in the problem of collective organization. Only within the framework of effective collective organization, which in an analytical sense is political, can the *interpersonal* conditions of efficient social productivity be secured. In this sense the organization at the collective level controls the performance of units at the role level. Similarly only when the interests of particular collectivities have been relativized to the level of a normative system more general than the interests of any one instance or type of such collectivity can a system of order be established which provides the conditions of a higher level of collective effectiveness. A legal order which, though upheld especially by one collectivity—the state—is in important respects independent of the latter's executive authority, is the prototype of such a normative order. Finally, through the legitimation of collective authority, as Weber so clearly brought out, and through the commitment to values in a more definitely cultural context, values exercise a control over the lower levels of the social structure in the sense that action in contravention of them produces conflicts precisely of meaning which can paralyze action unless an alternative pattern of values has been established.

The categories which have just been reviewed are predominantly analytical in reference. Every concrete society and every one of its concrete subsystems must be understood to involve all of them on both sides. There must then be hierarchies with respect to each category, e.g., the values common to the members of a total society must take precedence over those of a particular subunit like a family or a business firm. Taking account of the relativity inherent in the analytical status of such categories, however, we can say that the primary reference of the controlling elements, in the sense stated, is normative and cultural; whereas that of the conditioning "interests" is motivational, though at collective levels we must speak of typical motives and of patterned distributions of them, not of the concrete motives of particular individuals.

How, then, is the relation between these two sets of determinants —which can be taken to be a reformulation of the old "ideal" versus "real" dichotomy—to be conceived? I think it can now be said, in a sense in which this has not previously been possible to do, that a generalized answer to this problem is available. This is that in systems of a sufficient level of complexity, the relation operates through a set of generalized media which are so definitely media of communication that I think it is justified to treat them as specialized "languages of control." The best known of these is the much misunderstood—by social scientists—phenomenon of money. In my opinion political power, properly understood, is another such mechanism, and so is influence in the sense of which "influence on public opinion" would be an example.

One function of these media is to define the situation of action through the institutional definition of the "interests," *i.e.*, the categories of goals, which can be pursued and attained through them, and thereby also to define the limitations to which action in pursuit of such interests by such means is socially acceptable. Thus in the case of money, in a developed market economy a wide range of "acquisitive" interests is legitimately attainable through the use of money, *i.e.* control of goods and services and certain "intangibles" both as consumption items and as factors of production. Conversely there is equally an oriented or directed set of modes of action by which money in turn can be acquired, e.g., by work which results in occupational remuneration, by selling valuable goods, or for governmental units by taxation. Both sets, of course, are subject to important normative controls both formal and informal, and not only are there illegitimate ways of using and acquiring money, such as fraudulent representations about goods, but there are exceedingly important contexts in which the use of money is stringently prohibited, for example in inducing constituents to deliver votes.

Money thus serves to organize a wide range of activities and relationships within a society, including the control of physical resources and the output of physical objects of utility, in the service of a primary function for the society as a system, the economic one, which concerns the production and distribution of generalized facilities, or resources for other functional needs. The *goals* of units, so far as these are definable in terms of economic interest, are defined as related to the economic or productive *function* of the system, the two being primarily integrated by the values which are institutionalized in the system and its units and by the norms through which these values are spelled out in a variety of different contexts.

At the same time money is, for different units of the structure, a generalized medium of the implementation of the interests of the unit, which precisely because the medium is so generalized, can be defined as an interest in monetary resources without specifying the detailed subgoals or "wants" which lie back of the more general interest. The monetary mechanism, including the institutional framework of norms to which it is subject, and the complex of relational contexts, or markets, in which it operates, may thus be regarded as *one* (among several) crucially important mechanism by which the interests of units of a social system and the normative structure of the system come to be integrated with each other. This integration is of course subject to much strain, is always incomplete, and on occasion may break down seriously or even totally. It is also subtly involved in interdependence with other factors in the total system. These difficulties, however, do not alter the basic fact that it is only through the understanding of such mechanisms that it is possible in process terms to understand *how* rather than merely structurally *that* the "ideal" and the "real" factors of social systems are related to each other, including the disturbances to which their operation is subject and hence the conditions of their effective operation.

I would like to suggest without being able to analyze the problem here that political power constitutes another such generalized mechanism, such a language of control, operating in an analogous, though by no means identical way in societies. Power in this sense I conceive to characterize not only governments but all organized collectivities, the private as well as the public sector. I conceive it to be linked to authority in a manner similar to the linkage of money to property as an institution. Power is the medium through which generalized authority is used to bring about collective action effectively. Its exercise *binds* the relevant members of the collectivity to performance of the role, tasks which are necessary in implementing the collective commitments made.

Without going further into the intricate problems of the nature of power systems, I may then suggest for present purposes only that they have features parallel to those of money. The legitimate aspects of authority, private as well as public and including the limitations on its use and acquisition, define the ranges of goals which collectivities in a society may pursue and the ways in which they may pursue them. In this way the normative structure of the society is brought to bear on the crucially important sphere of collective action. But at the same time the power complex, which includes not only the generalized medium itself but the authority system within which it is exercised, the rules of access to power, the conceptions of its illegitimate use and of the spheres in which it may not be used at all—e.g., in a liberal society to enforce subscription to a religious doctrine—is, along with money, a second mode of the general structuring of interests in a society. Whatever the members of a given collectivity may want, they must operate through the power system or renounce certain basic advantages of membership. Hence, within rather broad limits, understanding of the institutionalized power system of a society can contribute to our understanding of the processes by which motivated action is channeled and hence of the ways in which the pursuit of certain interests can be understood to have certain orders of consequence for states of the system.

Such political analysis is, of course, subject to the same order of difficulties as is that of the economic aspect, difficulties which inhere in the incompleteness of integration and in variations in its levels. Above all only for strictly limited purposes is it safe to concentrate on the political complex in isolation from others; it is interdependent in very complicated ways not only with the economic but with at least two others which cannot be considered here.

In the last few pages I have discussed a line of extension of sociological theory which has been of special personal significance to me in recent years. It is a line which seems to me to have special importance in several respects, not least of which is opening the door to a much more advanced synthesis between sociology and economics on the one hand and political science on the other than has existed in the recent past. As a result of this developing synthesis, I think we are approaching a much higher level of generalized knowledge than has been true of earlier phases of theoretical development. Furthermore it seems to me that, with the abandonment of concentration on the type of purely structural analysis discussed in the beginning of this paper, with its resort to highly *ad hoc* accounts of process, theory has begun to evolve to a point where the older meaning of the term "structural-functional" is no longer very relevant. In this sense I tend to agree with my colleague Kingsley Davis that all good theory is functional.

II.

Since I am in a position to speak with most assurance of developments of sociology in the United States, I shall confine myself mainly to American materials. Here it is first to be said that explicit concern with general theory has been confined to a relatively small number of persons, most notably myself and a small number closely associated with me at some stage of their careers. However, stemming mainly from the same roots, partly through direct association, the work of Merton and his students is closely related. This does not, however, by any means mean that the underlying influence of such earlier movements as that of the "social psychology" of C. H. Cooley, G. H. Mead, and W. I. Thomas has ceased to be important. Indeed it has fitted in closely with the more structural-functional movement, particularly on the side of the analysis of motivation. Closely related to this in turn has been the influence of psychoanalysis, especially through the writings of Freud himself.

As I once heard Rene König state in a lecture, the American sociology of the 1930's and 1940's was particularly concerned with an understanding of the workings of their own society, with a strong emphasis on its smaller-scale aspects. Examples were the urban community and the impact on it of immigrants, ethnic groups and the racial issue, formal organization as it was appearing especially in the spreading industrial system but also in government, the small group and the social aspects of group decision-making. There tended in many of these studies to be a strong emphasis on psychological aspects, thus, in the field of organization, on "informal" relationships, indeed those which tended to frustrate the intentions of leadership.

In this whole connection very substantial contributions were made to the analysis of smaller-scale social structures and to the functional problems involved in them. But perhaps, with special relation to the family and to the field of mental health, the most important contribution to theory from this phase came in the sophistication of the analysis of motivation in *relating* the psychological and the social levels to each other. Here contributions from the anthropological analysis of kinship and from psychoanalysis were particularly important.

Seen in terms of the principal currents of theoretical tradition mentioned above, it may be said that this phase of development was more Durkheimian than Weberian. By this I mean that it was more concerned with the intensive analysis of the internal workings of particular subsystems of a particular society than with the comparative and developmental analysis of societies as a whole. Furthermore, it took a line which was Durkheimian in another sense; namely, the deeper one went in this intensive analysis, the more circumstantially necessary it became to probe into the problems of social motivation. It is not accidental that Durkheim's work converged with that of Freud in discovering and analyzing the crucial phenomenon of the *internalization* of social objects and cultural norms in the personality of the individual. I would then suggest that during this period there occurred a very major extension of empirical knowledge of the relations between social structure and the motivation of the individual. This empirical knowledge, purely as fact and empirical generalization, was very much shaped by the statement of problems in terms of the structural-functional scheme as I have outlined it, and in turn contributed to the elaboration of that scheme on the part of a number of authors.[3]

Two developments along these lines may be singled out as particularly significant. In the major empirical study conducted during World War II by S. A. Stouffer and his associates, *The American Soldier*, the concept of "relative deprivation" was put forward. This was a precise statement that under certain conditions the "absolute" desirability or undesirability of a situation gratifying to a motivational interest would be counteracted by the relative significance of variations within a situation meaningful to the actor. Thus, in a famous case, northern Negro soldiers preferred to be stationed in a southern rather than northern training camp, because they had a higher relative status in the southern than in the northern *Negro* community, which status more than counterbalanced the greater discrimination against Negroes in the south generally. This principle was then generalized by Merton and Kitt to other cases and became the basis of the important body of theory now known as "reference group theory."

Indeed this is a much more precise further development of Thomas' well-known concept of the importance of the "definition of the situation."

The second development is one in which I myself have been involved. This is an attempt to synthesize more strictly Freudian conceptions in the theory of personality with analysis of the social structure—in the first instance the family, but also, for example, the educational process. Besides my own *Family, Socialization and Inter-action Process* (in collaboration with Bales and Shils), and a number of essays, similar lines of work have been pursued by a number of authors, among many perhaps notably D. M. Schneider, Theodore Lidz and his associates and J. R. Pitts. This may be said to be the complement of the reference group theory in that the latter clarifies the significance of the structure of the particular situation in its bearing on the concrete motivation of the individual, whereas what I may call socialization theory attempts to show how experience of previous social situations becomes a factor in the structure of the personality itself so that concrete motivation must be understood partly in terms of this social experience. Adequate analysis on both sides of the relationship is essential to the building of a bridge which will make it possible to analyze social process technically and not merely rely on *ad hoc* imputations of motivation.

It must, of course, not be forgotten that the development of theory has been closely interdependent not only with the accumulation of empirical knowledge but also with the development of the techniques of research which have yielded such knowledge. The techniques of interviewing and participant observation on the one hand and of statistical analysis, especially of sampling, on the other have been critically important. Above all they have made possible a bridge, in a sense in which this did not previously exist, between the study of small scale systems—an important part of the appeal of which has been the feasibility of their direct study—and larger scale systems, ultimately total societies. There are two such fields in particular, the importance of which for present purposes is very great, namely ecology and demography on one side and survey research on the other.

The distinction between them corresponds to that between the structural and the motivational (process) references of general sociological theory. Statistical ecology and demography have been supplying us not only with far more extensive and technically refined data than before but with data far more closely relevant to major theoretical problems. The work of such researchers as Kingsley Davis, Philip Hauser, Donald Bogue and Leo Schnore will illustrate the point. Perhaps, in particular for American society, the monograph series based on the U.S. Census is especially notable. Thus one can have a far more accurate and generalized picture of actual household composition and its relation to the family than ever before. Glick's volume, *American Families,* in this series is a mine of information, very well ordered, for the sociological theorist.

Survey research then works on the other main side of the relationship. It gathers information about opinions and attitudes on a basis of sampling which makes possible generalization even for very large populations from small samples. In spite of the highly empirical character of its early phases, theoretically it is becoming progressively more sophisticated and has become an indispensable tool.

Karl Mannheim in the 1930's made a well-known statement to the effect that American sociology had been concerned with, as I noted, the smaller scale phenomena, whereas European has been concerned with societies as a whole and their great historical trends. One of the most significant recent American developments lies in the fact that this has ceased to be true on our side—as I gather the converse has ceased to be on the European side. However, largely because of the techniques just mentioned and some others, and the statistical information deriving from their use as well as information in other fields like the economic, the study of the large-scale society has become possible on an entirely new level of empirical detail and accuracy, particularly with reference to the distribution of the structural types and processes known to exist. Broadly this means that the pressures to comparative and developmental study of social structure, and beyond this of process of change which was mentioned earlier in this paper, have an opportunity for implementation on a more nearly adequate scientific level.

Besides the inherent logic of theory by which the society as a whole must be considered a system, various more specific foci of interest have been involved in the transition between the smaller and the larger scale of systems studied. Among these probably the most important has been the study of social stratification which first took serious hold in studies at the level of the local community, notably those of the Lynds and of Warner. Very quickly, however, the problems not only of the definition of classes but of the balance between conflict and integration were raised, and there has been lively theoretical discussion on these points. Empirical landmarks have been the studies of North and Hatt and of Centers, theoretical perhaps above all the controversy between Davis and Moore on the one side and Tumin on the other.

I am sure that other factors have been involved in the very noticeable recent growth of concern with these problems in American sociology. However this may be, there are, I think, four main areas in which this interest is to be expected. There are economic sociology, political sociology, the sociology of law and social control and the sociology of culture, especially religion and science.

Of these four the sociology of economic systems and of law are the least developed. In the former case two barriers may be suggested. First, for this interest to be developed very far, close integration of the work of the sociologist with economic science is essential, and unfortunately there has been a serious hiatus in this respect—contrary to earlier situations. One contributor to this has been the tendency of economists to regard their discipline as a closed technical system, relatively inaccessible to outsiders. A second reason is that the old dialectic controversy of capitalism versus socialism has come to be seen, on the whole correctly, as more a political than an economic problem in any technical sense.

However this may be, there are promising beginnings of a revived collaboration. Perhaps the most notable contribution so far is the study by N. J. Smelser of *Social Change in the Industrial Revolution,* which followed a theoretical study in collaboration with myself. Indeed I think it probable that the greatly enhanced attention now being devoted to problems of economic development in the "new nations" will prove to be the most important meeting ground of sociologists and economists in reviving this very important collaborative field on a theoretical level.

The beginnings of a sociology of law which were made a generation and more ago, mainly by European writers, have only very recently begun to bear fruit on the American scene. There are, however, unmistakable signs of an important development, though so far little major published work has appeared. There is a barrier in the tradition of the legal profession, including its academic branch, which is in some respects similar to that in relation to the economists. The barrier has been broken by positive collaboration, however, notably at the universities of Chicago, of Michigan and of California (Berkeley). At least some of the emerging work will be broadly comparative and historical, though that in the more microscopic fields is initially more prominent. This will, in my opinion, however, over a period prove to be one of the most important of the newer fields of both empirical and theoretical development of sociology. It should lead to generalization of the findings of the studies of deviance and social control which are already fairly highly developed.

The sociology of religion has been developing rather more rapidly. For a long time it seemed to concentrate almost exclusively on a somewhat sterile controversy over Weber's famous work on the relations of Protestantism and capitalism. More recently, however, there has been a revival of scholarly work with sociological perspective dealing with other cultures and societies—that of R. N. Bellah on Japan and of Clifford Geertz on Indonesia is so far outstanding. There is a whole series of monographic studies, many of them in Christian and Jewish historical fields and most still unpublished. At the same time modern sociological theory and empirical technique are being increasingly applied to the study of the religious situation internal to American (including Canadian) society. In all this the knowledge derived from anthropological studies of primitive religions has figured prominently.

The other field of the relation of culture and society where the greatest development has occurred has been the sociology of science. Here Merton, with his study of nearly thirty years ago of science in seventeenth century England, was the main pioneer. He has recently revived his historical studies on a broader basis, devoting his presidential address to the American Sociological Association in 1957 to this theme. However, the immense growth in the importance of science in American society has stimulated a renewed interest in the contemporary aspects of this field which is not confined to the United States as the work of the Israeli sociologist Joseph Ben-David makes clear. The German tradition of *Wissenssoziologie* of course stands in the background, but the theoretical framework of the field has been very much refined, precisely along the lines indicated, since Mannheim wrote.

The most active field in this process of transition to the study of the larger society as a whole and the comparative and developmental study of societies has been that of political sociology. Perhaps its most important point of reference in the earlier phase has been the study of stratification, and the basic discussion between those who have emphasized elements of conflict on the one side and integration on the other has been continued in this new setting. Also it is important that, as in the study of stratification, there has been a combination of treatment of smaller- and larger-scale systems. Thus many of the studies of formal organization and bureaucracy by such authors as Bendix and Selznick have been related by them to studies of larger-scale systems, as in the case of Selznick's book on communist tactics. A particular notable case of bridging this gap is the relation between the study by Lipset and his colleagues of *Trade Union Democracy* and the same author's broader studies of governmental democratic systems and their conditions of stability and instability. Also the newer technical resources have been extensively mobilized in this work, notably the results of survey research, of which the outstanding American example is perhaps the series of studies of Lazarsfeld, Berelson and their associates.

There have undoubtedly been matters of the personal political orientation of authors themselves mixed up in the movement. One can very broadly speak of a polarization between a more "leftist" position emphasizing conflict from a nondogmatic but more or less Marxist point of view, in positions taken by such authors as the late C. Wright Mills and to some extent Coser—a position at least related to that of Dahrendorf in Germany. On the other hand there have been those whose position has been more oriented to a functional analysis of how political systems operate, more or less successfully, and emphasizing the mechanisms which make this possible. Those on this side include Lipset, Kornhauser, Bendix and certainly myself. Our most prominent European colleagues are perhaps Stein Rokkan in Norway, and in some respects Raymond Aron.

This broad political polarization over left and more or less "center" positions is, however, not merely a matter of personal predilections for political action. It concerns major matters of orientation to the nature of theory. Though there are many nuances of difference, I should say broadly that the more "integrationist" group are more concerned with *analytical* levels of theory, whereas the "conflict" theorists—I use these ambiguous terms only as tentative labels for lack of better—tend to think more in terms of the development of irreducible complex structural totalities, like "classes," interest groups, and sometimes whole systems. Mills' conception of *the* "power elite" set over against *the* "mass" is a good example.

The challenge of the more concretely minded conflict theorists in this sense has served to pose essential problems to the more analytical ones. These are by and large restatements of the great political problems of our century, democracy and totalitarianism in both its fascist and its communist forms, the possible modes of participation of the masses of people in political process, and the role of bureaucracies, parties and the like. These old problems can, however, be seen in the light of a broader theoretical and comparative perspective than before; much more adequate data bearing on them can be mobilized, and a more critical analysis developed.

It should also be remembered that along with studies of other cultures than the Western, especially of religion and society, there have been other notable comparative studies relatively remote from the current political scene but bearing on the problems of political organization and process. Perhaps the most notable of these is by the British-trained Israeli sociologist, S. N. Eisenstadt, in his very recent book, *The Political Systems of Empires.*

Perhaps the activation of the above four foci of comparative and historical study of the large-scale society, and in particular the recent prominence of the political focus, justify saying that, in a sense parallel to that in which the previous phase of American sociology was mainly Durkheimian, the present one is in an important sense Weberian, a fact which if true makes the centenary of Weber's birth next year all the more significant.

In its earlier phases what has been called structural-functional theory would not have been very closely associated with Weber's name. What has happened is, it seems to me, that after the initial impact of Weber's influence which became important only in the 1930's, there has been a very extensive process of broadening and deepening the stream of development of sociological science, so that a new phase has incorporated the "Durkheimian" components as well as others and can now come back to the kinds of problems which were at the center of Weber's interest not only with greatly improved research techniques and an immense accumulation of empirical data, but with a considerably more refined theoretical scheme, which covers many of Weber's concerns and owes an immense debt to him, but which in many respects has gone far beyond Weber.

Whether or not this should still be called "structural-functional" theory seems to me to be a matter of taste of the individual. That it is the product of a normal process of scientific advance in the background of which structural-functional theory has played an important part seems to be beyond dispute.

NOTES

1. This paper was originally written as a lecture to be delivered at the Free University of Berlin. It was read there, in German translation, and subsequently at the Universities of Hamburg, Munich and Cologne. This circumstance of its origin will explain the sketch of what will be to

American sociologists and anthropologists some rather elementary developments in their own fields, since I did not think knowledge of these could be fully taken for granted for a European audience. It also explains, being written as a lecture, the absence of the scholarly paraphernalia of references.

2. A recent, interesting and significant attempt to treat the theory of social interaction in terms of general principles from which strict logical deductions may be drawn to yield a logically complete series of propositions, is that of George C. Homans in his *Social Behavior: Its Elementary Forms.* Much as I believe that this logico-deductive propositional form is that which a completed theoretical system must eventually take, it is my view that Homans sacrifices too much of the richness of reference and flexibility of the tradition of what is here called structural-functional theory and its sequels for his position at present to be attractive to the general theorist. Almost inevitably he selects one particular level, namely that of elementary psychological motivation, as that is defined in the following exposition. He might as well have selected a correspondingly simplified set of propositions starting from idealistic premises. The choice between them is not the issue, but rather whether this order of apparently logically rigorous conceptualization is empirically fruitful in the present stage of theoretical development.

3. When, earlier in this paper, I spoke of Max Weber giving more attention to problems of the motivation of the individual than did the initial tradition of structural-functional theory, I meant to refer to the earlier phase of the influence of the latter. Weber, however, did not develop *technical* analyses at the motivational level whereas, as I now suggest, the logic of the position of Durkheim pressed him strongly in the direction of attempting such technical analysis. This trend of Durkheim's thought then converged with that of Freud and of the American social psychologists. It is primarily from these sources that the more technical foundations of treatment of the motivation of social action which are current in American society have been derived. The more recent "Weberian" phase of our interests, then, does not consist in renewed interest in motivational problems but rather in the problems of the large-scale society as a whole, of comparison between societies, and developmental patterns at this level.

JOHN F. MANFREDI

Chapter X: Societal Complexity and Limited Alternatives

OUR ANNOYANCE with the ethnocentrism of the writers of the nineteenth century in dealing with cultural and social evolution has probably discredited the idea of societal convergence unduly. Hegel saw
man moving ineluctably toward the Prussia of the 1840's; Herbert
Spencer was used as a voice of empire and white man's burden;
Comte saw the positive society as within reach within his own century; even so respectable a figure as Durkheim saw his own society
as close to the apogee of human attainment and sought to dismiss
its most egregious social problems as normal. In all of these writers
there was a presumption of aesthetic, moral and social superiority
that contemporary readers may find a little disturbing. These writers
saw themselves as the voices of the nearly perfect society that was
to come through a systematic application of human intelligence to
technological and social problems. These same writers usually assumed that extant primitive societies and other civilizations were in
large measure identical with previous phases in the development
of their own societies. They have caused no end of annoyance to
anthropologists by underestimating the diversity of primitive cultures
and talking grandly about primitive man as though he were a creature
of but one mind and mold no matter how various were his incarnations in the particular. We must in fairness say that if any ethnog-
rapher of the nineteenth century saw such primitive homogeneity
it could only have been because he failed to read his fellows' work.
The specialist certainly knew too much to fall into this error but the
great system-building theoreticians were too concerned with writing
weighty organa under which *all* knowledge might be subsumed to
deal with minutiae that might detract from such master plans.
Perhaps we should not be too critical of this—a system-builder must
necessarily have some of the schizophrenic's ability to ignore data
that do not fit into his constructs if he is not to become involved
in the insurmountable chore of dealing with all phenomena. In general, however, one may say that the chauvinistic excesses of the
nineteenth century theoreticians did much to incline later scholars

159

toward dismissal of the notion that societal forms could converge and toward emphasis of diversity. It seems well to examine a proposition that as societies encompass more people and become more involved in their relationships the possibilities for diversification in institutional arrangements may become more limited and that for this reason institutional arrangements may tend to converge.

Professional ethnographers today, in marked contrast, incidentally, to most laymen, see primitive societies as displaying such diversity that it is practically impossible to theorize about them. They have been so insistent upon diversity as the most striking fact about culture and, it seems not unfair to say, so hostile to theory, that their pre-occupations are inevitably encyclopedic in scope. Inevitably, and justifiably, they become critical of generalizations that are presented as universal in their applicability. It is probably true that there is no imaginable social arrangement so *outré* that it cannot be found as a normal part of life in one place or another. One can give many plausible reasons why polyandry cannot work, but work it does in Tibet; one can give many plausible reasons why "the principle of legitimacy" has to be universal, but it seems not to apply among the lower classes in the British West Indies; one can give many plausible reasons why the *susu* cannot work, but work it does, too.

What lacks emphasis in these discussions is the consideration that the primitive society, with relatively few individuals or groups pursu-ing divergent, and therefore mutually limiting, activities, has a liberty for variation that cannot obtain in the large multi-group society. This variation is also a luxury of technological and social inefficiency. The adeptness of some primitive peoples at certain manual skills can obscure the fact that there is no important chore to which the devices of a scientific technology cannot be brought with some advantage. (Let us note in passing that once one introduces such technologies whimsical variations become subordinated to rationality of produc-tion.) Similar diverse complications and inefficiencies may be observed in some of the social arrangements of primitive societies with their complex laborious constraints upon interaction, such as for instance, those involved in ascription of status, with its age grading, clan divi-sion, moieties and phratries; in the elaboration of kinship systems; in magical practices and in the institutionalization of what Kroeber called "the infantile preoccupation with physiological facts."

This great "involution" as the late Clyde Kluckhohn called it cannot be carried on except at the expense of rationality of organiza-tion. The absence of rationality which permits divergence between primitive groups fosters *within* the primitive culture rigidity and conformity rather than diversity. Rigidity and conformity in their turn retard the development of rationality of organization. This is the primitive dilemma. Efforts of the Canadian government to introduce wholesale cooperative buying of food among subarctic Indians aborted in many cases simply because there seemed to be no way of preventing these Indians from inviting friends and kinfolk to a feast that lasted until the six-month supply of food they had purchased was gone. (Postponement of gratification is so much a part of life to people of the European complex of subcultures—at least when they are of middle-class status or better—that it is rather easy for us to forget that it is one of the prerequisites in developing a rationally organized society.) These subtle inflexibilities of primitive societies are as important in retarding progress as are low levels of technology. We may say that both factors combine to keep a society "primitive," "rural," "folk," or "*gemeinschaftlich.*"

It is now essential to the development of this paper to suggest some features that are necessary for diversity and growth within a society. Organization of a society on a large scale requires a technology capable of supporting at a high level of consumption a large population without involving the whole, or nearly the whole, in primary production. It must therefore have developed the division of labor sufficiently that there are special trades and professions. It must have economic trade in the sense that people exchange different kinds of goods on a large scale. It must also have a highly developed monetary system. Because of this division of labor and interests it must have some uniform system of social control that can mediate the unbelievably involved conflicting claims of divergent interests, both personal and group, within the society. It has been suggested by Roscoe Pound that this social control must be through law if it is to work at all. It must have an educational system that produces not only the normatively indoctrinated persons characteristic of all societies, both primitive and advanced, but also the technical specialists with *expertise* in almost infinitesimal segments of the culture.

These conditions are the manifestation of a high degree of rationality of organization—a rationality that brings into play certain mutually interdependent activities. Division of labor and large-scale trading operations are the obverse and reverse of the same coin. Before they can come about the society must learn to postpone gratification, and if the trading operations are to be effected without the assistance of some form of authoritarian distribution system or cumbersome records of barter a highly developed monetary system is necessary. As the conditions ramify it can be seen that they are imposing demands and restrictions upon the organization of the society and its groups.

In terms of technology this limitation of alternatives with increasing complexity is perhaps more obvious. We might, for instance, consider airborne objects. Nearly any thirteen-year-old boy will allow that kites and paper airplanes can be of a great diversity of shapes and sizes and still go aloft on whimsical breezes. But the thirteen-year-old who wants predictable results is likely to be yearning for a gasoline-powered model of more restricted design. The government seeking a military plane that travels faster than sound is bargaining in a technological area that leaves practically no gross variations in design open for consideration. Considerations of speed and safety severely limit the possibilities for diversity in design. This is a far more complicated case of the point Goldenweiser made in his much-quoted explanation of the similarity of oars all over the world.

However, let us consider the proposition again in societal terms, in the repeated occurrence of what Carle C. Zimmerman has called the "atomistic" and other writers the "particularistic" or "companionate" family. When one considers the common elements in the societies where such family systems have occurred one sees that the economy has permitted and encouraged high levels of consumption; that trade has increased; that population is too large and diverse for a *gemeinschaftlich* society; that forms of property rights other than control of land have become a significant basis for family and individual status determinations. When these conditions obtain, in fact, it is doubtful that any family system other than the "atomistic" remains an operable possibility. The "stem" family so intriguing to Frederic Le Play and his followers was shown in Thomas and Znaniecki's classic scrutiny to lack resilience under the pressures of modern society. Most of the features we see as characteristic of the family type that has arisen in modern industrial countries are those we might expect. Children are no longer an economic asset. In fact their maintenance and unconscionably protracted education constitute an extended reduction of the family's standard of living. It is not surprising therefore to find that limitation of family size is common. Success goes to the aggressive-manipulative person in these societies; so it is perhaps not surprising to find such traits encouraged in the young, often at the expense of the spontaneous affecting and consideration that can make children so satisfying (and surely to the confusion of children also enjoined to follow the golden rule). While many primitive societies foster a competitive mold of character this phenomenon cannot be regarded in any way universal among these societies as it is in complex societies that emphasize attainment, whether these be those of the Japan and the West of the twentieth century or that of the Rome of the second century.

Let us now consider the limitation of alternatives in the area of higher education—an area that one might like to regard as free of limitation and open to diversity within the bounds of scientific and philosophic truth. We have grown used to the standardization of lower and intermediate education. Compulsory education has, in producing normatively indoctrinated and usefully trained members of society, leveled and broadened, and, one must admit, for the brilliant student, probably lowered, publicly provided instruction. The demands of the society for persons reliably trained in more and more varied and specialized skills, in more and more widely separated geographic areas, have begun to impose on higher education the necessity for standardized courses, examinations and degrees in the applied arts and sciences. The demand for the higher degree is so universal in these areas and the potential student body so vast that few educational institutions can afford to resist the pressures. As more and more broaden the base of their instruction, more and more begin to assume a certain identity. The hordes of students impose an impersonality upon the instruction, an impersonality bolstered perhaps by the realization on the part of the professors that many students have but one object and interest—the standardized diploma. Because certain common standards must be met and because so many students must be graded by professors who have no close contact with them (or more probably by the professors' assistants), frequent objective examinations become the rule. The same general impersonality and standardized demands made by the society necessitate a more authoritarian discipline and reduce the choices open to a student once he sets his course. (It is fortunate for the survival of the values provided by a liberal education that the subjects pursued still enjoy a certain immunity from the pressure of the forum and the marketplace and still seem worthwhile to those who would enter the intellectual arcana of the elite.) Moreover these phenomena are not peculiar to the United States. They have occurred wherever a country has tried to come to terms with Western civilization in the nineteenth and twentieth centuries. The folk substrata have been as radically different as those of Japan, India, Russia, and Northern Europe; and yet the results seem always to have led to big classes, standardized, impersonal examinations and dictation of the curriculum from outside, either formally or informally, by the state or by professional organizations or by business. In fact it is only within the United States that there has been any alarm over these tendencies; in other advanced countries they have been more marked.

Another illustration of converging practice may be found in systems of bookkeeping and trading practice. In this area extensive similarities of procedure have arisen recurrently in times and places sufficiently isolated historically or geographically as to rule out diffusion as the critical factor. It is unlikely, moreover, that, with the social stigma that attaches to trade, such techniques have been preserved for their intellectual interest by the elite to the same extent as has, say, Roman law. The explanation seems rather to lie in the fact that commerce on a large scale imposes certain conditions for itself. As transactions become more complex and removed from the immediacy and finality of barter or even monetary settlement, records become necessary in order that a business may "account" in understandable, and therefore usually standard, ways at any moment to its customers but more especially to itself or its "shareholders" and, as things ramify, to the state. The very rationality of trade as a process lessens the possibility for the exercise of whim in any fundamental aspect of the activity. Variation in keeping satisfactory records is possible only in minor matters of convention and systems of notation.

As we have developed the argument supporting the proposition that increasing complexity within a society reduces the number of possible forms that social arrangements may take, it has become apparent that the convergence which results is not always that of simplification. In many cases it is due to duplication of more and more facets in arrangements of greater complexity. However, in the final analysis, it is the demands of the larger, more complex society that are more complex; not necessarily the answers to these demands. The rationality of organization required by the large-scale society probably dictates that the answers be as simple as possible yet without always forcing simplification unless incompatibility of some sort is involved; it may in the same instance make other aspects of the arrangement more complex to satisfy other demands. However, whether it is in simplification or in complication, convergence of patterns of social arrangement does appear to come with increases in size and complexity of the society due to a limitation of alternatives by that increase in size and complexity. A proposition similar to this has of course been suggested by many in answering the question, "Does history repeat itself?"

ERNEST BECKER

Chapter XI: The Validity of "Oedipus Complex" as an Abstract
Scientific Construct

VON BERTALANFFY has compared science, poetically, to the art of
painting—that is, the art of omission, which represents things by a
few characteristic traces.[1] It is enough for science to connect certain
traces of reality, to establish some orderliness in the relations of things,
without having to penetrate to the "innermost core of reality" (whatever that may be). Science does this by formulating the well-known
"abstract constructs"—bold theoretical conceptualizations which represent nothing in observed reality, but which nevertheless enable man
to get beyond everyday facts with a new, clear understanding.

Proponents of the construct called "Oedipus complex" have
claimed that this has the status of precisely the kind of bold abstraction which science fashions and with which it explains so much. And
psychoanalytic clinicians have amassed a half-century of case histories
to support the validity of their claim. Critics of the "Oedipus complex"
have countered by citing indisputable evidence from the history of
science which shows that the explanatory power of a construct has
no relationship to its truth or falsity: the metaphysics of man's sinful-
ness, for example, has a high and durable explanatory potential and
little relationship to the findings of science. The only way out of
the dilemma of validity, they claim, is to fashion abstract constructs
that can be connected to some form of controlled inquiry so that
these constructs may be proven "assertible" or false. It is the purpose
of this paper to contribute to a clearing of the air in this sometimes
acrimonious debate by suggesting a more comprehensive approach
to the problem.

The recent symposium of psychoanalysis and scientific method
reflected the apparent irreconcilability of the positions of most philosophers and the psychoanalysts.[2] In this debate, positions seemed
invariably to solidify around the "Oedipus complex." There is no
need to recapitulate the details here, except to say that the philosophers tended to protest that this concept had to be better defined

before they would seriously consider it; it had to be removed from its sacrosanct status of a merely asserted universal and submitted to possible falsification. It will not do, claimed the philosophers, to have a small band of experts asserting that the "Oedipus complex" is a universal phenomenon and then adding that those who have not been initiated into this core of experts naturally will not and cannot admit the concept to scientific status. The psychoanalysts, on the other hand, protested their aspirations to scientific method, their nonesotericism, and the indubitability of the "Oedipus complex" in *Homo sapiens*. It seems fair to say that, to an impartial reader, the philosophers seemed to unload the more impressive critical volleys.

There is perhaps nothing amazing in the opaqueness of communication among men of good will; but I daresay that in this case we are justified in pointing an accusing finger at that familiar scapegoat—namely, the narrowness of *expertise* that must usually result from the compendiousness of modern knowledge. This does not imply a megalomania on the part of the present writer but rather the hope that we can turn up a few corners that have been overlooked.

One understanding attempt to reconcile philosophers and psychoanalysts was made by the philosopher Arthur Danto. He pointed to the extraordinary difficulty that the psychoanalysts had in connecting the abstract construct "Oedipus complex" with the facts of observation. There are semantic rules for establishing this connection, he maintained, but

> . . . it is also clear that whatever are the semantic rules that they [the psychoanalysts] employ, these must be complex to an extraordinary degree. So complex, in fact, that a statement of the rule would very likely involve an enormously long disjunction of observation predicates, with each disjunct itself highly complex. But this means that it requires considerable training, responsibility, and experience ever to be able to apply that term (or any other theoretical term in psychoanalysis).[3]

This observation is true enough, and psychoanalysts would undoubtedly not hesitate to make it their own. Certainly, no uninitiate can proceed to wield the observation predicates of quantum mechanics. But anyone *could*—and without intuition—if they wanted to, learn to do so. Furthermore, and more importantly, they could proceed to controlled testing. Fortunately, Danto goes on to point out that the philosopher may wonder whether there is indeed any sense in which the "Oedipus complex" theory might be invalidated in view of the labyrinthine rules and partly intuitional procedure of a psychoanalytic practice.

FREUD'S CONCEPTUAL IMPERIALISM

When we look back at Freud's early formulation of the concept, two things stand out. In the first place, his procedure was scientific, in the way some understand the term. In the second place, Freud, flushed with the explanatory power of an imaginative abstract construct, succumbed to the fallibility of many theorists: he went on to claim too much.

Freud formulated the idea of an "Oedipus complex" at least partly in time-tested scientific procedure: he began with a real and vexing problem; he probed about for certain facts that would clarify it; he went beyond the meager and common-sense facts to an imaginative postulation that beautifully answered his problem by laying bare heretofore unsuspected relationships. In the widely familiar classical case of "Little Hans," for example, the clinical problem presented to Freud was a crippling phobia of a five-year-old boy, whose fear of horses kept him indoors. Communications from the patient, although intimating and revelatory of broader connections, were too crude or insufficient to determine the true cause of the phobia.[4] But Freud used his familiar entity—the "Oedipus complex"— to explain that the child's fear of his castrating father had been projected onto horses. Of course, the argument over the validity of the construct centers here: in the absence of the possibility of falsification, there is a danger of built-in circularity. But there seems little reason to impugn the aspiringly scientific nature of Freud's approach. Nagel, for example, has insisted that there is no logical difference between the data derived from "controlled investigation" and those derived from "controlled experiment." The scientist need not himself introduce "the observed variations in the assumed determining factors of observed changes in the phenomenon." He may simply find them in the phenomenon, providing that the inquiry is controlled with care.[5] Lest we get caught up here in the argument over the rigorousness of control and the validity of interpersonally communicated data in the psychoanalytical clinical situation, let me hasten on to further points which I hope will clarify the problem in retrospect.[6]

Now Freud, convinced that he had a good thing, undertook to make a real workhorse of "Oedipus complex." What took shape as an ethereal abstraction in clinical practice became truly protean: "Oedipus complex" was generalized to describe the crucial developmental phase of childhood. Every human child must pass through it on the way to adulthood. He must give way to castration threats and become a nonsexual performer. Thereby, he exchanges continuing biological dependence on his parents and (all this according to Freud) early sexual precocity for symbolic performance according to the commands of a social world. He becomes a social actor who must repress or otherwise defend himself against his biological tendencies. Thus, the "Oedipus complex" is postulated as a natural history description of human development in all cultures and in all times.

Secondly, Freud, in *Totem and Taboo,* made the "Oedipus complex" *an allegorical historical event* to explain phylogenetic development out of subhuman species. Freud postulated that over a period of time it was necessary for protohominids to suppress their natural, antipaternal aggressiveness in order for cooperative human society to take shape.

Finally, in clinical practice itself, the "Oedipus complex" took fatal reified shape as a *disease entity*. It was now less an abstract concept that imaginatively laid bare certain unobservable relationships between child and parents; rather, it came to be "thing"—a complex aggregate that the patient had to resolve and "work through" with the aid of the psychoanalyst—indeed with him alone. Everyone "had" an "Oedipus complex" if only he could be trained to see it or persuaded to avow it.

There is little wonder that contemporary philosophers, trained, for the most part, in rigorousness and parsimoniousness of thought, have found easy targets among the psychoanalysts, although one might suspect that the acidity of their attacks may have been motivated in part by the similarity of Freudian conceptual imperialism to that of certain speculative philosophers in their own historical ranks. However that may be, the philosopher would be wrong to imagine that vulnerability to attack is, in this case, indication of utter bankruptcy of concept. Freud's ambition attests to the very real importance of the basic abstract construct he has fashioned. However, only when the psychoanalyst is forced to retreat in his ambition does the full value of this concept become apparent. Furthermore (and here is the rub), when the full value of the "Oedipus complex" construct is revealed, it is no longer the legitimate property of the psychoanalysts! Freud's grave has been pillaged by needful—albeit respectful—social scientists.

Applied Problem versus Pure Historical Theory

The Olympian aspirations of psychoanalysts were in large measure responsible for the discrediting of their abstract constructs. The "Oedipus complex" became a logically untenable monstrosity: it could not claim to be—at one and the same time—an applied, recurrent clinical problem and a purely descriptive historical theory. To paraphrase a popular saying, the psychoanalysts could not have their historical Oedipus and treat it too.

Let us consider first the "Oedipus complex" as a natural history description of human development. It is to this formulation that the psychoanalyst reverts when a critic raises the question of the universality of the "complex." Thus, in the Hook symposium, Arlow takes pains to separate the "Oedipus" as a *phase*, from the Oedipus *"complex."* As the "Oedipus phase," the term refers to a universal developmental sequence in the human primates. The outstanding feature of this phase, which occurs between the ages of three and six (roughly), is that by means of language, the biologically dependent, physiologically performing child develops a behavioral style unique in the animal kingdom. During this period, he learns to pattern his conduct upon a symbolic code of rules transmitted by the parents; he becomes a value-responsive actor, for the most part, rather than a physiologically responsive actor. Biological systematization of his conduct is discouraged and symbolic codification is encouraged by threats, cajolings, and enticements to new forms of mastery. The end result of this process is the formation, as we noted above, of a responsible social actor—a potential "solid citizen" as common parlance has it.

Now the social scientist gladly accepts this redefinition of the "Oedipal phase" of human development.[7] It becomes an important concept to include in a unified theory of human behavior, a use to which Talcott Parsons, for example, has put it in his abstract theories. But it would seem that the psychoanalyst, by honest clarification, has met the fate common to the true scientist: his formulation has become the property of the scientific community at large, and he can no longer claim the unique possession of an esoteric insight. Furthermore, there is another consequence which the psychoanalyst has not seen and (up to now) *will not* see; and this consequence has more far-reaching implications.

The psychoanalyst has urged us to consider the "Oedipus" as a developmental phase rather than as a complex in order to stress its universality. So considered, he is unquestionably correct—the "Oedipal phase" is part of the natural history of all human actors. But in winning the skirmish he has done himself out of the battle. If we define the "Oedipal phase" as that behavior by which a potential *Homo sapiens* becomes human, where are we to observe it? In the style of behavior which we term human, of course: in other words, "Oedipus" becomes a behavioral style which everyone possesses. It is the human mold for action, an adaptation in the higher primates that permits symbolic action. "Oedipal phase" as a description of human behavior actually tells us much less than it seems to promise: that is, it is tantamount to saying, "All animals which undergo a stage of development in which proximal, biological relationships give way to relationships based on symbolic derivation of action-rules will manifest value-responsive, symbolic functioning." In other words, "All humans show human behavior."

If we accept this analysis, it becomes plain that the "Oedipus complex" can no longer be considered a scientific "problem." The "Oedipal phase" is like archaeology and evolutionary theory: it is an historical theory. As such it has, of course, full claim to scientific status. But in asserting this claim, the scientific status of the clinical problem must vanish. It is difficult to conjecture what the psycho-analyst might counter here. Perhaps he would say, as he has done, that the clinical problem represents the individual who is not actualiz-ing his full human potential—that is, one who experienced such great difficulties during the "Oedipal phase" of development that his consequent "neurotic" behavioral style represents an undesirable pattern of conduct. It is precisely at this point that psychoanalysts cause irritation and undermine further their own case. An historical theory cannot prescribe a desirable development on the basis of the descriptive history alone.

It is easy to understand how the psychoanalyst got himself into this dilemma. He is a clinician primarily who must justify his prac-tice, whose business it is to treat those in search of correctives for behavior with which they are not comfortable. But it needs no reiteration that the injunction, "You haven't resolved your 'Oedipus,'" as a clinical problem is a normative prescription for behavior. Either it is normative or it is a frank accusation of subhumanity, an enjoinder to come into the human fold. Obviously, the two are synonymous.

ALTERNATE ABSTRACT CONSTRUCTS

The "Oedipal phase," then, is a unique adaptation in the higher primates in which is fashioned human symbolic action. Therefore, a clinical appraisal of the other, more limited problem, the "Oedipus complex," is of necessity always an evaluative prescription. It calls for a type of desired action which would or should replace it in any given case. It is no longer tenable to hold that a term descriptive of a developmental phase can also serve to refer to a reified entity that would or should somehow disintegrate under analysis.

The broader construct "Oedipal phase" is potentially valuable because of the possibility it offers of disclosing invariant points of reference. Anatol Rapoport has observed that the success of the comparative method depends upon finding the right things to compare. The biologists, he says, had a windfall when the theory of organic evolution enabled them to distinguish homologies and analogies in the structure of organisms.[8] It would seem that the theory of human symbolic development would provide a similar windfall in making possible the isolation of invariants. But the principal difficulty up to now, has been precisely this.

Dissatisfaction with Freud centers on his attempts to define certain crucial invariants in man arising out of his clinical work with the "Oedipus complex." Considerable cumulative evidence is being brought to bear against his most favorite invariants.[9] Thus, his sexual instinct and aggressive drive theories are no longer widely supported, even among psychoanalysts. Freud's main difficulty in the formulation of invariants appears now to have been his carrying over of the nineteenth-century mechanism and essentialism. He clung tenaciously to a libidinal energy theory of human functioning that derived from nineteenth-century physics and viewed man in terms of irreducible energies, instincts and strivings.

It was this, in fact, that prevented him from carrying forward his sounder abstract formulations to the point where they would do full work in disclosing a broader pattern of relationships. His belated treatment of the crucial problem of anxiety and his later ego psychology remained bound to his earlier thing-in-itself framework. All of this is well known and needs no expansion here. Rather, I want to stress the full—and as yet insufficiently fructified—consequences of the recognition of the "Oedipus" as a phase rather than a complex. This shift in emphasis, combined with an abandonment of the instinct theory, makes possible the formulation of abstract concepts that are more broadly relational than perhaps Freud himself might have liked. Indeed, he seems to have revealed, in his early dispute with Adler, that psychoanalysis had the choice of merging with a broad social science or remaining a vested-interest clinical grouping. By excluding Adler and his ideas, Freud chose the latter course. A truly staggering output of work has since gone into modifying or refuting dogmatic Freudian notions that were untenable from the start but that retained vitality partly because of this organizational move. Thus, it is fair to say that thereby social science has been considerably retarded.

When "Oedipus" is considered as a developmental phase, certain other abstract constructs can be understood in their full relational scope. In the first place, the whole developmental sequence pivots on one key abstract entity—the self-system (or ego). This is the major psychological organ in the higher primates, by means of which the organism mediates responses to stimuli. It is a response-delaying mechanism which acts on the basis of information fed into the cerebral cortex. The self-system, or ego, thus permits man to hold constant in awareness several alternative responses and action possibilities and to choose among them. It makes possible a complete break from slavish stimulus-response reactivity characteristic of the lower animals.

Harry Stack Sullivan conceptualized the "self-system," and he preferred it to the Freudian legacy of id-ego-superego.[10] In Freud's tripartite schema, man is viewed as fatally divided against himself, an instinct-ridden creature who somehow establishes his *modus vivendi* with society and with himself. It has been argued, with good reason, that by viewing man relationally and interpersonally at all times, Sullivan tended to slight the core personality that each actor must develop and that is so forcefully conveyed in the Freudian model. However this may be, it is important to note that Sullivan had set himself the historical task of breaking out of a rigid Freudian intrapsychic mold, and strong accents in his theory were unavoidable.

The tremendous advantage of the self-system as an abstract construct has yet, I think, to be fully realized. The superiority of the Sullivanian over the Freudian model lies clearly in the number of relationships that are elegantly revealed by the construct. With the Sullivanian view, we are brought to understand the crucial fact that the self-system is largely a series of linguistic conventions. The personality, in other words, is constructed of words and the ability to use them. Sullivan went so far as to say that the personality is largely a series of linguistic tricks by means of which man conciliates his environment. But this view is perhaps too extreme.[11] The self-system is also a locus of linguistic causality, by means of which man animates his environment and lays the ground for action by others. It cannot be overstressed that that which we call "personality" is largely a linguistic style of behavior—a style of initiating communication and a style of reacting to it verbally.[12]

Phrased in these terms, it is already possible to see the conceptual fruits of the abstract concept "self-system;" let us develop this somewhat. For both Freud and Sullivan, the idea of anxiety was basic. Sullivan understood that the development of language was in large measure directed toward the avoidance of anxiety—thus, the self-system was conceived as a series of linguistic "tricks." In the child's helpless dependence for survival upon his parents, an undercurrent of anxiety over possible separation has to be overcome by loving care. Adler understood that it is this anxiety of helpless dependence that is used by the parents as a lever in training the child. Early anxiety in humans seems to be akin to primitive annihilation anxiety that one divines in animals. As long as it is allayed, the child can proceed securely to a development of his potential for symbolic mastery. Early ministrations from the mother provide for a warm sense of goodness in the child, which the psychoanalysts call the early supplies of self-esteem. Later supplies of self-esteem must be won by the child himself in the form of proper linguistic performance and symbolically-mediated conduct that meets the approval of the adults. Self-esteem is a constant factor in human development, because it reflects at all times a secure mastery of the environment—a triumph over anxiety.

The "Oedipal phase" can be understood then, from one point of view, as that developmental process in which the self-system achieves a radical reorientation with respect to keeping self-esteem. The "Oedipal phase," in other words, is a developmental training period in which the child learns to *switch modes of maintaining self-esteem* from an early mode of proximal, biological relationship to a later mode of symbolic, linguistic performance, according to an internalized code of rules. Thus, we can parsimoniously conceptualize two abstract invariants in human development: the self-system as a response-delaying psychological organ and the self-esteem as a basic quality within which the self-system develops.

Now, we can consider the self-system from still another point of view. If all the above is warranted, it becomes clear that the symbolic composition of the self-system is a series of codified rule-prescriptions for action capable of being held in awareness and of being put into linguistic form.[13] The self-system is largely an action-potentiating entity composed of symbolic rule-prescriptions for anxiety-free behavior. This is what Freud meant by the superego, although he did not use the term to include the whole personality. We undoubtedly slight certain accents by viewing the self-system as a codification of symbolic rules for action; but the gain in conceptualization is enormous. We are enabled to see man in his fully relational nature; that is, the very predicates for action that compose the self-system *are rules for viewing and treating the world.* In other words, *the ego is a precipitate of value prescriptions,* which marks the appearance of *Homo sapiens* on the evolutionary scene.

VALUE AND QUALITY IN SOCIAL SCIENCE CONSTRUCTS

The significance of this view is that it permits us to understand that the cultural constitution of the self-system is itself a symbolic value constitution. It is a prescription for attention and action in the world. This was brought out extremely clearly in Florence Kluck-hohn's detailing of the five common human problems. They are questions to which the individual must be oriented *if he is to act at all,* in fact, *if he is to exist at all* as we know him. These five common problems are:

1. What are the innate predispositions of man?
2. What is the relation of man to nature?
3. What is the direction in time of the action process?
4. What type of personality is most valued?
5. What is the dominant modality of relationships of man to other men?[14]

It is plain that these five problems are addressed to the fundamental orientation of the self-system. Answered, they provide the individual with the requisites for coming into being: a sentiment of primary value in a world of meaning, so that self-esteem can be constant and anxiety allayed (2, 4, and 5); a map of rules for navigating (1 to 5); and a cognitional appraisal of the world to be navigated in, which reinforces both the rules and the sentiment of being in a meaningful world (1 to 5).

This long but unfortunately hurried detour has been necessary to establish the crucial point in our appraisal of the "Oedipal phase": namely, that the self-system fashioned in this transition is fundamentally a value locus; that human action is value, or it is not human action. Thus, the self-system, like any good abstract concept, cannot be analyzed as a thing-in-itself. It has utility because of the relations which it establishes. A full break with Freudian essences was necessary in order to shift to what Von Bertalanffy would call a deanthropomorphization of the social world picture. With this deanthropomorphization, we have left far behind serious consideration of the "Oedipus complex" as a scientific problem. It is now abundantly clear that any problem dealing with the mode of functioning of the self-system is a value problem, and as such it is inseparably embedded in a broad sociocultural prescription for normative behavior. The mainsprings for human action are rooted in an extraindividual context, even though they may be manifest only in individual behavior. In passing beyond Freud, we have taken another step in deanthropomorphizing the individual as a central locus of natural causality.

At this point, it might be apposite to object that in ridding science of the "Oedipus complex," we have replaced it by vague and more abstract notions that seem hopelessly to complicate the picture—especially with the introduction of *values* and *quality* as invariant components of the self-system. Several defenses to justify this procedure come to mind and, although they are well known, they are worth stressing in this context. In the first place, we can say with Woodger that it is the elegant structure of a theory that is important and not the "meaning" of its concepts. The symbolic self-system need not be as "meaningful" as, say, the idea of aggressive and erotic man. In the second place, we can insist with Nagel that it is high time to stress that "having knowledge is nothing like having an image, however grand and unified such images may be. . . ."[15] Freud's masterful talent as an image-maker is not enough to earn his theories a secure place. Also, we can level the same criticism against Freudian theory that Max Black leveled against Talcott Parsons' fundamental social theory; namely, that its concepts are too close to common sense. Black observes:

> If the history of the development of the natural sciences is any guide, fundamental social theory will have to employ recondite notions, at a considerable remove from direct observation, in order to have any hope of providing an adequate framework for research.[16]

It may seem inept for us to accuse a theory of being too close to common sense, whose concepts did, in fact, so outrage common sense. But the common sense of Freud's time is not that of ours, and sexuality and aggressiveness have become banal components in today's world view.

But the problem of the introduction of quality—the idea of self-esteem—needs further justification. Goethe earned himself a foolscap for protesting the correctness of his theory of color as an antidote to Newton's utter abstraction from quality in his physical theory. While Goethe's tentative was anomalous in the development of physical theory, there is no reason to deny quality its proper place in the social sciences. The plain fact is (as it seems now) that it is necessary to introduce the idea of a qualitative self-esteem to establish relations of dependence between what we observe in human action and what we do not observe. The difficulty in fashioning abstract constructs in the social sciences has stemmed precisely from the fact that man, unlike atoms, is a qualitative organism in nature. As Dewey observed on the physical sciences, their ideal of knowledge is to eliminate precisely that which is dependent upon the distinctively human response. Thus, abstract constructs that establish relationships in social science must needs include human factors so recalcitrant to physical science method. One of the most important of these qualitative human factors is, as we repeatedly noted, the concept of self-esteem, the basic predicate for purposive human action. In addition, to complicate the problem even more for a physical science approach, self-esteem is invariably a function of symbolic value prescription for action.

Furthermore, self-esteem performs a task in establishing certain relationships that we would otherwise be at a loss to explain. Since it is symbolically animated, as it should be if the "Oedipal phase" was negotiated, it remains bound to symbols. It is a direct link to historical and social events. Self-esteem is a quality that can be demolished by a single symbolic event or immeasurably multiplied by another symbolic event. Stock market fluctuations can break lives, if point variations are great enough. Thus, self-esteem as an invariant point of reference is meaningful within a larger theory because it can be integrated into a logically coherent system. Perhaps social science has so lagged behind physical science in establishing invariant points of reference because it has shied away from fixing upon qualities. And perhaps we can only deal with qualities in social science when we include values as an integral invariant in our theories.

Psychiatrists, who are occupied with these things, are becoming increasingly cognizant of self-esteem as the basic focus for the behavioral ineptitudes they treat. To judge by their theories[17] as well as by their anguished scrutiny of clinical practice, the psychiatrists are becoming aware of the inseparability of self-esteem from their formulations and from value-prescriptions for action. The psychiatrist is becoming (perhaps uncomfortably) aware that he is a merchant in values, a judge of values.[18]

The use of self-esteem as a qualitative concept may lead to the formulation of deductions testable in controlled inquiry. It might be operationally predictable in the individual, deviant case which the psychiatrist treats.[19] Admittedly, this would have to take place within a value definition for normative behavior. The symbolic self-system cannot be otherwise than continually grounded in the fabrication of meaning appropriate to a particular cultural system.

But by all physical science criteria, an operationally predicated construct cannot at the same time be a purely normative derivative. It would seem, however, that in some areas of social science, this must be the case. The formulations of abstract constructs and invariants, linked operationally to behavioral styles and interpersonal events, are inevitably value-laden when we deal with individual human behavior. This realization, if it is not fanciful, bids fair to cause discomfort among both some psychoanalysts and some philosophers although there have been those, like Dewey, who would acknowledge it with a wink.

NOTES

1. L. Von Bertalanffy, "Philosophy of Science in Scientific Education," *Scientific Monthly*, LXXVII (November 1953), 233-39.

2. Sidney Hook (ed.), *Psychoanalysis, Scientific Method, and Philosophy* (New York: Grove Press, 1960).

3. Arthur Danto, "Meaning and Theoretical Terms in Psychoanalysis," in S. Hook (ed.), *op. cit.*, pp. 317-18. Quoted by permission of New York University Press.

4. I am using Northrop's conceptualization of the stages of scientific inquiry although I do not subscribe to his rigorous, sequential separation. See F. S. C. Northrop, *The Logic of the Sciences and the Humanities* (Cleveland: World Publishing Co., 1959).

5. Ernest Nagel, *The Structure of Science* (New York: Harcourt, Brace and World, 1961), p. 463.

6. It seems pertinent to add that in Northrop's conceptualization of the stages of scientific method, he cautions against bypassing stage 2, or the inductive stage, too quickly in order to pass on to stage 3, or the postulational stage, in which an unobserved and abstract entity is formulated. Freud seems particularly open to Northrop's caution but for a reason that Northrop does not himself indicate. Northrop claims that a too-quick bypassing of stage 2 leads to immature, half-baked and dogmatic theory (his words). Actually, this would not be an objection in those cases in which the theory is *testable by experiment*. All theories by definition are, of course, immature and half-baked. But they cannot be dogmatic for long if they are testable. With Popper we might say that the leap beyond stage 2 is justified in all cases where falsification is possible. But on the other hand, in those cases where the leap cannot be rigorously justified by experimental establishment of invariants, there must be extremely careful and self-critical lingering at the inductive, fact-probing stage of inquiry. On this account, Freud seems remiss. Popper, of course, would maintain

that no amount of inductive support could establish a theory, that theory can be meaningful only if submitted to falsification by testing. On no account does Freudian theory yet rigorously fulfill this criterion.

7.   In the reinterpretation of the "Oedipus" as a phase, the much-paraded idea of infantile "sexuality" takes on an entirely different connotation. Forced to maintain self-esteem in his continued, dependent relationship on his parents, the child may attempt to keep a biological definition of the situation. Thus, he would be alert for whatever cues he could pick up—uses to which the adults put their body parts which he might imitate. Furthermore, the child's mode of thinking is still largely concretistic, and he has considerable difficulty in appreciating the value of the abstract, symbolic performance upon which his parents insist. Sharp encouragements and discouragements of vaguely understood behavior force the child to a pattern of adaptation which is largely unconscious of the crucial elements in the situation to which he is adapting. This automatic behavioral style is called by the psychoanalysts "the characterological mastery of the Oedipus complex." Actually, this "mastery" is really a *standardized human mode of confusion* in which each individual makes his own peculiar resolution of a technique to keep his self-esteem. When all of these actors—each with a different unconscious behavioral mode for fending off anxiety—are released onto the social scene, there is, as we well know, hell to pay.

8.   Anatol Rapoport, "Comments on 'The Comparative Method in the Social Sciences'" (a paper by Gideon Sjoberg), *Philosophy of Science,* XXII (1955), 118-22.

9.   E. Becker, "Anthropological Notes on the Concept of Aggression," *Psychiatry: Journal for the Study of Interpersonal Processes,* XXV, No. 4 (November 1962), 328-38.

10.   Indeed, the legacy shows its true conceptual clumsiness in that it leads to the multiplication of concepts beyond necessity. Some psychoanalytic theorists are now talking about a "main ego" and several "subsidiary egos." With this luxuriation, Ockham's razor will need replacing by a multibladed electric shaver.

11.   Sullivan's thinking stressed continual anxiety avoidance by the organism and so seems to have given insufficient weight to an anxiety-free urge for mastery.

12.   The idea of "life style" is, of course, Adlerian. (See also, E. Becker, "Socialization, Command of Performance, and Mental Illness," *American Journal of Sociology,* LXVII (March 1962), 492-501.)

13.   The rule-prescriptions can also be "out-of-awareness."

14.   Florence Kluckhohn, "Dominant and Substitute Profiles of Cultural Orientations: Their Significance for the Analysis of Social Stratification," *Social Forces,* XXVIII (1950), 376-93.

15.   Ernest Nagel, *Sovereign Reason* (Glencoe, Ill.: Free Press, 1954), p. 265.

16.   Max Black, "Some Questions about Parsons' Theories," in *The Social Theories of Talcott Parsons: A Critical Examination,* Max Black (ed.), © 1961 (Englewood Cliffs, N.J.: Prentice-Hall, Inc., 1961), pp. 279-80.

17.   Edward Bibring, for example, makes self-esteem the crucial focus for the mechanism of depression. See Edward Bibring, "The Mechanism

of Depression," in *Affective Disorders*, P. Greenacre (ed.), (New York: International Universities Press, 1952).

18.   Thus the serious preoccupation with Existentialism and Zen Buddhism as somehow applicable to clinical practice. These idealisms offer the hope of getting *behind* the cultural distortions of perception that brought the patient to the therapist for relearning. They hold out the fallacious hope of somehow remaking man without using a culturally-determined ideology in the process. What happens, of course, in this impossible venture, is a proselytization of the agog patient into a new mystical idealism. For a critical treatment of this problem, see E. Becker, *Zen: A Rational Critique* (New York: W. W. Norton and Co., 1961).

19.   Thus we could have pure or limiting cases of self-esteem—a theoretically complete absence in catatonic schizophrenia or depressive withdrawal.

Part Four

Cultural Relativity

T. F. McILWRAITH

Chapter XII: Facts and Their Recognition Among the Bella Coola

FROM THE DAYS of Tylor and Morgan, anthropologists have realized the value of data drawn from diverse cultures, including those of nonliterate peoples; in fact it is this material which is the special contribution of our discipline to the social sciences. Information regarding beliefs and practices from all periods and all parts of the world are, of course, relevant in a study of mankind as a whole, but where there is contrast to our own life, they provide as well a mirror in which we may see ourselves more clearly. Most field workers will recall incidents which have served to throw into relief some element in our own culture which had been taken for granted; indeed, field work among nonliterate peoples is one of the best training grounds for the social philosopher.

This point of view was brought home to me many years ago when working among the Bella Coola of British Columbia.[1] An informant described casually an incident in which a bear had changed into a stump and added that a white man living in the valley had seen this happen. I knew the white man and asked him about it. He remembered it and laughed. He had been in a canoe with five Indians when they all "saw" a bear which, when they paddled closer, turned out to be a stump. His explanation was an optical illusion; that of the Bella Coola, a transformation.

No clearer example could be given of contradictory interpretations of the same incident by individuals of different cultures. But to attempt to explain *why* they were given requires an analysis of what the Bella Coola, as well as of what we, regard as facts, together with the evidence used in their establishment. Since, moreover, a *fact* must be regarded as something that is *true,* this could lead to a study of the basis of truth and of reality. Such is manifestly beyond the scope of this essay, in terms both of time and space. In general, however, it is possible to recognize that most "facts" of our society rest upon four types of evidence.

Four Kinds of "Facts"

I. Facts dependent upon the senses.

We know that the sun rises in the east because we *see* it, that a rose has a certain aroma because we *smell* it, that the pounding of a hammer makes a noise because we *hear* it, and that fire is hot because we *feel* it. No serious mental effort is involved in these conclusions; they are, indeed, "matter-of-fact" observations known to everyone.

In the same category as these observable phenomena may be included those dependent upon personal experience. Each of us knows that certain foods produce a pleasant sensation, that summer will follow the longest winter, that birds will return in the spring, and that a headache is soothed by certain drugs. No two individuals will have had precisely the same experiences, and, consequently, will not have the same set of facts, but each will have a sum total of factual information. It is reasonable to assume that a high proportion of what each of us knows is dependent upon commonplace observation and experience.

II. Facts dependent upon hearsay.

In a court of law, hearsay evidence is not, generally, admissible, but in the course of life it is of paramount importance. A child at school is told that Columbus discovered the New World in 1492, that kangaroos live in Australia, or, a little later, that the nominative plural of third declension Latin nouns ends in "a." These become items of factual information. Many parents can remember a child making some inaccurate statement on coming from school and stoutly affirming: "Oh, Daddy, it must be so. Miss Smith said so and she's a teacher. She knows." The child may have misunderstood, or perhaps the teacher has been in error, but much of our factual information is derived from those who are experts in their field, the equivalent of the teacher in the eyes of a small boy or girl.

With the increasing range and specialization of knowledge, this process must become increasingly important. I *know* that the sun is approximately 93,000,000 miles from the earth because of the conclusions of astronomers, but I would not know how to prove this statement. I *know* that the Arunta have (or had) a complex marriage system which I explain to my students, although I have never even seen an Arunta. I *know* the proper length of exposure to give when taking a photograph because I accept the findings of unknown experts who have devised a light meter which I use without more than a vague comprehension of the principles involved.

In our modern world we are fully prepared to accept findings, but not necessarily those enunciated by anyone. The protagonists of two political parties may put forward statements that are diametrically opposed; we recognize that both cannot be correct, and we try to evaluate the speaker as well as his message. Many of the facts of our civilization come to us in words or in writing; if we stop to ponder their accuracy, we may question their expositor or his methods, but not the basic premise of reliance on hearsay evidence.

III. *Facts established by experiment.*

To a physical scientist, most facts can be proved by experiment. In a laboratory a student learns the boiling points of various liquids, the force exerted by gravity, the reaction of positively or negatively charged electrical elements, or many other physical and chemical phenomena. Having set up some type of apparatus, he watches, measures, and becomes aware of results in these fields by seeing them occur over and over again. In theory, no fact is as well established as that which can be proved repeatedly by controlled experiments.

In practice, however, the matter is not as simple as this. Before starting his experiment, a student knows, for example, the rate of acceleration due to gravity. Unconsciously perhaps, he regards his experiment as a failure unless the result conforms to what he already "knows" by hearsay. As every laboratory demonstrator is aware, many an experiment which is inaccurate owing to faulty technique appears to produce the desired result. In other words, facts obtained by experiment are fitted into the straitjacket of information obtained by word of mouth or by reading.

Outside of the laboratory, experiment is an important, but not all-important, aid to the establishment of facts. A boy who is learning to ride a bicycle may deliberately try to find out how slowly he can move before losing his balance; a gardener may learn to grow larger and more brightly colored iris by the process of deliberate experiments with hybridization. To the successful innovator there is the reward of something which he has himself learned or made, an addition, however small, to his own factual knowledge. If he believes that what he has done is of interest or importance, he may publish his results, and his findings thus become the basis of belief by unknown readers. Many of our most significant facts have become known in this way, but the number of those who have made such discoveries is a small minority in our total population.

IV. Facts dependent upon belief.

In the realm of emotion many of the most important facts rest not upon evidence but entirely upon belief. An amorous youth "knows" that "she" is the one and only girl in the whole world for him; she is equally aware that "he" is the most wonderful male who ever lived. The future of each may well depend upon the accuracy of these convictions, but the usual methods of appraising facts—by observation, by experience, by listening to the findings of others, or by experiment—would be regarded as meaningless, or almost insulting, by the two people involved. So, likewise, is it with religion. The Christian knows that God is in heaven, the Mohammedan that such is the will of Allah, or the Buddhist that Nirvana may be attained after a cycle of incarnations. No element of observation or of experience, still less of experiment, is involved; the facts depend upon faith. It may well be that when first learned in childhood, the tenets depended upon instruction from a parent or a teacher, but this tends to be forgotten in the satisfying sensation of belief. Surely facts appreciated in this way have been among the most significant of all in shaping the course of history.

In the same category belong the sentiments of patriotism, of moral conduct, of parental obligations, or of adherence to tribal or national mores. When Horace wrote, *"dulce et decorum est pro patria mori,"* it was no idle phrase; to the Roman it was a privilege to die for one's native land. A father does not argue why he should provide for his children; he merely knows that this is what he wishes to do, even if it be by the provision of a fatted calf. We may speak of the present as the "Age of Science," but we must never forget that many of the things which we hold dearest are the fruits of an accepted code, based upon faith, and not upon a slide-rule.

These four criteria for the establishment of facts are not mutually exclusive. Belief is influenced by hearsay evidence as well as by observation; experiment is shaped by experience and the findings of others. Nor is it to be expected that the categories would satisfy either social scientists or philosophers. But they will suffice to provide a framework for comparing the bases of fact among the Bella Coola. When I was honored by an invitation to participate in this volume of essays dedicated to Professor Haring, I had first planned to attempt a cross-cultural survey of *facts* as recognized in various communities. I soon realized that this would be impractical. Moreover, the diversity which would have been brought to light would have made any comparison difficult. Instead I thought that it might be of interest to limit a study of these categories to those of the Bella Coola Indians as a single example of a community far removed from our world. I hasten to add that I do *not* claim that the Bella Coola are necessarily characteristic of any community other than their own. Their recognition of facts is merely one aspect of their culture, and so would it have been had I chosen to analyze the beliefs of any other tribe.

I. Facts recognized without conscious thought or effort through the medium of the senses are a commonplace of Bella Coola life. It is through the eyes and the ears that a child recognizes his associates; it is by these media, reinforced by experience, that he builds up his knowledge of the everyday world around him. But his observations are affected by his belief and by his acceptance of hearsay evidence to a greater extent than among ourselves. I remember stopping to talk to a man one evening by the bridge over the Bella Coola River near the Indian village. Quite casually, he mentioned that he had seen a ghost at this particular spot the previous evening. It was an unusual, but not an unheard-of, experience, described as an item of interest. I do not know what he saw; perhaps a swirl of fog. But though his eyesight was, as far as I could judge, normal, he interpreted what he had seen in terms of his tribal cultural pattern, which included ghosts.

Another example of a comparable interpretation of a visual experience has already been mentioned, the case of the bear and the stump. There is no doubt of the circumstances,[2] if the evidence of eyewitnesses can be accepted. Five Bella Coola with a single white man were in a canoe in a narrow fiord when they saw a "silver-tip" grizzly bear on the shore. To get within range, they went behind a point and paddled forward under cover. Cautiously emerging at the end of the point, with guns ready, they saw, not a bear, but a gray, water-washed stump somewhat resembling a bear. The explanation was obvious to the Bella Coola: they had seen a bear, but now it was a stump; therefore the animal had changed its form. It was equally clear to the white man that in the distance they had mistaken a peculiarly shaped stump for a grizzly bear. The possibility of an optical illusion was as unthinkable to the Bella Coola as was a transformation to the white man.

Two Bella Coola independently described to me incidents of a somewhat similar kind which each had observed. In each case a hunter had been following closely a mountain goat which, he affirmed, had "gone inside the mountain." Each was certain that the animal could not have moved in any direction without being seen; therefore the only alternative was that it had vanished underground. The possibility of attributing its disappearance to faulty powers of observation was never even considered.

Just as errors in eyesight are disregarded, so, generally speaking, are lapses of memory. One morning I found an old Bella Coola man greatly worried about the behavior of his pet dog. Before daybreak he had been wakened by the dog and had let it go outside. He went back to bed, but on getting up about 7:30, he found the dog curled up in its usual place on the floor beside him. The man's worry was simple and direct: he *knew* that the dog had been outside, but likewise he *knew* that it was now inside. The only way in which this could have happened was by the dog transforming itself into something flat and sliding under the door. According to the dog's owner, unusual behavior on the part of a domestic animal was a bad omen. I suggested that perhaps the dog had whined at the door and he had gotten up and let him in without remembering the act. But this (to me) plausible explanation was impossible; the dog's admission to the house could only have been in conformity with what the old man had known, and this postulated a transformation.

Interpretations of visual experiences according to Bella Coola cultural concepts lead inevitably to a consideration of seeing or hearing objects which do not exist. I heard repeatedly of fantastic creatures—of a bony flying bird with long flexible beak with which it sucked out the entrails of a sleeper, of an animal with bearlike fur and the talons of a bird whose eyes could rotate in their sockets to emit rays of light that would paralyze an enemy, and of an enormous man living under the ocean who wore a circular hat around which mice gamboled. The number of these *siut,* to use the generic Bella Coola term, was very large; in fact I doubt if any individual knew them all. They resembled the mythical beings of the folklore of many communities, of interest perhaps only on account of their number and diversity. I was impressed, however, with the number of individuals who had heard, and less often seen, such creatures which were as much a part of their environment as the mountain sheep of the distant upper slopes or the rarely seen caribou of the interior. The Bella Coola realized that these creatures were less common than formerly and had an explanation which I heard repeatedly. "Siut do not like the sound of the white man's guns; they have moved away to the lonely areas of the north, particularly inland from Kitimat." Parenthetically, this is the region of extensive engineering dams for the power plants of the aluminum works at Kitimat; the refuge of the *siut* has not remained a solitude!

Though some of the more spectacular *siut* have moved away, some have remained. Four of the younger men were awakened by an unknown sound at night when camped on a fiord near Bella Coola; they tacitly assumed that it was a species of *siut* and drove it away by starting the engine of their moored motorboat. When dictating a text to me, an informant once asked me to keep quiet because "something" was talking to him. A few minutes later he continued his dictation calmly, merely telling me that he had seen a large black creature in the corner of the room. Obviously, this could properly be described in terms of vision hallucination; my point is the simple one that to the individual concerned, he had seen a *siut,* and that experience had become to him a fact.

Concepts from Christianity, particularly those shown pictorially, are likewise "seen," and thereby recognized as facts. A devout Christian Bella Coola once asked me if I had ever seen the Holy Ghost. When I admitted that I had not, he pointed out that he was more fortunate than I, and I naturally asked him when and how he had had this experience. He explained that when he was a young man he had been a patient in "a white man's hospital" somewhere down the coast, and that a young Indian lad had been brought in, badly injured in a logging accident. Neither the doctor nor the nurses could understand his language (I got the impression that he was delirious), and my informant was asked to come in to try to interpret. My friend gave me a vivid picture of the scene: the badly injured patient babbling unintelligibly, doctor and nurses trying to help, and the young Bella Coola, himself a sick man in a strange environment, standing at the foot of the stranger's bed and trying to talk to him. He could not make himself understood, and it was apparent that the injured man was dying. My friend had recently become a Christian, and he wondered whether or not the sufferer was saved. As he looked up he saw four figures bending over the head of the patient's bed. He "knew"—how, I do not know—that they were Holy Ghost, Holy Spirit, Baptism, and Faith, and, therefore, that the dying stranger would be or was saved. The experience was perfectly clear and vivid to him after many years; what he had "seen" was as real to him as a porcupine which he pointed out to me in a neighboring tree. I asked what the four looked like and he told me that they were tall and handsome white men, dressed in clerical costume. It was clear to me that he had visualized in accordance with his belief but that having been seen, the experience became a fact of his life.

Comparably, an old woman told me that when she was young and attractive she had been accosted by a white man when walking one evening in Stanley Park, Vancouver. She claimed to have rebuffed him, and that, as he turned away, he took off his hat and she saw horns projecting from his head. She had heard of the devil, and perhaps had seen pictures of Satan. At any rate she was convinced, by the evidence of her own eyes, of his existence.

This tendency to "see" objects according to culture patterns, completely disregarding the possibility of optical error, is, I believe, an important factor in the rituals of Bella Coola secret societies. Members of the *kusiut*[3] organization are men and women who have a particular type of prerogative enabling them to enter into close association with a supernatural patron, who is spoken of as the individual's *friend* or *comrade*. It is unnecessary to describe how this power is obtained or transmitted; the essential fact is that a group, probably comprising in early days more than half of the population, becomes supernaturally endowed in the ceremonial season every winter. Before the breakdown of native culture, they met as a group in a house from which uninitiated persons were excluded, a house which was believed to be filled with "power." At the climax of every individual ritual, normally every fourth night, the uninitiated were summoned to the house where they observed some remarkable spectacle made possible by the supernatural strength of the performer. A fluent announcer "explained" what they were seeing, but the impressiveness of the ritual depended upon what was seen, not what was heard.

Without question the spectacles were striking and convincing, carried out with great dramatic ability. It might be that the performer introduced his comrade, Thunder. From a corner of the darkened house behind the central fire, Thunder strode forth—a huge masculine figure with bulbous forehead, deep nasal notch and sunken eyes, broad face and a powerful body from which wings extended. As a mark of deferential welcome, members of the *kusiut* society blew eagle down over him, while the reverberations of thunder were heard in the distance. Or it might be that the performer was afflicted with a craze for human flesh and rushed around biting people, partially restrained by his fellow-*kusiut*. Four, eight, or twelve nights later the uninitiated might see the same individual, emaciated through his failure to get sufficient human flesh and inability to eat other food, being finally "cured" by his fellows and a cannibalistic incubus forced from his body in the form of the head of a wolf. Or perhaps the uncontrollable power which had entered the performer impelled him to "die" by being disembowelled, beheaded or drowned—only to return to life a few hours later.

No one pondered in an abstract manner the reality of these

spectacles. There was no question: they had *seen* thunder; they had *seen* one of their fellow-villagers, perhaps a father or mother, become a cannibal and the actual power responsible; or they had *seen* one of their neighbours die and be restored to life. When I was in Bella Coola, although the old beliefs had largely passed away, I was repeatedly impressed by the attitude of even sophisticated Indians during masked dances. In a sense they realized that they were watching actors; yet, at the same time they were seeing supernatural beings. They were not interested in the problem of contradiction; they merely saw, and "seeing is believing."

On the basis of early descriptions, as well as information from elderly Bella Coola participants, there is no doubt that the dances were formerly elaborate and spectacular. Masks and incidental equipment were carved in secret and usually burnt after use. The actors were skilled performers; ingenuity of no mean order was used in such stagecraft as the reverberation of thunder by the rolling of stones in wooden boxes or by the use of hidden cords to move manikins in a lifelike way. Above all, the only lighting came from a flickering fire, while the audience had seen similar performances from childhood and was in a thoroughly receptive mood. The *kusiut* society flourished in Bella Coola; its powers did not rest on some vaguely recognized strength but on the evidence of what the uninitiated had actually seen.

It is more difficult to explain the attitude of the members. One controlling factor was the close bond between them. United for the purpose of the ceremonials, they lived together, worked together and had the incentive of carrying out the rituals which had been practiced by their forefathers. They all knew that Thunder was one of their fellows in disguise, but a good actor virtually became the being represented. Knowledge of the appearance of a being was in itself beyond the range of outsiders; hence there was an exclusive right even in the depiction. Each had the prized function of showing his particular power, and he used it in the most effective manner, by visible display.

I do not know whether, a century or more ago, a *kusiut* member might have been sceptical about some other type of dramatic performance. I am inclined to doubt it, though my only direct evidence comes from an old man who described a number of shamanistic performances at which he had assisted, including a number of ingenious sleight-of-hand tricks. One performance, however, he claimed to have been done by a supernaturally endowed shaman, whose power transcended that of ordinary mortals. The feat was of a type similar to those which he had described, but the difference was that he had never assisted this shaman and hence was ignorant of his methods. And, being ignorant, he accepted the evidence of his eyes.

To sum up: one of the most important means whereby the Bella Coola recognize facts is by seeing, and what they see is in accordance with their beliefs. It is not a question of deliberate deception or of self-deception; it is a simpler matter of disregarding totally the possibility of an error in visualization. This, I think, plays a prominent part in the vividness of their concepts of the supernatural; beings are real because they have been seen, whether they be (what a white man would call) figments of the imagination or even the elaborately disguised depictions of their fellows.

II. If visual observation furnishes proof of many Bella Coola facts, equally important are those known by oral transmission—that is, by hearsay. The Bella Coola affirm that their world was populated by groups of individuals sent down from the land above in the beginning of time, often in animal form. Each of these first settlers brought a ceremonial name; and most of them, special prerogatives. Every reputable Bella Coola is the owner of one of these prized names and owns or shares in the prerogatives. There is, therefore, a close and significant dependence of present status and of certain types of activity upon the distant past. Knowledge of these has been transmitted orally through many generations, and no one would think of questioning its accuracy. It is regarded as an obvious fact that because so-and-so's name is such-and-such, he has rights in the area occupied by his first namesake. Use of a name illegally was regarded not only as an offense but as a sin. Feuds have arisen through such thefts, but the pattern of behavior is that rights, whether in names, songs, dance steps, hunting areas and so forth, are heritable property; their ownership is a fact, thereby sustantiating the orally transmitted statement on which they rest.

Bella Coola folklore is unusually rich and varied. The tales are divided by the people themselves into two main categories, those of personal or family property on the one hand and of general knowledge on the other. Many of the incidents, in the Raven cycle for example, are preposterous; but the attitude of the hearers, who realize that the incidents could not occur today, is that the world must have changed, and not that the verbal account is inaccurate. In some cases the belief may be only tacit, but usually the events are accepted as fact and thereby add to the knowledge of the Bella Coola in regard to the behavior of beings which can be categorized loosely as supernatural.

Sometimes this insistence on the accuracy of oral tradition is clearly formulated. An elderly informant was once telling me a particularly impossible folktale and clearly wondered whether I was believing him.

"It is strange," he said, "but it occurred just as I say. You know me, and you know I wouldn't tell you a lie."

Having been satisfied that I regarded him as a paragon of all virtues, especially truth, he went on: "You never knew my father. He was a great man and as honest as I am. He would never have deceived his son. And his father the same, and his father, and his father. It came down the line of my ancestors."

This man was no mystic; he had lived an active life in rough surroundings with experience of lies and liars, and I have no doubt that on occasion he did not speak the truth. But it was unthinkable to him that a father would misinform his child; hence what was told was a statement of fact. The possibility of error through forgetting or through embellishment never occurred to him: the acceptance of oral tradition as fact was as undisputed as the transformation of a bear into a stump on the basis of visual experience.

Only once did I meet doubt regarding the accuracy of an ancient tradition. A sophisticated Bella Coola told me one of the obscene Raven legends and then began to wonder whether he should have done so. Rather lamely, he confided that he felt sure that one of his ancestors must have made a mistake in the transmission of this particular tale.

Generally, however, it is assumed that a tale is rendered accurately. Once, hearing loud laughter from a group of young men, I wandered over to join them. Two or three of them began to explain, all at the same time, the joke:

"So-and-so had been telling about Caribou and Porcupine. He was so stupid that he mixed it up."

An informant once told me a long and detailed story involving a description of a mighty hunter carrying home an enormous load of meat in a bag slung over his shoulder. A few days later the man came to me in some embarrassment and began to apologize for his stupidity. He had made an error; the game was carried in a sack supported on the back by a tumpline across the forehead. The detail was inconsequential, but any deviation is improper. He explained that this was a story which he had not thought about for many years and that he began to wonder, after leaving me, whether he might have been at fault. He consulted his wife and a number of the older people, and they corrected him. That which is handed down by word of mouth is a *fact;* deviations are assumed not to occur.

This unquestioning acceptance of orally transmitted information can lead to contradictory conclusions. One of my most reliable informants one day described to me the being who was responsible for bringing the salmon each year to the Bella Coola River. He was an anthropomorphic creature, endowed with the ability to travel under the ocean and conduct the salmon to the river. The description was clear, and after I had asked a few questions to clarify some details, I wrote down the name of this *siut* being and his functions. There was no doubt in my mind that I was recording a well-known belief; in fact my informant mentioned that the Salmon-Bringer had been seen, though not for several generations. A week or two later I happened to be talking about salmon to the same informant who, quite casually, told me why the fish came to the Bella Coola River. These were brought, he explained, by a *siut,* whose name he gave me, and added various other details. But the designation was not the same as that of the Salmon-Bringer previously mentioned, nor were his appearance, attributes or functions similar except in the most general terms. Puzzled, I asked my informant why he had previously given me an entirely different account. He looked completely nonplused, listened again to my question, and began to laugh.

"Why, I never thought of that," he said.

He went on to explain that the first description was imbedded in a legend (historical tale to him) transmitted in his father's family, whereas the second came from the family of his mother's father. To him each was correct, and he had no reason to think of both simultaneously.

This faculty of accepting statements without question and without considering their implications has been of importance in the process of Bella Coola cultural adjustment in the last century and a half. When they heard of the white man's god, they accepted him with only slight hesitation; this did not mean giving up their own beliefs but merely the addition of Christian figures to their own pantheon of supernatural beings. That if one belief was right, the other must be wrong, was a point of view completely unthought-of. When I was in Bella Coola, many years after the almost complete adoption of Christianity, it was still customary to hold two funerals, one Christian and one non-Christian. No one appeared to consider this incongruous; no one even considered the logic involved.

I have little direct information about the acceptance of verbal statements in the ordinary course of life. My impression is that information given by an older Bella Coola or by a white teacher, official or other prominent person is accepted without question, particularly if it pertains to an aspect of life in which the narrator is considered to be an expert. But unfortunately, I did not make observations on the trivial but basically important daily routine of the passing of information from, for example, parent to child.

One seeming paradox should be considered. Although the Bella Coola accept orally transmitted statements as facts, it does not follow that every statement is believed. Liars occur in every community of the world, and the Bella Coola are perfectly familiar with deliberate falsehoods. In the abstract, lying is not a serious offense; in fact, clever lies were used repeatedly by the culture-hero Raven in the distant past, and a recital of them is a source of amusement coupled with admiration for Raven. But lying within one's family or within one's own social group is antisocial and reprehensible. The possibility of something being forgotten is not even considered; an oral statement is accepted as a fact unless it be deliberately altered. The basis of acceptance has nothing to do with the transmission of a fact through one or more intermediaries; the only criterion is the reputation of each for honesty. And with regard to the distant past, or in matters of religion, complete honesty is assumed. I am inclined to believe that dishonesty is considered as a possibility only when an element of self-interest is involved.

III. Recognition of facts by the process of experimentation, the third category which I made in our own society, is relatively unimportant in Bella Coola. There are no deliberate experimental techniques comparable to those used in a laboratory. On the other hand, experiment occurs in the normal course of life. A carpenter, a canoe-man, a hunter, a singer, each increases his skill by constant repetition. A skilled craftsman is respected, and it is recognized that his proficiency has been built up by years of practice. I have had an old man tell me how his fluency improved in the course of making many speeches over the years. Comparably, I have watched young men when poling a canoe look for guidance from the captain in the stern, a veteran of many years of experience in handling a dugout on the rapid and dangerous Bella Coola River. Proficiency thus acquired, however, is hardly comparable to a technique of acquiring factual information by deliberate experimentation. At most, it is practical expedient in the course of a lifetime, premeditated perhaps, but never a direct experimental approach.

IV. Factual knowledge dependent purely on belief, the fourth category, is difficult to analyze in any community. Among the Bella Coola there are no attitudes comparable to those of believing that one's country is always right, that one's religion is the only true faith, or that one's wife or husband is perfect, to use three common emotional statements of faith from our own society. Although many personal social and religious beliefs, particularly those in which there are prerogatives based on incidents in the distant past, depend upon statements transmitted orally, there is a core of beliefs for which no direct basis of information exists. These include cosmological beliefs, the powers and functions of the more important beings of the pantheon, and the fate of the dead, all of which are matters of general knowledge. Even with these, however, there is a tendency to look for substantiation in an oral tradition. Many times when I asked a question about a well-known being, I was answered by the recital of a legend (an historical fact to the narrator) in which the being appeared; it was unusual to be given a summing-up of the being's functions or powers. The contrast to the type of explanation which would have seemed normal in our own society was evident repeatedly. It would not be unfair to say that even in matters of universal Bella Coola knowledge, an informant tended to think not only of the factual information but of how he had acquired it. Of course this became of little importance in the case of items learned in childhood, but the tendency should be noted.

Once realized, however, whether on the basis of an oral tradition or by visual experience, there is no doubt of the complete belief. As I have said, beings unknown to any zoologist are as real to the Bella Coola as wolves or mountain goats; intermarriage between bears and human beings is accepted fact; everyone knows that the body divides into two parts at death, one going to a sky land, the other to a subterranean world. These are matters that every Bella Coola child learns—or at least that he learned prior to the breakdown of native culture. His attitude towards the concepts is somewhat prosaic; there is little evidence of the emotional inner feeling of the devotee.

In the important field of magical beliefs, however, this attitude of the recognition of fact dependent purely upon belief warrants further consideration. The Bella Coola accept without question processes of cause and effect which, to the white man, are completely fallacious: a child can be made a singer by placing a thrush against the infant's throat, a puppy can be trained for hunting beaver by immersion in a stream when wrapped in the hide of a beaver, the application of a wasp's nest will engender a warlike disposition, or a child can be made a carpenter by being placed in contact with an adze accompanied by proper procedure. Such methods are common knowledge and were still used, even in my time, to a considerable extent by thoughtful parents and by beaver hunters. Nor were they vague "superstitions"; they were practices in which there was firm belief. I knew one man who had been made a singer in infancy through patting his throat with a varied thrush, regarded by the Bella Coola as the best songster. The man was not efficient and consequently was not a practicing member of the choir, but his prestige as a singer was greater than that of more proficient performers; they might be able to sing, but he was regarded as rightfully entitled to do so. And when I once asked a woman who had given her a black eye, she casually replied that it was her husband and added by way of explanation to an ignorant outsider that he could not help it since he had been made a fighter by the application of a wasp's nest in infancy, and she was the only person with whom he could fight. She was rather proud of his propensity which she accepted as an obvious fact.

Many similar examples could be given. Undoubtedly a person who has been treated in this way is generally recognized as having the capacity in question, and this in turn affects his own attitude and behavior. Knowing that he is a carpenter, a lad is more apt to develop skill in woodworking than his brother who lacks this knowledge. A large number of beliefs of this type, conforming to the stereotype of sympathetic magic, are held by the Bella Coola. Their purpose includes the causing or curing of illness, the bringing of love and pregnancy, and the development of professional skills, covering, indeed, the whole range of human desires.

Much of the native culture had passed away when I worked in Bella Coola, but not the belief in magic. Fear was still present of those dreaded and loathed individuals who caused death by placing a victim's hair, spittle, a fragment of clothing, or exhaled breath in contact with a malevolent brew of human blood, wolf droppings, and other ingredients. Legend after legend told of the justifiable killing of a sorcerer, and I have no doubt murder was the usual fate of anyone accused of black magic. I knew one old man in his dotage whom everyone believed to be a sorcerer; I am sure he would have been killed except for the necessity of obedience to the white man's laws.

Using, in a loose and general manner, the term "magical" for the type of practice just described, it is obvious that it rests on an undisputed belief in power. When something is done, it is followed by an inevitable result, there is no question of probability, and it is a matter of accepted fact. There are, however, other ways in which power can be obtained and used in ways comparable to magic. By ostentatious giving at potlatches, a man makes himself "strong"; such a person is able to give orders, to take a dominant role in public affairs, and even to participate in secret society rituals for which he had no specific authority. It was even claimed, more or less seriously, that such a man was invulnerable in war. Even in my time it was accepted as an obvious fact that the influential giver of many pot-latches could cause the death of another merely by thinking and wishing. A case occurred in which I knew the participants intimately. A woman had died and her father, Captain Schooner, an old man who had given many potlatches, claimed that she had been poisoned by Willie, a fellow-worker at the cannery where both were employed. He planned to kill the alleged murderer and was dissuaded with some difficulty. He finally agreed that his daughter had not been killed but that the man whom he accused had wanted to kill her and that he, Schooner, knew that the man would die within a year. This statement spread rapidly through the village, and I heard a number of people express the opinion that Willie would die; Captain Schooner was so strong that if he made a prediction, his strength would be enough to bring it about. Willie came to me about it, very worried about what had been said. He knew "the strength of Schooner's mind," as he put it. It might be added that Willie was a sturdy man in his forties; Schooner, a feeble elder in his seventies.

A year later, when I was in the east, a friend wrote me from Bella Coola giving me local news, including the death of Willie. A week or two later I heard of the death of Captain Schooner. When I returned to Bella Coola I naturally made inquiries. Since Willie had died in the hospital, I consulted the white doctor who told me that he really did not know the cause of the death; his patient had not seemed seriously ill but seemed to have no vitality and gradually faded away. There was no uncertainty in the Indian village; there everyone accepted Willie's death as the result of the power of Captain Schooner's thoughts. Before going to the hospital, Willie had told several people that if Schooner "got him," his ghost would "get" Schooner. The old man knew this and tried to protect himself by obtaining a fragment of clothing from the corpse. Willie's sons pre-vented this, and Schooner died within a few days. His widow assured me that her husband told her that nothing could save him. According to her, he simply lost his appetite, wasted away, and died.

Needless to say, the relationship of these incidents could never be proved to the satisfaction of a legal mind. But there is no doubt that the Bella Coola regarded them as a case of cause and effect. Both Willie and Schooner believed that the other had the wish and the power to kill. In each case there was a verbal statement, the acceptance of the spoken word, but behind that was the pattern of tribal belief. Each *knew;* how he knew was irrelevant. But the belief, regarded as a fact, was dominant in the death of each.

This factor of unquestioning belief is particularly important in illness. A patient knows that he is helped if treated by a skilled shaman or by a white doctor who is assumed to have limitless power. Comparably there are remedies for various maladies and aids in childbirth which are widely known; the person using them gains comfort thereby. Belief is the keynote of the practices involved.

This type of belief is even carried over to the behavior of animals. I was once bitten by a dog, and when I complained to its owner, I was told politely but flatly that the dog was a chief which could do as it liked. Further questioning brought out the information that a considerable amount of money had been distributed at a potlatch to "strengthen" the dog. Thus endowed, the animal was regarded as entitled to behave like a chief. Though I did not appreciate being bitten, at least I had the advantage of a specific (and personal) example of an interesting point of view.

In summing up, it may be said that although the Bella Coola rely on verbal statements and on visualizations, there is a core of knowledge, particularly in fields which may be described as magic, which rests firmly on the basis of unquestioned belief.

This study of Bella Coola concepts concerning facts and the means whereby they are recognized does not reveal attitudes or approaches fundamentally different from those of the Western world. The differences are in degree rather than in kind. The Bella Coola are interested in facts; and their affirmation of the accuracy of oral traditions and the display of prerogatives based on these show that facts are of vital concern in their culture. Their reliance upon hearsay evidence and upon inaccurate visualization may strike a white observer as peculiar, but our society likewise gives credence to verbal reports and to what is thought to have been seen; we, too, tend to adjust what we see or hear to the norms of our culture pattern. Deliberate experimentation is the only one of our techniques lacking in Bella Coola. Though belief plays a large part in Bella Coola life, the same applies in our society although the aspects in which it is prominent are not the same. As I stated earlier, I do not imply that attitudes in this or any other respect are universal or, indeed, are characteristic of any tribe other than the Bella Coola. I think that similar studies in other communities might lead to a wider understanding of how man looks at facts and how he concludes that they are facts; this paper is merely a step in this direction.

NOTES

1.   Field work among the Bella Coola was sponsored by the Victoria Memorial Museum, now the National Museum of Canada. Much of the material presented in this paper is included in a monograph on Bella Coola ethnology, namely, *The Bella Coola Indians,* by T. F. McIlwraith (Toronto, 1948).

2.   I am relying on hearsay evidence, the basis of much of our ethnological data.

3.   The word is a derivative of *siut,* having the implication of *supernatural, learned,* and *powerful.*

MORRIS E. OPLER

Chapter XIII: Cultural Context and Population Control Programs in Village India

THERE HAS BEEN a good deal of discussion, both within and outside of India, of population growth, population control, and their relationship to India's economic development. Often opinions about the advisability of foreign aid or estimates of the possibility of industrialization and the time required for it hinge on judgments regarding India's ability to control demographic factors. It is well known that the Indian government is concerned about overpopulation and that relatively large sums have been included in the present five-year plan to disseminate birth control information and to experiment with methods for achieving family limitation. Many of the proposals seem to assume that it is mainly ignorance and poverty which stand in the way of a solution and that if simple, direct educational techniques can be devised to bring knowledge to the local level and if a cheap, effective method of birth control can be taught, general acceptance and progress are assured.

It is true, of course, that ignorance and poverty are extremely important in the situation. With poverty and crowding goes a lack of privacy and facilities which makes it very difficult to carry out the directions of a family planning adviser. The illiteracy which is usually linked with poverty prevents the use of written instructions and puts a premium on expensive and slow methods of personal contact. Yet, too often the analyses and the plans which see ignorance and poverty as the prime obstacles assume that there is a vacuum of need and receptivity which can be filled once these first barriers are overcome. Actually, there is no facet of Indian life where there are more profound and solid convictions than in the area of procreation and family life. It is only by taking into account this realm of practice and belief that those who are concerned with population control can appreciate the currents of thought and action which can aid or hinder them and which they will have to utilize, counter, bypass, or ignore.

201

Opinion varies concerning how important a knowledge of cultural factors is to a solution of practical problems. There are those who believe that involvement of administrators and planners with complicated social science data leads only to excessive timidity and postponement of decisive action. They argue that a technological or economic breakthrough or a firm directing hand forces whatever adjustment is necessary in ideology and customary usage. Others argue just as stoutly that the inability or reluctance of planners to take deeply rooted, traditional practices and convictions into account deprives them of sources of support for their programs and blinds them to centers of resistance for which they could be prepared.

Without entering directly into the debate at this point, I should like to present material about family life and population control in a village of north central India. The village in question, which we shall call Madhopur, is located in the Jaunpur District of the State of Uttar Pradesh. The great majority of the residents of the village are Hindus. The Muslims number only seventy-nine. They are believed to be descendants of converts to Islam during Mohammedan rule. Whether or not this is true, they carry out Hindu practices in many of their activities, and even their religious behavior is influenced by Hinduism. The material upon which this highly condensed résumé is based was collected by me and by associates in the Cornell University India Program from 1947 to 1957. From our own comparative work and from the literature, we know that many of the traits and views described are found throughout most of the rural sections of India. I leave it to the reader, and, hopefully, to the planner to decide how much of this general picture is pertinent to the programs which are now being initiated.

The particular community we are considering has a population of about two thousand people. The actual number in residence fluctuates. Most of the time approximately one hundred men of the village are involved in outside employment, primarily in urban centers. They seldom sever their village ties and often return seasonally to aid when agricultural work is heaviest. There is a movement of women in and out of the village, too; girls leave the village in marriage, and married daughters return to visit their parental homes. As this suggests, there is village exogamy and patrilocal residence; girls are expected to leave the village at marriage and to become identified with their husbands' families. As we shall see, there is a strong accent on the importance of the male and of the male line. Traditionally, property has been inherited by males, and this practice persists in ignorance or defiance of recently enacted inheritance laws which entitle the widow and daughters to inherit equally with the sons.

Another prominent feature of the social organization is the joint family. Not only do sons remain in the village of the father after marriage, but, if possible, they continue to share the same household. In fact, it is considered a serious affront to the father for a son to live separately from him. It is more common for brothers to separate after the death of the father, but even here it is thought desirable that they remain together. In 1956, of 316 families in the village, 211 were joint. Of these, 149 were composed of males of more than one generation and their families, and 62 were made up of brothers who had cast their lot together. The elementary, or nuclear, families of the village numbered 105. Not only was there a larger number of joint families than elementary families, but it must also be remembered that the joint families are on the average larger. Consequently, well over two-thirds of the people live under the influence of a joint family system. Moreover, some elementary families exist by necessity rather than by choice. These are cases where a solitary individual is the sole representative of a line or where a line has shrunk as a result of deaths or the failure to produce male issue. In fact, the latter exigency is one of the gnawing fears in Indian thought. It should also be remembered that the term "joint family" indicates more than simply living under one roof. It connotes that land and property are held jointly and that a manager (*malik*) acts in business matters for the whole group. It means that a common kitchen and storeroom are maintained and that the women of the household share the domestic labor. It implies that the children of the household are entitled to the affection and support of all and can expect equivalent treatment and education according to sex. Because there is so much loose and unfounded talk about the disappearance of the joint family in India, one further observation may be in order. As a result of the death of the father who has been the nucleus of a joint family or because of disagreements between brothers or their wives, joint families are often dissolved. Yet, because of the marriage of sons and their continued residence with their fathers, it is just as common to find joint families becoming newly established. A quarrel which destroys a joint family is more dramatic and conspicuous than a number of uneventful, conventional cases of patrilocal residence. Consequently, observers, especially foreign observers, are sharply conscious of such disruptions and have been predicting the imminent disappearance of the joint family for some seventy-five years.

Because the central and state governments of India have shown concern about excessive population growth and are providing funds and personnel for family limitation programs, it is sometimes assumed that the people as a whole are worried about population size and are prepared to welcome birth control programs for patriotic reasons. The thinking of national leaders and of a highly educated urban elite should not be confused with the outlook of the villager. India is a country of intense regionalism and local separatism. Until recently India was subject to foreign rule, and independence and national unity were realized only yesterday. Americans can identify prominent Indian national leaders more readily than can most Indian villagers. Even national elections are contested locally on village issues. Consequently, it is scarcely realistic to expect that population size will be thought of as a national problem or that the dimensions of the question will be anything but local or personal. In fact, perceptions, because they are so local and circumscribed, often belie statistics. For instance, despite the fact that village population has greatly increased in the last fifty years, some villagers have actually told us that they think the population is decreasing. They claim that there are more deaths than there used to be and that families are smaller, and they point to certain lines that are dying out. A person who belonged to a large family which became segmented, who becomes more conscious of death as he grows older and his responsibilities in death rites multiply, and who hears continual lament about lines without male issue is likely to form such an opinion. Pressure on land, which should have been a clue to population growth, was often explained instead as a consequence of the rapacity of the landowning caste or the failure of land reform programs. Even when population growth was recognized as a problem, the blame was projected upon others. Members of one caste conveniently tended to see other castes growing too fast and acting incontinently. Seldom did caste fellows see themselves as the culprits or even see themselves involved. This inability to conceive of a national problem and the reluctance to accept responsibility or even to admit involvement on the local level increase the possibility that lip service to population control programs is likely to outstrip genuine participation in them.

One of the factors which cannot be ignored in discussing family size or population growth in India is early marriage. Here a distinction must be made between marriage and the initiation of sexual relations between husband and wife. Prepubertal marriage in India is common; prepubertal cohabitation is rare. Also, there is considerable variation in the age of marriage according to caste. The general pattern is something like this: The marriage of children, especially of daughters, is a solemn and, indeed, a religious duty. So strong is this feeling that persons without daughters sometimes symbolically participate in the giving away of a girl in marriage. Parents and grandparents are apprehensive until this obligation is discharged. In a country where the span of life is short and where widespread sickness and disaster strike suddenly, they feel relieved if they have performed their function early. In addition, they are particularly anxious about the prospects of the daughters of the household. In a situation where marriage is an arrangement between families and where a woman's sphere is traditionally restricted to domestic work and to sharing the caste work of her husband, it is absolutely essential to arrange a secure future for her in a household to which she will go in marriage. In spite of the recent law which sets a minimum marriage age of fifteen years for girls and eighteen years for boys, most of the low caste girls are married between the ages of five and ten, and most of the boys are wed when slightly older. Among the high caste groups, which do not permit widow remarriage, the unions take place when the girls are twelve years old or a little older and when the boys are approximately fifteen years old. The marriage rite is held at the home of the bride; and if the girl is immature, the groom and his marriage party return to their homes without her. She may, however, come for a token visit to her husband's home and may come to his home to live and work for several years much as a daughter of the household without intimate relations or much contact with her husband. These practices take account of the fact that marriage means a totally new environment for the girl and affirm the belief that she can become best adjusted to it by coming to it when she is young and malleable. Whatever the arrangement, it is very likely that the young husband and wife will not be allowed to have intimate relations until the girl is mature. Even so, the young couple are very likely to begin living as man and wife somewhat earlier than their counterparts in Western cultures. There are various other rationalizations and sentiments which tend to justify and promote early marriage, such as that India has a hot climate in which young people mature quickly and that parents and grandparents have a natural wish to see their grandchildren before they die.

There is, however, especially in the contemporary setting, an important countercurrent to early marriage. Because of the esteem for the male, the dowry in marriage goes to the family of the groom. The amount is based on the status and prestige of the family of the boy and is increasingly becoming related to his degree of education. This, of course, is associated with his potential earning capacity; it is assumed that a more highly educated youth will command a better position and salary. But education takes time, and the more highly educated grooms are certain to be older on the average. Their brides, too, will be older, for there should not be too great an age difference between mates; and, though the groom should be better educated as well as older than his bride, there should not be too great a discrepancy between the two in education, either. Thus it is likely that the drive for education is doing more to advance the age of marriage than are legal enactments. Nevertheless, it is very difficult to depart too widely from the prevailing practices in regard to age of marriage. If relatives of some eligible girl have not asked for the hand of a boy in marriage by what is considered a reasonable time, it is assumed that the young man must have some defect or that the record of his family is wanting in some particular. If the marriage of a girl is not arranged by the time she is mature or shortly thereafter, her desirability may be suspect; and, moreover, the list of males who are eligible and still available steadily shrinks. Recently the family of one young man who had reached the age of eighteen without marrying, instead of receiving a dowry, had to pay 200 rupees to arrange a marriage.

It is all very well to talk about population control and the right of the husband and wife to determine whether they can afford to have children, but any careful study of village life impresses upon one the degree to which women are conditioned to see their success and their destiny in terms of procreation. An older woman meeting a younger one says: "May you be fruitful." "Get a good husband." "May you have sons." "May your family grow and increase." Even anger and curses point to the same values. One of the most baneful things one woman can say to another is: "May your children die!" In interviews both men and women stated that the mark of a good wife was to bear children, especially boys, and to be faithful. Consequently, once marriage relations are initiated, the most fervent hope of the young woman is that she prove her worth to her husband's family by producing a healthy male child. She knows very well that she will have little standing in her husband's home until she bears him a son. Nothing is more frightening to her than the specter of barrenness. The word for a barren woman is the same as the term used for a parasite on a tree. It is seldom that a young woman escapes emotional disturbance if she has not become pregnant within five years of marriage. On the other hand, we noted a number of cases of childless women who had constantly complained of chronic ill health or persecution by malignant spirits, who miraculously recovered health, poise, and confidence after giving birth to a son. The practical reasons for this attitude on the part of the young wife are not difficult to find. The birth of a son entitles a woman to respect and status and exempts her from much hard work. She and her baby are likely to be pampered for some time after parturition. Henceforth she is referred to through the name of her child; she becomes "the mother of so-and-so."

The woman who bears no children receives markedly different treatment and lives in a different atmosphere. Among the low castes, where divorce is permitted, barrenness usually terminates in divorce. Among the high caste groups, which do not permit divorce, most cases of polygyny in the village of which we could learn occurred because the first wife had borne no sons. Information on the religious practices of women indicated clearly how important the desire and need for children, especially male children, loomed. The prominent shamans of the region acknowledged that much of their activity was on behalf of women who desired sons. Many of the offerings made at the shrine of the goddess Kali in Madhopur were by women who were imploring the goddess to grant them a son. If appeals to local shamans and the goddess failed, the women of the village traveled even farther to obtain help. In the city of Banaras, 25 miles distant, is a well famous for bringing sons to the childless. Near the well is a shrine to Lolarak Baba, the presiding deity of the place. Madhopur women, often accompanied by their husbands, visit this place for a ceremony which they hope will result in pregnancy. So great is the general concern over a wife who does not have children that women outside the family have been known to make offerings on her behalf to the local gods. If many years pass and a woman does not become pregnant or if two or more children born to her have died in succession, she may vow that, if a certain deity will grant her a healthy baby, she will have its hair-cutting ceremony performed at a shrine or temple dedicated to the helpful god. Also, if a woman feels that the ceremonies of a shaman have helped her achieve pregnancy or give birth to a son, she may have the hair-cutting ceremony of the child performed at the shrine of the deity to whom the shaman appeals.

When a young woman bears a first child who is a daughter, this is disappointing; but it at least proves that she is fecund. No matter how many girls she bears, she will probably attempt to have children until she has borne a son. Consequently, there is little use trying to determine from the number of children in the family whether the parents are likely to favor limitation of family size; it is the number of sons that counts. If one asks why sons are considered so important, the answer is that daughters marry, often very early, and are lost to the family. Moreover, their marriage entails great expense. It is the sons who bring the dowry, who are needed to inherit the land and continue the line, who are present to aid in the work and to take care of their aging parents, and who finally carry on the funeral rites for the repose of the souls of their parents.

The need for a son is considered so great that one son only is deemed an insufficient safeguard. Childhood diseases take such a toll that safety is sought in numbers. As a village proverb phrases it: "One eye is no eye, and one son is no son." And another proverb tells us: "No one is satisfied with the amount of milk and the number of sons." After the continuity of the line is assured by the presence of at least two sons, a daughter is desired. As was mentioned before, it is a religious duty to give a daughter in marriage. Even here the emphasis is on the welfare of the man. "Girl babies are wanted so men can marry," villagers told us. The very word for marriage means to give a daughter in religious alms. Therefore it is said that when a daughter is born, the womb of the mother becomes sacred. When interviewed concerning ideal family size, most informants, no matter how poor, asserted they would want at least two boys and a girl.

Next to being barren, the misfortune that a young woman dreads most is to lose children by stillbirth, miscarriage, or in infancy. A woman who consistently loses children either is considered somehow remiss and therefore culpable or is thought to be persecuted by ghosts and malignant spirits. If a woman who has lost young children becomes involved in a heated argument, she may be charged by her opponent with having "eaten" (*i.e.*, caused the death of) her children. In one instance, a young woman who suffered a miscarriage ordered away two unmarried girls who came to her assistance. She feared that her bad luck would be communicated to the girls if they touched her while she was in this unhappy and polluted condition. But an older married woman who was present hesitated to become involved, also. She was afraid that any contamination she suffered would be projected on to the young, unmarried girls of her own household. Even a low caste midwife, who was called to massage the abdomen of the sufferer, found excuses for avoiding this task until the period of pollution was over.

As might be expected in such an atmosphere of concern, women go to great lengths to insure a safe delivery and a healthy child. For instance, a midwife with "good hands" is chosen, one who has had no mishaps or failures in her work. Persons from other families are excluded from the room and area where the birth is taking place so that no possibility of unfriendly intentions will cause trouble. The low caste woman who assists at the birth shakes her clothes over the protective fire that guards the door so that no evil forces will gain entrance. One woman who had several children die in her husband's village went to her parents' village to give birth in the hope of breaking the chain of bad luck.

There are still other means by which a woman who has been unable to raise boys seeks to preserve her newborn son. She may have his nose pierced, as is done for a girl, and thereby deceive malignant spirits into believing that a mere girl, whom they hardly need bother to persecute, has been born. Or, to divert the jealous supernaturals, an opprobrious name such as "He-who-has-been-thrown-away," "He-who-has-been-driven-away," "He-who-is-worthless," "He-who-has-been-sold," etc., may be bestowed on the child. As one of the names suggests, a boy may be symbolically sold by a woman who has failed, in the past, to rear sons to maturity to a woman who has been conspicuously successful in this. The baby boy is weighed, and his weight in barley is given by the "purchaser." In return, the mother of the child gives the purchaser a sari. If the boy survives, the grateful mother continues to give gifts to the "purchaser" on various occasions until the boy marries. Still another practice is to make a cookstove of clay and place the baby boy on it for a few minutes. Then the stove, which, of course, has never been ignited, is broken. Presumably the mischievous spirits are expected to believe that the child has been destroyed and that they need not seek him out for their unkind attentions.

It is quite evident that in these attempts to mitigate anxiety and to guarantee the birth of children it is the welfare and the perpetuation of the male which is emphasized. Despite the importance, for religious reasons, of having daughters, the feeling in regard to girls is reflected in the village saying: "If God gives daughters, he should be so kind as to make a man rich." The differential attitude toward boys and girls is noticeable in beliefs and practices that even antedate birth. For instance, it is considered a good omen if the fetus is carried directly in front of the woman; then a son is likely to be born. When the low caste woman who is called to cut the umbilical cord is on her way to the room where a birth has occurred, she is escorted by one or two men who are considered a guard to repel evil influences. If the newborn child is a boy, two men accompany the woman; if a girl has been born, one man suffices. Needless to say, she receives more for her services if the infant is a boy. At the time of birth the midwife picks up the newborn baby and places it on a winnowing tray. The tray is covered with a new piece of cloth if the baby is a boy; an old piece of cloth suffices if the infant is a girl. If a son is born, the midwife is generally given a sari and some money; she receives nothing if the baby is a girl. As soon as the birth of a boy is announced, the women in the house immediately begin singing a *sohar,* a type of song associated with birth and infancy; if it is a girl who is born, there is no singing. If a boy has been born, an older woman of the household goes about the neighborhood spreading the news. A band may be summoned to play. At the very least someone will beat a brass tray. A man of the household may discharge a gun. This clamor is partly in celebration and partly to discourage evil forces that may threaten the newborn child. These activities do not take place at the birth of a girl. When a woman gives birth to her first son, the barber who serves the family and who has ceremonial as well as practical functions is sent to inform her parents. If it is a daughter who is born, no messenger is sent; eventually a visitor to the woman's natal village or a letter will carry the news. If a woman gives birth to a son during a visit to her parental home, the barber is immediately sent to her husband's village to notify her in-laws. There is no haste if the newborn infant is a girl. Women of the neighborhood gather in the evening for twelve days to sing *sohars* in the courtyard of a home where a son has been born. For a girl, they appear on the sixth and twelfth evenings only. Again, if an infant has been born in an unlucky sidereal period, an elaborate ceremony, called Mul Shanti, is performed to remove the curse, providing it is a boy. During the hair-cutting ceremony of boys, a rite that takes place during a child's first, third, or fifth year, the women present sing *sohars;* in the case of girls, they sit impassively and do not burst into song.

It is not only in ceremony and symbol that the male baby receives favored treatment. One of the conclusions which was drawn from the work of a small dispensary and health center which we maintained in the village for some time was that the illness of a male infant was likely to receive more prompt and anxious attention than that of a girl and that families were willing to spend considerably more on medicine and medical aid for a boy than for a girl. One can sense this attitude in the lecture of one of the older women of a joint family to a young mother. She climaxed her remarks by saying: "Because of your carelessness, you killed two daughters. Now be careful with this one. He is a boy and he needs proper care and attention. Boys need more care than girls. Don't you see, girls survive nicely; but if a little thing happens to a boy, he dies." Again the traditionally guided perception clashes with fact. Actually there are approximately fifty more males than females in the village population. Moreover, this superior survival record of males is duplicated throughout the region and the state. At the time of the 1951 census, there were three million more males than females in the State of Uttar Pradesh. The greater concern for the health, nourishment, and safety of the male certainly has some bearing on these figures, although the confinement of *parda* (*purdah*) and the hazards of delivery in unsanitary surroundings undoubtedly are contributing factors.

There are a number of calendrical rites which embody features associated with the preservation of the married state and with the health and longevity of husbands and sons. These rites are extremely complex and cannot here be described in detail. A few of the practices especially germane to our topic may indicate the attitudes they support, however. One, called Chotka Basiaura, which occurs at the onset of the heat, is meant to ward off the epidemic diseases brought by a goddess. It is performed only by families which have requested the goddess to grant them a son. About two weeks later there is a companion ceremony, Barka Basiaura, which is observed by all families. This, too, is directed mainly toward protecting the children of the family against the diseases sent by the goddess Bhagavati Mai, especially smallpox and cholera. Again, the protective attitude toward males is conspicuous. Small figurines of silver, one for each male member of the family who has ever had smallpox or chickenpox or who has been vaccinated for smallpox, are used in the rite. Figurines of this kind are not made for girls. Yet it is the women of a household who conduct Basiaura.

Roughly similar concepts and practices are found in the worship of the goddess Bani which takes place in late summer. After a son is born, a family usually requests a goldsmith to make a ring of silver called a *thos;* these are never made for girls. If a son has been born in answer to a vow to the goddess Bani, the *thos* is square in shape with a human figure molded on it. If a *thos* is not made after a son's birth, two must be obtained at the time of his marriage. A *thos* made at a boy's birth is not kept by his family but is given by his kin to a Brahman priest who serves them. The priest puts it with others in a container in his house, and the whole collection from the many families he serves represents or personifies Bani. On a Monday or Friday during the month of Savan (approximately July–August) following a son's birth, Bani is worshiped. For the occasion the Brahman comes and brings his box of *thos* with him. Unmarried girls may not witness ceremonies to Bani or be connected with them in any way.

Soon afterwards Cauth, or Kajali Day, is celebrated by the women. This ceremony is connected with the worship of the elephant-headed god, Ganesh. On this day unmarried women fast until noon, but women who have sons fast the whole day. The women sing *kajali*, or songs with romantic themes. They take seedlings from barley they have planted some time before and tie one of these to the pigtail of each male member of the family. In the early afternoon the women gather at one of the houses and continue to sing *kajali*.

In early fall comes Tij, a women's fast and festival which honors the husband and acts as a supplication for the continuance of the married state. Parvati, the devoted consort of God Shiva, is worshiped on this day. Wives and unmarried pubescent girls keep the fast and carry on the ritual; widows are exempt from participation. Married women receive presents from the homes of their parents on this day. They go together to bathe at a tank, singing *kajali*. In one of the songs a woman mentions her husband by name, the only time of the year that this kind of reference to her husband is permitted the wife.

Soon after Tij there are ritual observances in honor of Shashthi Devi, the goddess who presides over married women and children and who gives and protects sons. In this ceremony, Lalahi Chath, only married women with sons participate. One woman of each household keeps a strict fast. She collects certain foods and places them on a brass tray. The arrangement of food is somewhat different for households where a son has been born within a year. The women meet and go together to a tank near which a protective circle of buffalo dung has been traced. In its center a figure is molded of the dung to represent Shashthi Devi. Stalks of a sacred grass are fixed on the figure. Each family representative tries to tie a knot in a stalk of grass, using only the thumb and little finger of the right hand. To succeed is to add to the lives of the sons of the family. One of the women tells six stories. Most of these tales recount how a son's death was thwarted by faithful observance of this fast and ceremony. On the way home women sing *sohars*. A gesture of hospitality attends this rite; curds are offered to anyone who comes to a household in the morning.

A little later in autumn falls another important ritual occasion, Jiutia. The word is probably related to the term *jiu* (life). Jiut Baba, the god of this occasion, especially blesses sons. Again, it is the women of the household who are responsible for the events. A woman begins to observe the rite only after she has borne a son. If she has borne only daughters, she may keep the fast in the hope that Shitala Mai, another deity worshiped on this day, will grant her a son. At least one woman in each family keeps a total fast for twenty-four hours in connection with Jiutia. When a woman observes Jiutia for the first time, she keeps her fast a secret to everyone except women of the family. The female head of each family has in her keeping a necklace of small, elongated gold or silver beads strung on a red and yellow cotton thread. There is one bead for each male in the family. This necklace, too, is called *jiutia,* and it is brought out and displayed at this ceremony. Toward evening on Jiutia the women go together to bathe at a tank, accompanied by a band. Nearby a large sacred circle has been prepared. At its center a mound of cow dung representing Jiut Baba has been shaped. An altar is prepared at this spot and offerings are made. The women offer water to the ancestors, saying: "Old ones, this is for you." Some women hold baby sons over the altar of Jiut Baba to secure blessings for the infants. A Brahman who is present tells stories appropriate to the occasion and kindles a sacrificial fire. It is expected at this time that women who have no sons will try to steal something, especially the *jiutia,* from more fortunate participants. Before she starts for home, each woman lights the wick of a little earthen lamp from the sacred fire and tries to reach her destination with the light still burning. The flame is associated with the life of the sons of the family. On the way the women talk to themselves in a stylized manner, saying: "Go tell God that the mother of (naming her son) has kept a very strict fast and therefore he should guard and protect my family." At dawn the women break their fast and worship the female ancestors of the family, because Jiutia falls within the half-month set aside for honoring the ancestors and is the day on which female ancestors are particularly remembered. These ancestors are, of course, the mothers of the male members of the line. Previously women have prepared foods which are especially associated with their sex, and they dine on these.

Godhana and Piria are two related ceremonies. The first occurs in early winter, and the second a month later. They are entered upon by girls to lengthen the lives of male relatives, especially the brothers, and they involve an exchange of gifts between sisters and brothers.

Still later in winter comes Magh Cauth. This ritual is observed only by families in which a son has been born or married during the past year. In the ideology of this ritual, Ganesh, the elephant-headed god, is associated with the moon. Once more a woman of the family fasts all day. A place in the courtyard is purified and ritually designed. A figure of a lamb, made of sugar, is brought to the sanctified place. When the moon is rising, the younger brother of the father of the boy, or a Brahman, sacrifices the lamb by decapitating it with a knife and offers the head to Ganesh. As he does so, he may pray silently, saying:

"Oh, God, we are offering you all this. Keep our children safe." The one who has made the sacrifice then rushes out of the house, taking with him the head of the lamb. The next morning the body of the lamb is distributed to family members and friends as sanctified food. The woman who fasts lights a lamp and circles it in the air five times as if moving it around the moon. It is believed that this observance will bring blessings and good luck to the boy in whose name it is carried out.

Finally, Shiva Ratri, another winter ceremonial occasion, may be mentioned. There are conflicting legendary explanations of the day, but most think of it as the anniversary of the marriage of Shiva and Parvati. Unmarried girls fast this day in order to obtain good husbands. Women go to the shrines and temples of the vicinity, especially to those associated with Shiva, to pay their respects to this deity.

These are only a few details of some of the rituals carried on for the purpose of assuring a large and prosperous family. It is obvious that women are central in the conduct of these observances and that this aspect of the ceremonial pattern offers them an exceptional opportunity to identify themselves with the husband's line and to take responsibility for its welfare. It is evident, too, that this affirmation and identification are achieved largely through sons and that the contribution of the woman, both ritual and secular, depends greatly upon being the mother of sons. It is very likely that birth control propaganda picturing a national population crisis will have little effect until Indian women have some avenue of achieving status and security equivalent to the consideration they now receive from demonstrating their fecundity and ability to bear sons.

Thus far we have stressed the factors of status, religion, and tradition which support the desire for a large family. There are a number of less abstract and more earthy considerations that have a similar effect. In general it is assumed that it is desirable and advantageous to have a large family. In fact, prosperity and a large family are linked in the villager's mind. "As the harvest grows from the work of the farmer, so the family grows from the good *karma* (actions) of its members," runs the village proverb. "Who doesn't want children? People want as many as they can have," said one of the villagers. And there are reasons why this attitude has grown up and persists.

For one thing, rural and agricultural life tends to obscure overpopulation and underemployment. On an unmechanized farm there are always chores to occupy everyone. At times of preparation of the fields, irrigation, and harvest all hands are desperately needed. In fact, at these times women and children are pressed into service, and men return from urban employment to participate. It is the image of these peak work periods that lingers in the mind of the villager when he discusses population size.

In the second place, a good many villagers are sent by their families to work in cities and towns on a seasonal basis. These family members remit a good deal of their earnings to the village, and this supplies a cash income with which the families can undertake new projects, educate sons, buy land, and in general advance their status. Families with surplus members are in the best position to take advantage of the possibilities of both the village and urban center. The wives of those who are working in the cities almost never accompany them, partly because of lack of facilities, partly because of their own timidity, and also because family members wish to be sure that the young men retain their ties with the village and will return.

Another practical advantage of a fairly sizable family relates to involvement in the *jajmani* system, the network of hereditary work obligations and exchanges. A barber family, for instance, serves a number of families of other castes and occupations. The arrangement is one between families and not between specific individuals. Consequently, if one member of a barber family is ill on the day when certain *jajmans* are to be visited, his brother or his father can substitute for him. When there is but one person available to honor the traditional work obligations, sickness or some other emergency may be a great inconvenience.

In seeking credit, too, the larger family may have a decided advantage. Debts are considered a family obligation; and if a man has brothers, sons, and grandsons who can be approached in case he dies or defaults, he is much more likely to receive financial consideration.

Nor can the familism, the factionalism, and the rough-and-tumble of village life be ignored in interpreting the desire for a large kin group. Disputes over land and other issues are common. To be a member of a flourishing joint family gives security of property and person which is not enjoyed by those identified with a small or weak kin group.

The factors which have been reviewed to this point are mostly those which glorify parenthood and underline the importance of a large and strong family. There are, however, traditional ideas and restraints which work in the opposite direction. Moreover, it is quite possible that westernization, technological development, and new programs are doing more to undermine these internal checks of the social system than to counteract the forces that have created enthusiasm for large families.

It will be remembered that the bride, especially if she is young, often does not go to her husband's house immediately after the marriage and that several years may elapse before she takes up regular residence with her in-laws. Even after she has come to her husband's village and home, the marriage most likely will not be consummated for some time. It is only in a wealthy family with a large house that the girl will have a room of her own. The wife and husband do not see each other alone and have a virtual avoidance relationship in the presence of other members of the household. In fact, their communication is conducted through older women, and the young man risks ridicule if he shows too much interest in his young wife or is seen too much in her company. The formality between the two is a measure of the respect owed to the older members of the house, and the young bride of a joint family is usually in *parda,* or seclusion, and has a respect relationship with the elders of her husband's family. Consequently, at least for some time, meetings for intimate purposes are determined by family elders to suit the needs and convenience of the family. It is traditionally the wife of the husband's elder brother who makes the actual arrangements, who tells the younger woman where to go to receive her husband, and who directs or leads her younger brother-in-law to his wife's room. Later on the couple may take more initiative; when his wife is serving food to the men, the husband may whisper a request that she leave her door unlocked that night. But in many joint families arrangements through intermediaries continue for some time. Even if a man succeeds in indicating his desires, he may not be able to visit his wife. An unwilling woman can feign that she has not heard the message and bolt the door or send word pleading illness. Of course, in nuclear families husband and wife relations are necessarily much freer, and even in joint families the husband and wife feel less diffidence as they advance in age.

Even when the husband has reasonable access to the wife and where children and the continuation of the line are desired, there are strong philosophical and psychological restraints on sexuality. Hindu philosophy and doctrine have contrasted the intellectual with the physical and have encouraged asceticism. The average villager does not know too much about this in the abstract, but he has not been untouched by these currents of thought. He has many times heard that semen is highly purified blood and that it takes up to 10,000 drops of blood to form one drop of semen. Consequently, he takes a grim view of the debilitating effects of incontinence. It was pointed out to us that the best wrestlers and athletes were young, unmarried men. One respondent said to a field worker: "If I had reached your age without being married, I would be so strong that all I would have to do is touch a tree to make it fall down." A ninety-year-old man solemnly attributed his longevity to the fact that he was thirty years old when his first child was born and that, although he became a widower in middle life, he never remarried. A well-known dance, a specialty of one of the castes, depicts weakness from sexual over-indulgence. One of the arguments frequently offered for vegetarianism is that meat stimulates sexual feelings. Sexual indulgence not only allegedly produces weakness but is accountable for serious sickness. The heat generated by sexual intercourse can supposedly lead to tuberculosis. Since sexual activity is so distracting and dangerous, it is considered incompatible with educational progress. The name for the Indian student who is receiving an orthodox Hindu education is *brahmacharya,* a term that has come to be synonymous with "chaste" or "continent." As we have already mentioned, marriage is now often delayed in order to permit young people to complete their education. It was explained to us time and again that boys are not considered fully developed until they are twenty years of age or older and have to be careful and, if necessary, strictly controlled in matters of sex until then.

With this background of disparagement of unbridled sexuality, it is not unreasonable to expect that physical intimacy is felt by many to be proper for procreation only. The heroes and strong men of village tradition are those who visited their wives until the family had a son or the requisite number of children and then lived a life of continence thereafter. Even the gods do not indulge in sexual activity overmuch. There is a taboo against uttering the name of a Hindu month on the first day of that month. The explanation given is that this is the day of the month when Bhagavana Rama (the name by which the Supreme Deity is known in the village) visits his wife for sexual relations. To call attention to the day will remind people of this. Just as God keeps man's intimate secrets, so should man refrain from embarrassing God. This custom suggests the control, the shame-faced attitude, and the secrecy with which sex is attended for God and man in the eyes of the villager.

While it is admitted that few attain the ideal and it is lamented that "men go to their wives too often," the doctrine does have an effect. One family was severely censured because it was considered that a young bride became pregnant too soon after coming to her husband's home. The family elders were taken to task for allowing the young couple to come together for intimate relations so early in their married life. Yet to judge from the date of delivery, the girl must have been at her husband's home over six months before pregnancy occurred. Once a woman is pregnant, intimate relations should cease. One explanation for this is the fear of incest. It is said that if the fetus is that of a female, a man would be having relations with his own daughter. Possible injury to the fetus is another reason given for the postpregnancy taboo. The head of the fetus is soft and vulnerable until birth, it is explained, and could be damaged during sexual intercourse. Properly, the abstinence should continue not only until childbirth but for two years beyond. Weaning is late, and it is felt that the health of the nursing child will be impaired if the mother becomes pregnant again. Therefore it is a disgrace if children are born too close together. In a case where a child was two-and-a-half years old when a sibling arrived, the family was roundly criticized throughout the village. Another element in the situation, less a matter of constraint than of belief, is the notion that the period of greatest fertility immediately follows menstruation. Often, when a child is wanted, the young couple bathe and carry on ritual and are brought together at this time.

In the Hindu view a person's life is divided into four *ashrama,* or periods, and it is to the second of these that sexual activity is appropriate. The first is the period of studentship, *brahmacharya,* when chastity is so strictly enjoined. A person enters the third *ashrama, vanaprastha,* when all his children are grown and he has a grandchild. It is the general feeling that sexual activity should cease by this time or, ideally, before this. One woman, who had conceived nine times and had six living children, told how embarrassed she was to breast-feed her youngest child in the presence of the oldest of his siblings. Another woman was the subject of much gossip and criticism because she bore a son even though her daughter and her daughter-in-law already had children. We were assured that a woman of thirty-five years of age, whose husband had died four years before, will probably never marry again, although she belongs to a caste which permits widow remarriage. She has two married daughters and therefore, as we were told, "is getting too old to marry."

It is the consensus of the villagers that remarriage must be entered upon cautiously. Divorce and widow remarriage are forbidden among the high castes, though separation does occur. Even separation is a grave blow to the high caste woman, for her sons will undoubtedly remain in their father's house. A high caste widower may remarry and will almost certainly do so if he is fairly young and if his first wife had borne daughters only. If he has sons and there is any kins-woman to help him care for them, he will be much less inclined to remarry. The harsh stereotype of the stepmother in Hindu lore is a sobering influence. In a second marriage the man is likely to be considerably older than his bride. Among the low castes divorce and remarriage are possible for both sexes. There is no bar against widow remarriage, either. However, a woman who seeks separation or divorce or a widow who remarries faces almost certain loss of her sons.

Another custom that separates married pairs and acts as an indirect check on population is the visits of the woman to her parental home. It is assumed that marriage will be a difficult transition point for a girl. After all, she has had no contact with the family with which she will become so closely associated. In fact, it is considered bad manners to discuss a girl's impending marriage in her presence. The ex-pectation is that the girl will be lonely, frightened, and homesick when she takes up residence with her in-laws and will want her own kin to call her home for a visit. A girl who is not invited back to her parents' or her brother's home soon after marriage is likely to feel deserted and aggrieved. Actually her solicitous kin seldom disappoint her. These visits of the married woman to her former home and her return to her husband's family are often major undertakings. Cere-monious messages must pass between the two families; an escort must attend the woman; and expensive presents, upon which family status and honor rest, accompany her. Consequently, the visits are prolonged ones, seldom less than three months in duration and often lasting a year. During the first period of a woman's married life, she may spend as much time in her natal village as in the home of her father-in-law. As she grows older, has children, and acquires greater status and responsibilities in her husband's family, the number and duration of the visits to her village of origin diminish. By this time, however, her period of childbearing may be over or drawing to a close.

Present economic practices and conditions also separate married couples for significant periods to some degree. It will be remembered that according to our census figures approximately one hundred male adults are engaged in work in urban centers at any one time. Although some of them return for a month or two every year and although few of them continue in their urban jobs permanently, many of them remain away for a continuous period of from one to two years. Not all of these migrants are married; but, because of early marriage practices, most of them are wed, and it is predominantly the younger married men who are to be found in urban employment.

It should also be recognized that the villager is not a complete stranger to population control measures; in fact, on occasions he has used rather drastic ones. Among the Kshattriya of the village, infanticide was practiced until the last quarter of the nineteenth century because of the expense of arranging marriages for daughters and because of the humiliation in seeking mates of higher status for the girls of the household. Infanticide formerly existed and is rumored to occur occasionally now in cases of illegitimacy, for the growing outside employment of men has resulted in an increasing amount of extramarital relations involving the wives who have been left behind. Abortion, too, takes place when a girl is faced with disgrace. There are a number of specifics in Ayurvedic medicine which are used to prevent conception by those who are engaged in unsanctioned liaisons or to induce abortion when an unwanted pregnancy occurs. Mercury is obtained by the drop at high prices from goldsmiths for these purposes, and the root of a giant milkweed is used in a concoction with the same ends in view. A number of respondents have admitted to the withdrawal technique, and others have acknowledged that they use condoms, which they obtain in towns and cities. Condoms are probably more often used in connection with illicit relations than in ordinary married life. Most of those who attempt to prevent conception do so because their children are grown or married and because they already have grandchildren and fear the embarrassment of now having additional children of their own. It was suggested to a number of village women who sought to avoid further pregnancies because of an already large family or poor health that they seek help from a birth control clinic in Banaras. The fear that they might have to undergo a physical examination was the chief deterrent in these cases.

It is often said that there is nothing in Hindu religion which would prevent the dissemination of birth control information and practice. In this connection the cooperation and affirmative stand of the Indian government is cited. But some cautions need to be observed here. After all, no less an Indian leader than Mahatma Gandhi urged, on religious grounds, that no method be used other than the self-restraint doctrine we have already discussed. And the concept of noninjury to living creatures, *ahimsa,* is strong. In discussing birth control, many respondents made it clear that they would want assurance that any practice they used would not destroy life. There is good reason to believe that a method that prevented fertilization would be much better received generally than one which destroys the fertilized ovum. One has to take into consideration, too, the large section of the population which is enthusiastic over naturism and which insists that the only medicines which should be taken by man are natural products and not chemical agents. In all plans for population control that are contemplated for the present period, the dependence and enforced modesty of the young girl in village India and her reluctance to contradict and lead her husband must also be kept in mind.

A thorough knowledge of the more subtle aspects of culture frequently reveals the weaknesses of opinions arrived at from more superficial observation. There are those, for instance, who assume rather easily that the replacement of the joint family by a smaller family unit would surely have a depressing effect on population growth. Usually such judgments are pronounced without an understanding of the internal controls on sexuality and childbearing that have developed in the joint family. A consideration of these factors suggests, instead, that a weakening of the joint family and of the restraints which the presence of adults of different generations in the same household mutually imposes might well result in an initial rise in the birth rate.

A close look at Indian culture and at Indian rural life in particular impresses one with the degree to which thought and behavior in intimate family matters are shaped today by early marriage, the dependence of women, the limited means at the disposal of women for achieving status, and the economic and social advantages of a large and strong kin group. It is certain that more education, the greater control of disease, further industrialization, and the implementation of laws now on the statute books will alter existing relationships and concepts. But programs always begin in a present among determined people and not in a timeless expanse populated by automatons obedient and responsive to the wishes of the technician. Consequently, any population control plan that does not take these cultural realities into account initially and does not respond to whatever changes occur in them as time goes on is adding psychological and cultural difficulties to the ordinary mechanical problems that confront any large-scale effort.

Chapter XIV: Active Vulcanism in Kau, Hawaii, as an Ecological Factor Affecting Native Life and Culture

THERE WERE four chiefdoms or *moku* on the island of Hawaii[1] which were affected by active vulcanism of Mauna Loa and Kilauea: Hilo at the northeast and east end of the island, Puna along the southeast coast, Kau in the south, and Kona in the west. Hilo, Puna and Kona have endured and still endure lava flows, Kona with greatest frequency; and Kona was and is subject to severe earthquakes. Kau it was, however, that was affected most by the complex of phenomena caused by active vulcanism: violent and devastating earthquakes, lava flows covering some of the best habitable land, tidal waves, and windborne volcanic dust from the eruptions of Kilauea, which is located in eastern Kau. It is not to be wondered at, then, that the culture and lore of the natives of Kau reflected their awareness of vulcanism as an ever-present environmental reality.

THE TERRAIN

It is undeniably true that the coast of this district as seen either from the sea or from the uplands presents a peculiarly forbidding aspect, due to the effects of vulcanism. Lieutenant James King on the ship "Resolution" recorded the impression which a view of the coast made on him when he sailed alongshore in 1779:

> The coast of Kaoo presents a prospect of the most horrid and dreary kind: the whole country appearing to have undergone a total change from the effects of some dreadful convulsion. The ground is everywhere covered with cinders and intersected in many places with black streaks (lava flows). . . . The southern promontory looks like the mere dregs of a volcano. The projecting headland is composed of broken and craggy rocks, piled irregularly on one another, and terminating in sharp points.[2]

In 1823 a party of hardy missionaries made a tour of Hawaii on

222

foot. As they entered the district of Kau from Kona, proceeding along the shore of the area called Manuka, they traversed difficult terrain, seeing only

> here and there, at distant intervals . . . a lonely house . . . with a solitary shrub of thistle struggling for existence among the crevices. . . . All besides was one vast desert, dreary, black and wild.[3]

However, after leaving this land of desolation they went up a trail leading to the somewhat elevated plain called Pakini and found themselves in what appeared to be an area ideal for habitation:

> A beautiful country now appeared before us, and we seemed all at once transplanted to some happier island, where the devastations attributed to Nahaorii and Pele (volcano deities) had never been known. The rough and desolate tract of lava, with all its distorted forms, was exchanged for the verdent plain, diversified with gently rising hills and sloping dales, ornamented with shrubs, and gay with blooming flowers. We saw, however, no streams of water during the whole of the day; but, from the luxurience of the foliage in every direction, the rains must be frequent, or the dews heavy.[4]

DEMOGRAPHY

The problem of livelihood was very acute in this country. Fishing was hazardous everywhere: there were no lagoons, and hardly any bays, due to the rugged coastline of basalt and lava. This was directly the result of vulcanism. There was no net fishing in which groups of canoes or shoreline fishers worked together. Right offshore was deep water, where roamed big fish like the *ulua* (crevalle or jack), for which this coast was famous. *Ulua* were caught from shore or canoe by casting with heavy lines and large hooks. Smaller fish that grazed or hunted along the rocks were also caught with hook and line.

The soil in the lowlands was disintegrated lava or accumulated ash and dust blown by the winds. In crevices and holes in the rock there was some accumulation of humus. Farming was seasonal in the lower drier areas, where sweet potatoes were planted after the winter rains had soaked the earth, carefully cultivated and sometimes watered by hand during the summer months. On the plains of Pakini and Kamaoa, which were described as so verdant by the missionaries, at an elevation of about one thousand feet, there was sufficient good soil and enough moisture from occasional showers and dew to make sweet potatoes flourish; while in the damper sections of Pakini there flourished a form of taro peculiar to the area that could prosper in soil that was moist the year around.

The controlling factor in the matter of subsistence was fresh water. Only at Waiohinu, at the base of an escarpment on the southern flank of Mauna Loa, was there a stream that made it possible to develop a few acres of leveled terraces upon which irrigated taro was cultivated. At Ninole, close to the sea, were abundant springs, but almost at sea level and surrounded by rocky land offering only very small pockets of soil that could be used for potato planting. Beyond Ninole, at Punaluu, was a swampy area watered by springs, where a little wet taro was grown. It was inland, just below and within the margins of the forest zone at altitudes of from one to two thousand feet, where rains could be counted on the year around, that mulched taro was extensively cultivated in deep, moist soil ideal for such planting. This was the backlog upon which the population of Kau depended for subsistence. The crops grown here were not sufficient, however, during those periods when drought, field fires and volcanic eruption deprived the folk who lived on the plains, lowlands and seashore of their expected crops of sweet potato.

Kau was the only area in the Hawaiian Islands which periodically suffered severe famines. In 1830 or 1831 there was much starvation because of the fact that during a period of drought the land was swept by field fires. For anyone familiar with the area, the dryness of the lowlands through half the year, and the incessant, powerful winds, it is easy to visualize these burning times. Starvation was again widespread in 1845 and 1846 due to drought, and again fire swept the land. Chester H. Lyman, in his journal of 1846 and 1847, observed through two-thirds of the district in which he had previously seen lush, habitable land, only "the black roots of tufts of grass, the wilted and blackened shrubs and the smoked stones (presenting) a most dismal prospect for many miles."[5] This fire had destroyed not only vegetation but whole hamlets of native houses, which were in those days thatched with dried grass. In 1867 came another drought and another famine. Immediately on the heels of this, in 1868, "came the great disaster, the overturning of Kau with the earthquake and the tidal wave destroying the villages from Punaluu to Kaalualu."[6] These were all the sizable coastal settlements of the area. The catastrophe was equally as violent inland, though not as destructive of life and property. For three weeks the earth quaked night and day, culminating in an upheaval which opened a great chasm running for miles into which fell horses and cattle. There was a flow of lava and volcanic mud west of Waiohinu in which some human beings and many cattle, horses and sheep were killed.

These cataclysms destroyed the old demographic pattern of the area and set adrift a large part of the population. Many, when and as they could, left the district to earn a livelihood elsewhere. The old economy was one in which households of related relatives by the shore, on the plains and on the slopes below the upland plantations had maintained continuous exchange of foods and other necessities.[7] As it happened, the stage was all set for the emergence of a wholly new pattern, namely, that of the industrial sugar plantation combined with ranching. In 1867 an American had planted ten acres of sugar cane as an experiment, at Naalehu just below Waiohinu, the largest town in the district. Many of the victims of the disasters of 1868 first took refuge in the sugar cane fields. And when further planting was undertaken, and a mill established, many of the survivors who remained in Kau found employment with the plantation.

IDEOLOGY

Hawaiian mythology dramatized the forces of nature as a hierarchy of deities identified with the sky, the sea, rain and rain clouds, the forest, springs, etc. Taro, dependent upon flowing water as it was generally cultivated, was identified with Kane; the sweet potato, with Lono. As taro god, Kane was referred to as Kane-of-the-water-of-life. As sweet potato god, Lono (whose name means "to resound") was seen in the rain clouds. Clouds of fumes, steam and water vapor are always associated with eruptions of the volcanoes. Sometimes rain clouds have the appearance of huge animals. Lono was, therefore, seen as Kamapua'a, the giant hog god; and it was believed that wild hogs rooting in potato patches were Kamapua'a. Lono was referred to as the uncle of the goddess of the volcano.

In view of the dominant role of vulcanism in the life of the folk of Kau it is not surprising to find that there Pele, the volcano goddess, who was not one of the primal deities in the native pantheon, was worshipped as a major deity. Traditionally, Pele with some of her relatives migrated to Hawaii from the south in prehistoric times. Tahiti is named as the island from which she came, but neither her name nor those of her relatives are to be found in Tahitian lore and mythology. An elder sister named Kapo-ula-kina'u came to Hawaii from Tahiti before Pele. Kapo appears to have been mainly associated with sorcery. On the same migration with Pele came an uncle, Ka-moho-ali'i, the lord of sharks, to whom a cliff on one side of the crater at Kilauea is sacred; and Wahine-oma'o, who is embodied in the foliage that clothes the slopes of the volcano. With her also was Hi'iaka, her beloved youngest sister, who is described by many epithets having to do with the heavens, with the sea, with "waters of life," and with the glow of clouds reflecting the crimson of molten lava. As Pele's most beloved sister, Hi'iaka is referred to as Hi'iaka-i-ka-poli-o-Pele or "Hi'iaka-in-the-bosom-of-Pele." Always beneficent, Hi'iaka is a life-giver, healer and dancer. With the migrating voyagers came a younger brother named Kane-apu'a who dwells in the fringes of the forests on the slopes of the volcano. Other members of Pele's family identified with the volcano were Ka-poha-i-kahi-ola (The-explosion-in-the-place-of-life), Ka-ua-o-te-po (The-rain-of-the-night), Kane-he-kili who was seen as lightning, and Ke-o-ahi-kama-kaua (The-fire-thrusting-child-of-war).

According to the legend or myth of Pele's coming, she landed first on Kauai, then moved southeastward on Oahu, then on Maui and finally on Hawaii, seeking a home in which to dwell. Finally she dug the crater of Kilauea volcano, and there she took up her abode. It was there that she was venerated; there were never any shrines or temples dedicated to her. The skeletal remains of the aristocrats of Kau, who considered themselves to be descended from Pele, were cast into the crater, and offerings were made of pigs and flower garlands.

The ritualistic *hula* dancing peculiar to the Hawaiian Islands was intimately related to Pele worship. An epic legend belonged to the *hula,* whose verses, chanted by the masters of the rite, were dramatized in steps, postures and gestures by maidens trained from childhood. Some stanzas describe phases of vulcanism in Puna and storm in Hilo. The main theme of the legend has to do with Pele's love for a handsome young chief of Kauai. While she lay asleep in Kilauea, the spirit of Pele journeyed to Kauai and there saw Lohiau dance. She fell madly in love with the young chieftain. Her soul returned to her body in Kilauea; and Lohiau, who had become infatuated with the spirit of Pele, died of grief. His body was laid in a cave on the mountain high above Haena, on Kauai. At Pele's solicitation Hi'iaka undertook the dangerous ordeal of journeying to Kauai in order to revive Lohiau and bring him back to Pele at Kilauea. She was given magical powers by Pele and was sworn to chastity. Reaching Kaua'i, Hi'iaka discovered Lohiau's body in the cave and restored it to life, aided by the chanting and dancing of the folk of Haena on the shrine dedicated to the *hula,* a stone platform the remains of which are still to be seen by the sea below the cliffs at Haena. Returning to Hawaii with Lohiau, Hi'iaka saw, as they traversed the uplands of Oahu, that fires started by the impatient Pele were consuming the beautiful forests of Puna. And when she came to Puna she learned that her beloved friend Hopoe, who had taught her the *hula,* had perished in the flames. In her frenzy of rage Pele killed Lohiau again. This so angered Hi'iaka that she threatened to quench forever the fires in Kilauea by releasing the waters in the bowels of the earth; but her sister Wahine-oma'o, she who clothed the uplands with foliage, persuaded her not to do this. Instead, she again restored Lohiau to life by her magical powers of healing. Then boldly she embraced him, standing upon the very rim of the volcano, Pele's home. So the drama has its climax in the triumph of virtue over passion.

THE CULT OF PELE

The lore of Hi'iaka and Pele's other relatives survived only as a part of the literary heritage of native Hawaii. There is today no active belief in the continuing existence of the benevolent little sister or of Kapo or Wahine-oma'o or the rest. Pele, however, as the animating spirit of vulcanism, remains very much alive. She appears in dreams, she is seen in flames in the crater and over the incandescent flows of molten lava, and there are numerous stories that tell of her being met within the uplands of south Hawaii, sometimes in the form of an old hag, sometimes as a beautiful young woman dressed in white. It is believed that when Pele is reported to have been seen or has been met with, an eruption of Kilauea or Mauna Loa is imminent.

Until quite recently the cult of the volcano goddess and her sisters survived in mediumistic séances in which Pele and two of her sisters, Kapo and Hi'iaka, have "sat upon" or "dwelt in" (*noho*) a medium, who was referred to as the "perch" (*haka*). This aspect or phase of the cult is not reported at all in early literature, but this is in no way strange since it would have been concealed from missionaries and other whites.

The séances were by no means casual or informal; and they were strictly private, within a family who traced their ancestry to "the Pele clan." In every detail the séances were formally ritualistic, and the ritual was entirely in accord with Hawaiian religious practices. There is no reason to believe that this mediumistic phase of the cult was a result of any extraneous influence. The medium was dressed in a robe whose color denoted which sister was invoked (Pele, white; Kapo, red; Hi'iaka, pink). There was a special mat on which the medium sat, and there were offerings of food and drink. The medium had a helper who was responsible for all the arrangements, and this helper was also the chanter whose invocation invited the spirit to enter or "sit upon" the medium.

The cult of the volcano goddess is traditional in the sense that it conforms to the ancient patterns of pre-Christian Hawaii. It is more, however, than the perpetuation of a traditional pattern. It continues because of experiences, actual or imagined, which are to her devotees clear evidence of the continued existence of Pele and of her concern with the affairs of her relatives (as evidenced in dreams); and of course the dramatic phenomena of vulcanism and the reports of Pele's being seen at times of eruption, a popular theme even among whites in the modern folklore of this community, produce repeated revivals of the cult which would undoubtedly lapse if vulcanism ceased.

In this cult, involving lore, *hula* dancing, dreaming, visions, encounters, mediumship and prayer, there exists a specific, purely native cultural complex which perpetuates itself in the region where the active volcanoes exist, namely, south Hawaii, where the cult had its origin. Here, then, is a single and unique cultural phenomenon based upon a dynamic ecological or environmental factor which continues to motivate a set of beliefs and practices that are in complete accord with ancient Hawaiianism in a community which otherwise is wholly American and Christian.

POSTSCRIPT

During the eruption in January 1960, near the village of Kapoho in Puna District, a group of behavioral scientists of the University of Hawaii made a study of the attitudes of people in the affected area. A brief report in *Science* gives a factual picture of the persistent worship of Pele during these crises. The report says in part:

> One unusually interesting class of "security seeking" behavior emerges consistently during Hawaiian eruptions: rituals and offerings are made to the Hawaiian Volcano Goddess, Pele. . . . [A photograph shows] a Hawaiian language chant to Pele being read by a Chinese-Hawaiian. The traditional offerings of breadfruit, bananas, pork, and tobacco are at his feet. The Western influence is manifested by the Christmas gift wrapping and green ribbon for the box of offerings to Pele. The throwing of the offerings upon the lava flow was accompanied by the singing of a Chinese song.
>
> Preliminary data indicate that this behavior and especially the related beliefs are not limited to any one religious creed, ethnic group, age level or degree of educational achievement.

Among the believers in Pele are some highly educated individuals and some prominent citizens of the island.

The old Hawaiian beliefs are remarkably rational and provide an apparently consistent explanation for geological growth processes. The beliefs appear to be reinforced by a number of factors. One such factor is the very sight of the fountains which are often over 1000 ft in height. . . . This magnificent phenomenon is accompanied by auditory, olfactory, and tactile stimulation produced by the fountain and its accompanying fallout.

Another source of reinforcement for belief in Pele is the inability of science and technology to cope with the destructiveness of the lava flows.[8]

NOTES

1. Geographical names are spelled in accordance with general usage. Spelled phonetically, with glottal stops, they are as follows: Hawai'i, Ka'alu'alu, Kamao'a, Ka-'u, Kaua'i, Na'alehu, Punalu'u.

2. James King, *A Voyage to the Pacific Ocean*, Vol. 3 of Captain James Cook's *Voyages* (Third Voyage) (London: G. Nicol, 1784), p. 104.

3. William Ellis, *A Journal of a Tour around Hawai'i, the Largest of the Sandwich Islands* (Boston, 1825), p. 95.

4. *Ibid.*, p. 100.

5. Chester Lyman (MSS in the Hawaiian Mission Children's Library, Honolulu), Book IV, pp. 10, 14.

6. "MSS report of the pastor J. Kauhane at Kapaliiuka, Ka'u, for 1867-68." (In the Hawaiian Mission Children's Library, Honolulu.)

7. E. S. Craighill Handy, Elizabeth G. Handy, and Mary Kawena Pukui, *The Polynesian Family System in Kau, Hawaii* (Wellington, N. Z., 1958), pp. 132-36.

8. Roy Lachman and William J. Bonk, "Behavior and Beliefs During the Recent Volcanic Eruption at Kapoho, Hawaii," *Science*, CXXXI, No. 3407 (April 15, 1960), 1095-96. Copyright 1960 by the American Association for the Advancement of Science.

ALFRED RODMAN HUSSEY

Chapter XV: The American Official Overseas

I. The Problem Stated

EVERY SOCIETY works out its own system for training and educating its members—but no society has yet worked out a satisfactory system for easy, much less automatic, integration of the stranger. Indeed, without any capabilities for developing such integration, some of the more primitive societies solve the problem simply by killing the stranger on sight.

Similarly, few societies, even today, have accomplished much in the way of preparing their individual members for life in another social climate. Perhaps the seafaring peoples have done more than others, but once the necessity is supplanted by metropolitan power the need for easy adaptation disappears.

At the same time accommodation to alien societies has varied widely. Both the integration of national societies and the effective accommodation of individuals between national societies has become a pressing necessity. A glance at the Congo where both individual leaders and national groups are striving for a peaceful and constructive solution to the problem of building a nation illustrates the complexity of such an effort. The fact is, we are in the throes of developing not a true world society, but a series of regional or international societies. The nineteenth century concept of the national state is slowly giving way to a broader concept. Integration is first political, but eventually it must be completed in the cultural and social spheres. Economic integration is already well advanced in many areas. A necessary first step toward achieving a world society is the training and educating of the individual for effectively playing his part on the larger scene. Indeed, it is an essential element of survival.[1]

For us in the United States, the problem is one of successful adjustment to the interacting pressures and influences of a novel and continuing situation in which an individual's trained and tested responses no longer offer assurances of validity and in which one's known and familiar methods of communication no longer work. The problem is further intensified by differences in representational role.

230

Extremes of representation range from the one-day tourist in Mexico to the prisoner of war whose captors will try to utilize him for their own purposes. When physical and psychological pressures are used the process is called "brainwashing," although today it is becoming increasingly evident that the traumatic effects of capture and imprisonment are more likely to be astutely utilized than are the mysterious treatments referred to in the realm of fiction. Especially is this true where the culture of the captor society is markedly different from that of the prisoner, as, for example, was the case in Korea.

The traitor, the defector—and even the expatriate—experience traumatic results, usually greatly magnified by the psychological effects of their own actions. All too frequently melancholia, hypochondria, insanity or suicide is the probable result.[2] The fact is that for the ordinary individual role-playing in one's own familiar surroundings is quite different from role-playing in an alien environment. Rarely are the familiar guideposts, the cues, the sanctions and the promises present; and if they are present, they are in a seemingly familiar form that is almost invariably deceptive. To an American, a policeman's uniform in Bonn or Rome or New Delhi does not have the same significance that it does to the same person in New York. Its impact upon the traveler or the businessman overseas is considerable. The added pressures upon the prisoner of war, traitor, defector, or expatriate, whose moves are only partially voluntary, are far more severe. Everyone who goes or is sent overseas wears the vestments of our culture, the imprint of our heritage, as well as the infinitely diverse influences of physical, emotional and intellectual individualism.

Cleveland, Mangone and Adams,[3] Adams and Garraty,[4] and many others have discussed in detail the problem of Americans overseas in their varied capacities. Others have considered the equally important problem of the foreigner visiting America. I shall confine my remarks here to the particular problems of the official American—the influences, beneficial and detrimental, which affect his conduct abroad.

The problem of adjustment to an alien society is difficult in itself. How much more difficult is it for one charged with both direct and implied representational responsibility to accomplish effectively the aims and objectives of his government? He may go as an ambassador plenipotentiary or as a guide in a trade fair pavilion; the quality of the responsibility may differ radically, but the problem in essence remains the same. Whatever the situation, the individual must successfully cope with all of the complex problems of adjustment to unfamiliar physical, social and mystical surroundings without benefit of the guidances and supports with which he is familiar in his home environment.

Three major elements are present in the particular problem of the representational individual: (1) his historical role in the service of the United States; (2) his societal background—the particular imprint of American society on him; and (3) the personal problem of individual adjustment to his surroundings. To begin with, the individual is representing the United States at a specific time in the nation's history, and the nature and extent of his responsibilities are directly related to the growth and development of the United States— up to that particular point in time. One must consider also the shifts in impact and influence from the days of the sailing vessel to the age of traveling in excess of the speed of sound.[5]

The traditional role of the thousands of United States nationals working for our government overseas in 1961 is still related to that of their predecessors of one hundred years ago, but today it is markedly different from what it used to be.

The problem of varying cultural backgrounds is also important. There is a wide divergence between the atmosphere of Beacon Hill and that of New Orleans; yet the men we send abroad, whether they come from Massachusetts or Louisiana, are all Americans and represent American cultures. The question might well be asked: Do differences in views concerning the institutions of our society impair our effectiveness abroad? Do we possess such implicit faith in the excellence of our system of jurisprudence that we are prepared to export it, as the British exported the common law to Burma?[6]

The problem is one not only of understanding ourselves but of understanding the view others have of us. It is not only that we are shaped and guided by our social education, but that we must somehow bring into meaningful alliance what we are as Americans and what the people in whose culture and society we are working think we are—or should be—as Americans. One is impressed by the recall of President Eisenhower's visit to India in 1959. He considered it a personal triumph. But was it not in actuality a tribute to the concept of the United States of America and its President held by most of Asia? Here is the real problem.

Lastly, what is the nature of the problem from the point of view of the individual himself? What changes does he undergo? One can, of course, consider only the general elements of adjustment and adaptation, but a knowledge of them is essential in enabling the several departments and agencies of the executive branch of govern-

ment and of Congress itself to select with increasing care the men
and women sent abroad to represent the United States of America.
If this is particularly true for those whose duties relate to policy
commitment, it is no less true for members of the Peace Corps. Both
the Congress and the Executive should have a clearer awareness of
the demands they put upon their representatives overseas than they
have at present. In the long run the effective discharge of duties
abroad must be determined in terms of human and social realities.[7]

The whole problem of effectively representing the United States
overseas has been considerably complicated by the very nature of
the times in which we live. The modern world is, ostensibly at least,
a pragmatic world, a world of science and technology, a world of
economic enterprise on a vast scale, a world of vast dependence
upon the machine.

Even more serious is the great and persuasive fear that someone
will in error press a button that will launch World War III, starting
a chain reaction beyond control or recall that could wipe out all
of us. The sole control—the sole safeguard—the world has to rely
upon is the discipline implanted in trained individuals by the society
to which they belong. Is this wholly reliable? What of the physical
and psychological stresses operating upon these human beings during
the long periods of complete detachment and isolation, sealed in an
unfamiliar element? Whether in a nuclear submarine, a supersonic
bomber, or a space capsule, the problem is the same. With the
added element of risk in these latter cases—in both bomber and
space vehicle—the reality of space and time may be lost. Detachment
is even more complete, and social controls are to that extent more
tenuous.

The plight of the individual in a position of responsibility today
is to be faced with the necessity of making decisions in a relative
social or political vacuum and under the pressure of time, measured
not in days and weeks but in minutes and hours. This is so of the
official in a representational capacity on behalf of the United States
as much as it is of an officer in the armed forces. Each is trained
in a given culture with all of the implicit and explicit rules of conduct,
the habits, traditions, disciplinary processes bred into him or passed
on to him through the more formal and overt means of education
and training, but without the tangible symbols of the sanctions and
values that keep him on a balanced course at home. Under such
circumstances, he is expected to discharge his responsibilities effectively and adequately in an atmosphere and under pressures which
are to him completely alien. What happens to him, and what are

the guarantees and assurance of his effective performance? These are among the questions which merit careful consideration.

II. THE UNITED STATES' INVOLVEMENT IN WORLD AFFAIRS; 1789–1961

The United States, in the first developmental period from 1789 to 1865, was devoting itself to internal growth, to the acquisition, exploration and exploitation of a continent. It was also concerned with the long struggle between national and local loyalties, institutions, and concepts which ultimately had to be resolved in the bitter conflict that forged the federal union and left scars still visible today. Its external affairs were those of protection of its sea commerce and prevention of encroachment of European states upon what it regarded as its own special preserve. Washington's advice, in his *Farewell Address*, was clearly aimed at keeping his country from becoming involved in European rivalries, not because political association was dangerous per se but because there were real dangers for a new, weak country in taking sides. Monroe's position was against encroachment, the more because he preferred to face and deal with the young and struggling South American republics rather than with European powers based in the Western Hemisphere, than because of any altruism for the late Spanish colonies. We fought the Mexican War largely to keep Mexico below what we considered a natural boundary—and out of Texas. We forced the reopening of Japan not so much because we desired commercial relations with the Japanese as because we resented the mistreatment of our sailors shipwrecked on Japanese shores. We also needed harborage facilities on the other side of the Pacific and close to China.

Under these circumstances, our diplomatic and consular representatives had strictly defined and limited responsibilities. Our ambassadors and ministers quite formally represented the young United States, negotiating treaties, conveying official messages of felicitation or protest, and attending affairs of state such as coronations and royal weddings. The demands upon them were rarely heavy—there were few deep personal individual responsibilities. There was no need for them to become involved with or even to understand the culture and social climate of the national state to which they were accredited, and the rules of diplomatic conduct were clearly established—protocol was universally accepted. The ambassador was the formal representative of the President of the United States. What sort of an individual he might be did not matter, so long as he conducted himself in affairs of state in the correct manner.

Either he had been carefully instructed in Washington on the nature of his mission or sufficient trust was reposed in him by Washington so that he could act with a free hand according to his own discretion.

Moreover, events tended to move slowly. There was always time for correspondence, if not a formal request for an official position, at least for an informal letter to a member of the Cabinet, to a senator, or to the President. This was the great age of correspondence, of thoughtful exchange of ideas as well as formal exchange of compliments. The men in positions of authority in the government were largely drawn from one segment of American society. They understood each other, even if they did not agree. Most of them also thought they understood the people with whom they were dealing overseas, an assumption which worked well in this earlier period and was, within limits, founded on fact.

By and large, matters were not greatly different in the consular service. Dealings were on a somewhat more personal and local level and the work involved commercial dealings and a wide range of other duties related to travel and trade. Consular affairs did not involve the representation of the United States except as an agent in what were strictly personal matters. A knowledge of local customs was obviously useful as was a knowledge of the local language, but they were by no means essential. Basically, as with the diplomatic service, dealings were at arm's length and required little more than formal representation based on legal status.

This general state of our foreign representation and the mission of our overseas representatives continued virtually unchanged until after the Civil War. The end of the epoch came in 1865. Lee's surrender at Appomattox marked the dawn of a new day. We had, at terrible cost, proved to ourselves and to the world that we were a unified nation and not a loose confederation of semiautonomous states. We began to look outward beyond our shores, and at the same time we began to consolidate internally.

That war had already forced upon our attention the necessity for establishing new relationships with foreign states. Indeed, our far-flung shipping interests had begun this trend, as witnessed by the forced reopening of Japan. But the Civil War made us aware of the dangers of ignoring the demands and interests of Europe. For one thing, there was the question of recognition—would England and the Continent recognize the South?—a question resolved only after much negotiation, many setbacks, and strong support from diverse elements in England and France. It was then also that France took advantage of our domestic preoccupation and intervened in Mexico.

Ours was an increasing involvement in many other ways as well. At every cultural level exchanges were on the increase. At the same time, citizens and subjects of other countries were flowing in to participate in the expansion of our economy, and our citizens were beginning to tour Europe and write books about foreign countries.[8]

Queen Liliuokalani paid a visit of state to this country, and our ships and sailors were seen with increasing frequency in ports the world over. But with all these changes, we were still largely bystanders on the world scene, having small influence and few responsibilities as a nation among nations.

In the economic sphere also, with the growth and development of our economy—of corporate business in the United States—we were not only accepting foreign investment, we were also looking beyond our shores for new opportunities, for new markets, for new sources of raw material, and all the while developing a new form of economic enterprise. Entering late upon the scene, we were slowly moving toward full involvement. "Manifest Destiny" became the hue and cry of the new expansionists. Before we knew it we were involved in a foreign war and had acquired both colonies and vastly expanded overseas responsibilities. By the turn of the century we spanned the Pacific, one of our two major national parties was split into two camps—the imperialists and the anti-imperialists—and Mr. Dooley questioned whether "the Constitution followed the flag" or the "election returns."

This was the period in which Theodore Roosevelt instructed his Secretary of War, William Howard Taft, to discuss informally with Count Katsura of Japan the demarcation of zones of interest in the Western Pacific between Japan and the United States. It was also the period in which the United States emerged as a naval power, when the Great White Fleet made its slow if impressive circumnavigation of the world, and Captain Alfred Mahan made his notable contribution to international political thinking, *The Influence of Sea Power upon History*.

Little by little, we became so inextricably involved in world affairs that we were forced to assume entirely new and far-reaching responsibilities.

After World War I we found ourselves even more involved than ever in world affairs, but we backed away from joining in the first serious attempt at world government—the League of Nations. As a nation we were not yet psychologically ready for such a commitment, but we participated in the affairs of other nations and in matters of world interest as fully as if we had formally joined the League.

Our concern with China and our assumption of direct responsibility in Turkey are witnesses to this participation as were the joint interventions at Archangel and Vladivostok. The Dawes and Young plans for the resolution of Germany's economic difficulties were further evidences of direct and intimate participation, and the influence and widespread activities of the Foreign Policy Association and the Institute of Pacific Relations during this period revealed our global interests and concerns.

In growing numbers and increasingly diverse capacities our representatives were being sent abroad. Two million and more men under arms had reached Europe during the war, while naval contingents participated in joint operations the world over and we gained valuable experience by sharing in the occupation of the Rhineland.[9] Our reaction to participation in World War I was not only a marked urge to return to "normalcy" but fully as well a swing toward a new form of isolationism. We also sought to prevent recurrence of a similar catastrophe. We actively promoted disarmament or rather the limitation of arms. At the same time, we began seeing foreign shadows under the bed.

There were many who saw what lay ahead and knew the measure of our international involvements. One of the first indications was the merging of the diplomatic and consular services into a single career foreign service. The service academies were broadening their curricula, and the general academic field was beginning to concern itself with the training of public servants.

The problem of representation overseas had become immensely more involved and complicated, and the world at large was facing deepening crises. The major causes of anxiety and unrest were the Depression of 1929, the rise of naziism and fascism, and Japan's trend toward military totalitarianism. No one wanted war, and those nations whose governments were responsive to their people backed away from provoking it, while fully realizing that a line had somewhere to be drawn. The extent to which the United States had become involved is well illustrated by President Roosevelt's "Quarantine Proposal."

In this period our representatives overseas had two grave responsibilities: first, to represent effectively the policies of the United States and second, to report accurately to Washington what was happening abroad. They had also to protect the persons and property of American citizens, a task which was becoming increasingly more difficult in certain countries. The last responsibility was of course a traditional one, and precedents existed which could be followed. The effective representation of United States policies for the first time included the promoting of international cooperation and the providing of accurate reporting, the latter a relatively new addition.

But even so, representation of the United States was restricted to its formal officials, by and large; that is to say, members of the Foreign Service, officers of the Army and Navy and senior members of the administration in Washington. Negotiations were still carried out with governments-in-being as a general rule, although as we got into World War II, we began to become involved with factions and elements of foreign societies not associated with and frequently in conflict with the formal regime. Our involvement was steadily deepening. We were operating with the hill tribes in Burma. We were being forced to choose between Tito and Mikhailovich in Yugoslavia. There was the problem of de Gaulle, Darlan and Giraud in North Africa; Chiang Kai-shek and Mao Tse-tung in China. Our soldiers, our sailors, our fliers were going ashore in India and Sicily; we were assuming responsibility for administering civil affairs in Micronesia.

Still, the numbers involved were microscopic in terms of the whole country, and few people in what the military used to call the "Zone of the Interior" knew or felt concern for what was going on. Few of those involved had anything in the way of serious and formal training for their duties. True, extended training programs in military government (and paramilitary operations) were initiated, but generally speaking, the men and women involved had to rely upon native intuition and professional knowledge and experience rather than specifically defined programs. Selection was making strides: the idea was growing in Washington that there was a relationship between what an individual had been—what he had done in civilian life—and what he could be expected to do in his particular assignment, although this awareness was generally restricted to professional or technical competence, with little reference either to "area knowledge" or to ability to work with peoples of different cultures.[10]

The year 1945 was both an end and a beginning for the United States. Gone forever was the traditional dream of insularity, although it has taken over fifteen years to realize the truth of such an assertion. At long last foreign aid has become an integral part of our international responsibility and is being put on a long-term basis through formal institutional reorganization. Gone also is the notion that we could settle any time and any place an international crisis without careful preparation and without serious consideration of cause or consequence. Korea taught us a valuable lesson. We learned that combat effectiveness requires something more than men in uniform and military material in quantity. We also learned that our "American way of life" was not preparing our troops—officers or enlisted men— to withstand the pressures of captivity in a country harshly schooled in the drives and disciplines of an alien ideology. The world has become a complex place, closely knit by modern systems of transportation and communication and widely separated by anciently rooted concepts and beliefs. The simplicities of pre-twentieth century life in America upon which most of our institutions and much of our thinking are still based are no longer valid bases for decision.

If 1945 ended an epoch, it also began one. With the surrender of Japan, we appeared upon the world stage as the most powerful national state in the world. Since then we have been forced to concern ourselves with responsibility for the political stability and economic recovery or growth of national states in both hemispheres, for the support of our wartime allies and for the defense of the noncommunist world against further encroachment or subversion by the U.S.S.R. or the People's Republic of China.

It was a short step from aid to Greece and Turkey to the Marshall Plan. Then came Point Four and the concept of broad aid to the underdeveloped countries. We were also a prime mover in the organization of the United Nations and now, in its period of challenge, the leader in its support and defense. Today we participate in a far-flung network of international organizations. Perhaps there is no better illustration of the extent of our involvement than a recent Department of State press release entitled "Current International Conferences and Meetings in which the United States Government is Participating" which lists twenty-seven international conferences concurrently in session.[11]

Who carries out these myriad activities? The burden falls upon men and women drawn from every segment of our society and not just upon members of the Foreign Service. The degree of their total success must be measured by the extent to which they carry out the nation's policies and their ability to adjust and adapt to life and work beyond the scope of their own culture. Cleveland, Mangone and Adams describe them:

> Thus it is that the overseas Americans carry with them not only the responsibility for their own behavior but also the guilt for intolerance in Arkansas or bumbling in Washington. They likewise bask in the reflection of great achievements at Cape Canaveral or of inspiring acts of leadership in Washington. Businessmen or missionaries, airmen or soldiers, "experts," or diplomats, they are all, like it or not, surrogates for the United States. . . .[12]

The role of the United States in the world today is immense and complicated, and there are few in Washington who fully understand it. In the above outline I have sought merely to suggest the quality and size of that role and the progress of its development. Even more important is the problem of understanding the nature of our society and the contribution it has made toward its members for service abroad.

III. What is an American?

The United States is the wealthiest and most technologically advanced free political society in the world today. It is also unique in two marked ways. It is the first truly federal national state in world history, and at the same time, it has developed a society in which social movement is relatively unhampered and uninhibited. This is not to say that there are not sectors of our society in which barriers to social change do not still exist. True, there are certain so-called power elite groups representing efforts to turn the clock backward to an imaginary time when everyone knew his place and Americans were secure from "alien" influences. But these represent attempts at imposing checks and barriers of which we have been historically so notably free. Our culture covers a wide range, from ancestor worship in Brahmin Boston and Shinto Charleston to Zen and the beatniks on Telegraph Hill, all freely accepted as part and parcel of our unique society. We have an organized labor movement that equates in size and power Big Business itself. We are one of the most totally and minutely regulated countries in the world. Our political structure is costly and inefficient, and yet, for all of this, few really feel imposed upon or feel seriously restricted. We consider ourselves living in a flexible society, one in which we can move freely anywhere and at any time.

Age, religion, national origin, family status, financial condition—none of these has any significant bearing on the ability of an individual to move ahead, to change his social, economic or political status. Perhaps the major segment of our population whose freedom is seriously hampered is the women. Sexual bias has been a deterrent, and in spite of great accomplishments on the part of women they are still treated by the law and by society in a special category. Women remain subjected to severe discrimination—particularly, I might suggest, in Washington.

We are a nation of paradoxes. We are on the whole deeply religious and moralistic. "God" in name and concept plays an important part in our daily lives. Legislative proceedings are opened with prayer. One of our most basic social motivations is the belief that man was created in God's image and that we owe it to Him to conduct our lives according to His principles; yet, we insist upon the formal separation of church and state and have decreed this in the Constitution.[13]

The historic conflict between Protestant and Catholic is a legacy inherited from Europe. Also, much of our emotionalism concerning communism stems from the Judaic-Christian origin of our values and beliefs, immensely augmented by the influence of Calvinistic pragmatism that confused religious virtue with property ownership. Middle-class values in the United States during the late nineteenth and early twentieth centuries tended to equate morality with property and role with status in what was deemed a settled society. Any movement that appeared to profess differing standards of ethical conduct or supported concepts of human relationship not in accord with the accepted norm or with conventional family life (including an owned "home," a bank account, and other symbols of middle-class security) was a threat to society. Socialism became an identifiable threat to the so-called American way of life. The October Revolution and the subsequent adoption by the Communists in Russia of the terminology previously utilized by Socialists created confusion in our concepts which we have yet to outgrow.

The wartime alliance of Great Britain, the United States and the U.S.S.R. following Germany's sudden attack upon Russia served to soften somewhat our distrust of communism or at least of the Soviet Union, but a deep-rooted basis remained to flower anew when we suddenly discovered in the immediate postwar years that we had not achieved either peace or security. Where did the fault lie? Who was to be blamed? We had to find an answer—a scapegoat. Aided greatly by the forces of conservatism and isolationism, we entered the tragic period of McCarthyism in which all our failures, real or imagined, were blamed upon the conspiracy of international communism and qualified and responsible citizens in and out of government, including some occupying important positions of authority, were literally hounded out of office or public life because of their alleged treasonable adherence to or softness toward the tenets of an alien ideology— alien, that is, to our complacent acceptance of a traditional point of view.

That there was some infiltration of the government cannot be denied, but that the small number of true Communists in government had any effect upon decision-making is highly questionable. Secrets were stolen, and technological leaks occurred, but in the most famous case of the Chambers-Hiss affair and the "pumpkin papers," the stolen evidence was devoid of any real value to any foreign power. Yet we seized upon this case as tangible evidence of how badly we were being mistreated and mistrusted.

In an extreme case of jitters between 1945 and 1960 we sought to blame specific people and specific things for a state of affairs which we found unacceptable and inexplicable. We settled on communism and Russia, to be quickly followed by communism and China, as the compendium of all that was wrong. Unaware of the great and significant changes within our own society producing elemental conflicts between geographical sections as well as social and economic groupings, we readily found explanation for the hurt and tension in what others—"aliens"—were doing or trying to do to us. The picture is not unfamiliar to the student of our recent history.

As a society we are still in the process of change, and our uncertainties reflect this change. Particularly is this true on the political scene. It is not without significance that in the popular vote total there was a hairline difference between the victory of Kennedy and the defeat of Nixon. There are no longer clear lines of distinction between the platforms of the two major parties. We are also shifting our major economic emphasis from agriculture to industry; we have become an urban rather than a rural society, yet we still give more support to our farmers than to our railroads.

Significant also are the changes taking place in our political institutions. The rigid line of demarcation between state and national government is fast breaking down. As our people become more closely integrated and our economy becomes national, the significance and adequacy of local self-government become more and more open to question. Within the federal field, the doctrine of the separation of powers no longer holds validity in practice. Our courts today are not only passing on the validity or applicability of statutory law, they are administering it.[14] The executive branch of the government has long since entered the legislative field, building up a body of administrative regulations which have all the force and effect of statutory law. Our regulatory agencies are acting as courts of law. The legislative branch has also stepped into the fields usually reserved for the executive and the judicial branches. It is a tribute to the wisdom of American leadership between 1775 and 1789 that a political system of such flexibility was devised, and if our representatives overseas discharge their responsibilities effectively they must have knowledge and understanding of what these changes mean.

In this period of change under the pressure of both domestic and international developments, both the strengths and weaknesses of our society tend to sharpen and to be reflected in our thinking and action as individuals. One of the strengths lies in our flexibility—our ability to meet and cope with any situation, relying upon the worth and availability of every other person involved. We may be too trusting, and often when we fail to rally support we are likely to undertake some course of action single-handedly. We are inclined even as individuals to attempt the unknown, to essay a solitary course of action unpremeditated and untested.

This characteristic has often been the despair of our friends and allies, but it has also caused confusion to our opponents. What most non-Americans fail to understand is that we are no more than acting out the long-established tradition of the pioneer, the colonist. Faced with the necessity for direct decision, the pioneer was forced to act alone without benefit of past experience—to devise his methodology from day to day or even from hour to hour.[15] Although a strength, this is also a weakness. It may call for reliance upon ingenuity and expedience rather than upon planning and training. And yet, in terms of dealing with individuals, our tendency to rely upon people rather than doctrine serves us well. Leadership is still equated with competence.[16]

The ability to mobilize human resources, to work with others toward accomplishment of a common purpose, is one of our great resources. In recent years, the molding of American manpower into a highly complex military machine, involving not only selection and training in the ordinary sense but also the setting of equals over equals in terms of military hierarchy and making it work, was indeed unique. In previous wars, selection (as, for example, between officers and enlisted men) had been based generally upon predetermined status, e.g., wealth, education, or community position. The occupation of Japan was another comparable instance of far-reaching consequence. I venture to suggest that this will be regarded by historians as one of the truly great contributions of the United States to world history. Ruling a distressed national society through the medium of its own political, economic and social institutions in a way that would preserve national unity and basic culture and at the same time encourage the growth of democratic institutions was a formidable task under any circumstances and yet, generally speaking, one successfully accomplished.[17] On more than one occasion, observers, both Japanese and foreign, commented that the Americans who directed and administered the Occupation were acting as though they were elected public officials responsible to their constituents, their constituents being the Japanese.

Sometimes, however, we Americans tend to barge ahead with a plan of action because we believe it technically feasible and practically beneficial regardless of local cultural limitations. Time and again we ignore, because we have not thought through or do not understand, the immediate local protest. We fail to perceive that the native superstition is usually based upon a substantive social reason. We also tend to forget that we are dealing with human beings, not cases, and that whatever the reason for doing things in a certain way, social practices are part and parcel of the lives of people and cannot be altered overnight.

Our society has exhibited and developed a capacity for growth that has enabled us to enlarge the thirteen original colonies of the eastern seaboard into fifty states. Our strength is our capacity for expansion, adjustment and absorption; our weakness, that we have not yet adjusted our social and intellectual processes to the fact that we are not a simple, Calvinistic, Anglo-Saxon, common law society, but a polyglot of races, tongues, institutions and traditions which we have yet to mold into a common pattern.

We have elected a Hindu, a Japanese and a Chinese to Congress and we do not find this any more remarkable than electing a woman or a Negro. Abroad, we tend to treat other people in other societies as we treat members of our own complex of cultures, forgetting that within our own country, social, political and economic institutions have established a pattern of conformity that makes our society work despite its diverse coloration. We fail to realize that beyond our shores other influences are controlling and that we must work within the pattern of conformity of these societies and not that of our own.[18]

Dennis W. Brogan's volume on the subject of the American character is useful.[19] Bruckberger's "Letter to Americans" at the end of his interesting and unconventional study of the growth of our character contains a frank appraisal of our many-faceted national self.[20] Julian Marias' article on "The Unreal America" deserves careful study.[21] And the following two quotations, one from an articulate and understanding Indian, the other from a gifted and experienced political scientist who served in the State Department under Dean Acheson, state, I think, much of the case:

> . . . America, with its driving energy, its earnestness, its kindness, and its extraordinary beauty, half deploring its ignorance of con-

ditions in the rest of the world, its smug *self-righteousness, and its assumption of privilege.*[22]

One of our national characteristics is admiration for doers, respect for action (rather than words), contempt for passivity. It doesn't matter that, in international relations, as in love, knowing how to wait may be as important as knowing how to act. We believe in seizing the initiative, in offense rather than defense, and so forth.[23]

IV. The Problems of Adjustment

Against this background of a world situation in which economic, political and social patterns are changing rapidly; of a society seriously encumbered by the necessity of absorbing and integrating complexities of color, of culture, of tradition into what was until quite recently a one-culture society; of a national state operating under a legal and political system devised at the end of the eighteenth century and an economic system erected in the twentieth century; of a political entity which has grown from a sparsely populated and loosely allied community of former English colonies to a super state spanning a continent and wielding enormous power—against this background, what are the problems of adjustment and adaptation faced by the individual who works for and represents the United States overseas? To what conditions and situations does he have to adjust in order to be effective?

Much of the answer to this question applies to everyone working overseas, whatsoever or whomsoever he represents, but the special considerations which apply to those working for the government will be emphasized in the course of the discussion.

The problem should be considered under two headings. There is first the individual's own personal adjustment in terms of himself as sentient and physical man. Secondly, there is his adjustment in his representational capacity—his adjustment in his relationships with others, familial and official, formal and informal.

In the first category, that of personal adjustment, let us consider some of the problems. While many of them will seem obvious, others either are not as apparent or have received little attention, as the erroneous assumption that whatever happens to us physically we can take in stride without having our effectiveness impaired. But there is actually a relationship between the physical condition under which one is working and one's effectiveness. In flying to a distant foreign country there is, physiologically speaking, a radical change, and the differences in physical impact are varied. A new climate, a new diet, strange plumbing, odd smells—these are only a few of the changes.

Social adjustment, too, has many aspects. There is the problem of adjusting to people—people who differ not only in dress and physical appearance, but in habit and manner, in the way they speak and the way they do things. The problem is one of adjusting to new institutions, new values, new beliefs. There is the difficulty not only of learning a new language but of learning and understanding the usages and symbolism which give the language meaning. There is also the problem of social ritual and social obligation. Americans tend to take the question of social relationships lightly. Most societies, however, and particularly the older and more traditional ones, take a different point of view.

Political adjustment also presents a related and similarly difficult problem. By *political* I do not restrict myself to the usual, more limited meaning of the term. Cleveland and Mangone use the term *organizational* in stressing the requirement of being able to build and utilize local institutions. This involves far more than a knowledge of the law and the formal political and economic institutions of a country. It involves a knowledge and understanding of the mechanics of social organization—how people relate to one another, how group action is accomplished, how decisions are made. One rarely deals with men as individuals—indeed, in some countries, the word is unknown.[24]

Traditionally, Americans are experienced in working together despite divergencies in background, education, and cultural origin. We have, I think, an instinct for organization. However, abroad our methods are not always acceptable or understood, and we are all too frequently puzzled if not hurt by the failure of immediate response.[25]

Then also the problem of intellectual adjustment is rarely recognized by Americans. It is probably based upon our popular belief in the "common man" and relates to the social flexibility so characteristic of our culture. We feel an innate sense of superiority because we broke free from England and Europe. Because of this sense of freedom and superiority, we tend to forget that it is vital in one's overseas relationships that he learn something of the intellectual coloration of the other country. One must learn a new approach to the processes of the mind and obtain a new understanding of the symbolism and imagery of the arts and of the religion(s) locally significant, for these are the ways by which the culture is expressed and communicated. It is a demanding task but a rewarding one. When one understands the frames of reference within which the people with whom one is dealing speak, write and act, one can begin to communicate and open wide a door to acceptance.

Lastly, and perhaps most importantly, there is need for psychological adjustment. Psychological adjustment requires a new insight into an individual's motives and attitudes—a new understanding of one's own ability and willingness to meet new situations, new conditions, new thoughts, new emotions.

The problems the individual faces as an individual in making the necessary adjustments are probably the most important aspect of the whole problem, and certainly the one that has received the most attention. But no individual lives within himself alone. However successfully the adjustment in terms of self, an individual is always faced with the problems of representational adjustment. Upon going overseas an individual immediately assumes a whole new set of responsibilities. He is subjected to a whole new set of demands. It is the rare situation, for example, in which the wife is as fully prepared as her husband to meet the problems with which she must cope. In the usual situation, the husband is working all day in a Western-style office with associates who speak a common language and are engaged in the same type of work. Unless the family is lodged in a compound with other American families, the wife is usually alone for the entire day in an unfamiliar house with servants who not only do not speak the same language but also do things differently.[26] She is surrounded by all of the tangible and intangible evidences of an alien land. Both, then, must learn new roles of guidance, support and understanding. Neither can rely upon the built-in aids to living provided in one's home community.

There is also the problem of office adjustment. There is an absolute necessity for close teamwork. The newcomer finds that the older members of the team have developed a pattern of life and work into which he is expected to fit without any real time for adjustment. Moreover, the work patterns are in most cases imposed by local conditions. There is an immediacy to one's operational activities which is not usually found in Washington. At home one lives and works in a familiar social atmosphere which tends to submerge individual differences and to set up a pattern of commonality. Overseas, this is missing and when it is discovered that a special pattern does in fact exist, it is usually peculiarly intense and warped. One suddenly discovers that the man with whom an office is shared at home is now a complete stranger. Under such circumstances one is left alone with his own problems which he must solve by himself.

Especially difficult are the problems involved in dealing with those with whom intimate relationships have not been established but with whom one must work in a representational capacity. These are admirably discussed in *The Overseas Americans,* which also contains an excellent bibliography.[27] The problems of relating to and adjusting to both the general American community and the rest of the foreign community, while important, are beyond the scope of this paper. There is, however, one aspect of the problem of adjustment and adaptation which must be emphasized.

The problem is a compound one. First of all, there is the question of communication. Overseas, one seldom deals directly with a person who is known to him at home. In Washington, on the other hand, one is among familiar acquaintances even though he can rarely exercise his own judgment freely. He has to consider and be guided by his supervisor, by the policies established by the White House, by the necessity for keeping peace on Capitol Hill, and not infrequently by an awareness of the temper of public opinion. Communication involves the use of words as symbols, and even within the framework of one's own culture two people rarely use words with quite the same meaning.

Furthermore, overseas the conception of urgency may well differ from that in Washington. Perhaps one has neglected to convey to Washington all of the information upon which a judgment must be based—indeed, this is too often the case. In the same way, the official in Washington may be reacting to information not available to the person overseas.

Thus, adjustment of one's relationship to Washington is perhaps the most significant problem one must face in serving abroad as a representative of the United States government.

In the above summary, I have attempted to outline some of the problems of individual adjustment which the official representative faces when he goes overseas. Perhaps the situation is best summarized by saying that, overseas, one is not only faced with all of the diverse problems of personal adjustment to life in a strange and unfamiliar environment, both physical and personal, but he is also faced with adjustments to his own government and his country in terms of his immediate surroundings and responsibilities. Throughout the period of adjustment, one is deprived of the directions, understandings and insights provided at home by the customs and habits of the society with which one is almost automatically familiar.

V. THE AMERICAN REPRESENTATIVE OVERSEAS

Who, then, is the representative of the United States abroad, and what is he representing? What are his problems, personal and official? In the foregoing, an attempt has been made to assess some of the elements characterizing the role and status of the American official overseas and some of the factors influencing the effectiveness of his performance. The present-day significance of his role as a representative of the United States reflects the immense changes that have taken place in the recently acquired world position of the United States as well as the continuing growth and alteration of the character and appearance of the United States as a nation. The complex interplay of stresses and influences—the pressures of tradition and custom and belief which in their totality make an American what he is today—significantly affects and largely controls his actions and reactions.

Under normal conditions and in the absence of strong pressure toward aberrant conduct, the individual tends to remain tied to his own environment, to accept the social disciplines he began being subjected to the moment he first drew breath.[28] The motivations and pressures that impel the defector, the expatriate, the deserter, the rebel to reject the aims and values—and the prohibitions—of his home society are many and diverse, but where no physiological factors are involved the choice of revolt is planned and conscious. Indeed, it does not necessarily mean total rejection, but it certainly means rejection of certain phases or aspects of the individual's home society. The late Frank Lloyd Wright is an excellent example of the conscious rebel. His partial and intellectual rejection was intended not to serve selfish aims but rather to make plain his passionate concern with social growth. He felt the need for outspoken protest against trends and developments in his own society of which he disapproved.

The rebel makes his own conditions, his own choices, admitting the risk that they will not be accepted by his own society and hoping that another society will accord him membership. Not so the individual who moves from his own society into another in a formal representative capacity. The American who goes abroad in the service of his country has two missions: to serve the best interests of the United States—to reflect its aims and beliefs and to interpret its words and actions—as well as to accomplish effectively the specific task or tasks assigned him.

Remaining an American while at the same time adjusting and adapting to the environmental atmosphere of the new society about him in a manner best calculated to give him real insight into its workings is one of the major responsibilities of his mission. This is no easy task; on the other hand, this task is today more difficult than at any other time in our history. We are living in the midst of change and transition. Under the pressure of his search for a better life and for a deeper understanding of the world in which he lives— a pressure gravely magnified by the threat of extinction the world faces today—man is once again revising the rules that order and shape his future. Nationalism, that political concept that was the natural outgrowth of eighteenth century rationalism, the translation of individualism into politics, is slowly but surely giving way to new concepts of sovereignty and the relationship between national states. Communism, socialism, regionalism, federalism—there are many terms, many theories, many doctrines. They all point in one direction, toward a reversal of the political fragmentation of the nineteenth and early twentieth centuries, when the multiplication of independent states came close to creating a state of chaos.[29] This, then, is a period of ferment and uncertainty. The changes that are taking place in the United States are reflected in those which are taking place in the world at large. Technical facilities for the exchange of ideas as well as ideologies, of individuals as well as products (exchanges in per-sonam as well as *in re*) have begun a new revolution in the affairs of man. Neither political ideology nor national doctrine will catch up for some time with the changes in faith, in understanding and in aim which are so clearly taking place among the people as in-dividuals.

We, as Americans, have experienced "culture shock" in our progress from Plymouth and Jamestown to San Francisco and Fairbanks and Honolulu. This is, perhaps, our greatest strength in serving our country overseas. Yet, because we have been successful so far, because we have overridden the hopes and ambitions of the minorities we have conquered or absorbed without too serious an impact, we tend to regard lightly our ability to cope with any situation, to represent our country according to our own lights, without regard for the faiths, the beliefs, the convictions—the social and political inhibitions and complexes—of the people to whom and within whose culture patterns we represent officially and formally the United States. Our great weakness is our confidence in our ability to overcome all obstacles, personal as well as physical, and our greatest strength is, perhaps, our faith in the essential workability of our system. We are indeed right in that faith. But we have much yet to learn about our own country and what is happening to it as we have much yet to learn about the countries and areas to which we send our representatives. Both are prime requirements. We Americans, like human beings everywhere, have much yet to learn about ourselves.

NOTES

1. The United States, in forming the first successful federal union on a large scale, took the first long step toward development of a successful international society. India and the USSR are in the process of doing this. The British Commonwealth has been, perhaps, less successful. European integration is proceeding with excellent prospect for eventual success. A comparison might be made between the present situation in Europe with that which existed in the United States between 1783 and 1789, when the pressure of internal and external events forced the forging of a lasting federal union.

2. Both Durkheim and De Grazia have examined the problem of *anomie*—the social disintegration that takes place when value and belief systems are destroyed or lost. Our problem is essentially an individual variant of this concept of social maladjustment.

3. *The Overseas Americans* (New York: McGraw-Hill Book Co., Inc., 1960).

4. *From Main Street to the Left Bank: Students and Scholars Abroad* (East Lansing: Michigan State University Press, 1959); *Is The World Our Campus?*, East Lansing: Michigan State University Press, 1960).

5. To many Americans, place names of the Far East had, at one time, a much deeper significance. The heritage of that significance is today important to us. Its influence on our attitudes was recently well explored by Harold Isaacs in his *Scratches on our Minds* (New York: John Day, 1958).

6. "For Burmese custom, Mr. Maingy substituted the rule of law." J. S. Furnivall, *Colonial Policy and Practice* (New York: New York University Press, 1956), p. 30. In actual fact, in this instance we do, as witness the American contribution to the new Constitution of Japan, written during the Occupation, with particular reference to judicial reform.

7. For an excellent discussion of these realities, see "The Unreal America" by Julian Marias, *Foreign Affairs*, XXXIX, No. 4 (July 1961), 578-90.

8. In many ways, Mark Twain's *Innocents Abroad* could well be considered the first treatise on "Overseasmanship," as his *Roughing It* was one of the early wry looks upon ourselves as pioneers.

9. *The Hunt Report* which became the Bible of military government training in World War II.

10. This was more true of the Army than of the Navy. The basic concept of the Army CATS program was selection on the basis of professional or technical competence, e.g., banking or public health; it provided training in techniques of civil administration while the Navy undertook area and language training in depth.

11. Department of State Press Release No. 317 of May 15, 1961.

12.   Cleveland, Mangone and Adams, *The Overseas Americans* (New York: McGraw-Hill Book Co., Inc., 1960), p. vi.

13.   Actually, only once in the Constitution itself and once in the Bill of Rights is the subject mentioned and then only in purely negative terms. Article VI of the Constitution provides that "no religious test shall ever be required as a Qualification to any Office of Public Trust under the United States." Article I of the Bill of Rights provides that "Congress shall make no law respecting an establishment of religion, or prohibiting the free exercise thereof. . . ." See Charles Warren, *The Making of the Constitution* (Boston: Little, Brown & Company, 1928), pp. 127-29.

14.   It would be difficult to deny that, in the field of desegregation of schools, the district courts of the United States are actually administering school affairs.

15.   Joshua Slocum's signal to the battleship "Oregon" in May 1898, "let us keep together for mutual protection," is far more than the dry wit of a salty New Englander; it is deeply illustrative of this native sense of commonalty of need as well as purpose. Captain Joshua Slocum, *Sailing Alone Around the World* (New York: The Century Company, 1919), p. 264.

16.   Cf. Murray Kempton, *Part of our Time* (New York: Simon & Shuster, 1955), footnote p. 88.

17.   Cf. Kazuo Kawai, *Japan's American Interlude* (Chicago: University of Chicago Press, 1960), especially Chapter I. Kawai says (p. 31):

> With comparatively few exceptions, Americans apparently found it contrary to their nature to harbor their wartime hatred for long. Very quickly the officers and men of the Occupation came to look upon the Japanese as fellow human beings rather than fiendish enemies and treated them with decency and consideration. p. 13. "The most that any military occupation can hope to accomplish in a conquered enemy country is to remove the obvious physical obstacles in the way of the desired conduct, set that country in the desired direction, and guide its first faltering footsteps. From there on, progress can be made only by the independent efforts of the nation itself. By this standard of what was possible, the (American) Occupation did about all it could have done, and in many respects it did more than could have been expected. In this sense the Occupation was justified in the pride it took in its accomplishments."

18.   Cf. John D. Montgomery, "Crossing the Cultural Bias," *World Politics*, XIII, No. 4 (July 1961), 544-60.

19.   See Dennis W. Brogan, *The American Character* (New York: Vintage Books, 1959).

20.   R. L. Bruckberger, *Image of America* (New York: The Viking Press, 1959), pp. 261-77.

21.   Julian Marias, "The Unreal America," *Foreign Affairs*, XXXIX, No. 4 (July 1961), pp. 578-90.

22.   Santha Rama Rau, *Gifts of Passage* (New York: Harper & Row, Publishers, Inc., 1961), 27. Italics added by present author.

23.   Louis J. Halle, "Lessons of the Cuban Blunder," *The New Republic*, CXLIV, No. 23 (June 5, 1961), p. 14.

24. In Japan, traditionally, the word for person refers to the family group, not the individual; the word for people refers to people collectively, not to a group of individuals.

25. Some relevant points are made by Colonel Lyndall Urwick, a British management expert, quoted in *Is The World our Campus?* by Walter Adams and John A. Garraty (East Lansing: Michigan State University Press, 1960), pp. 120-21:

> Do not be disappointed . . . if the results (of American efforts) at the moment fall short of your expectations. They are there all right, fermenting under the surface. But the gestation period for new ideas, the waiting time before they issue into action, is necessarily longer in older societies than in your own. How would it be otherwise? The people of the United States are conditioned by ethnographic make-up, cultural selection, geographic circumstances, and historic accident to be more ready to adjust themselves to the postulates of an adaptive society. . . . So do not be surprised if the European countries fail to accept as readily as you have done, or as quickly as they should for their own advantage, the truths about how to make the most of an economy based upon power-driven machinery, which seems too obvious to you. You have no monarchial or feudal past to persuade employers that divine inspiration or seigneurial privilege give them an inalienable right to govern wrong, or that those who suggest that they might manage better are guilty of a kind of blasphemy. . . . Believe me, I can see how very clearly frustrating to your enthusiasm and to your good-will is much that is happening in many European countries. . . . But in older societies you cannot sweep and start again as quickly as you can here.

26. There is actually an added problem here. In our society, we have substantially done away with the use of household servants, except perhaps for a weekly cleaning woman. The presence and utilization of not one but usually several servants, frequently living in, poses a very real problem for most American housewives.

27. For useful accounts of personal experiences in dealing with this problem see *Voiceless India*, by Gertrude Emerson Sen (1st Indian ed.; Benares: Indian Publishers, 1946); and *Hunza*, John Clark (New York: Funk & Wagnalls, 1956).

28. Cf. Erich Fromm, *The Sane Society* (New York: Holt, Rinehart & Winston, 1955), pp. 30ff.

29. A recent survey of the New York-New Jersey-Connecticut metropolitan area disclosed the existence of over 1400 separate political entities.